Belonging in Healthcare

PRAISE FOR
BELONGING IN HEALTHCARE

"The vital need to diversify our healthcare workforce has been palpable for a long time. Now, through Karen Catlin's research and stories, we have a practical guide that can help get us there."

— Eric Topol, MD
Author *DEEP MEDICINE*, Professor, Scripps Research

"Ms. Catlin did her research when taking on the healthcare industry after tech. I applaud her attention to the lack of racial and ethnic representation of frontline professionals and the need for white healthcare workers to practice allyship with their colleagues of color. What is especially concerning is the persistent elimination of diverse talent from the medical workforce at a time when retention should be of paramount importance to mitigate an impending workforce shortage, eliminate healthcare disparities and optimize public health."

— Pringl Miller, MD FACS
Founder and Executive Director of Physician Just Equity

"*Belonging in Healthcare* is more than a great book; it's a clarion call to action. Karen Catlin is a shoulder angel with practical advice for the privileged in healthcare to sponsor, champion, amplify, and advocate for their colleagues with less access. The book is a must read, and being a better ally is a must do. We can't hope to tackle inequity and disparities in health outcomes for patients without fostering inclusive workplaces for those who care for them."

— Murray Brozinsky
CEO of Conversa Health (now part of Amwell)

"In *Belonging in Healthcare*, Karen Catlin offers a wealth of poignant observations and practical advice that anyone who works in a healthcare-related field can use to make their work environments more welcoming and inclusive to our patients, students, and colleagues. This is a powerful book that is full of wisdom about issues that can often be difficult to discuss, while also leaving the reader feel inspired and equipped to help address those same challenges."

— Kyle Pusateri, MA, MPH
Chief Operating Officer, Global Brain Health Institute

"*Belonging in Healthcare* is an important read for all healthcare leaders seeking to understand how to shift the workplace culture to one of inclusivity and belonging."

— Resa E. Lewiss, MD
Professor of Emergency Medicine and Radiology,
Founder of *The Visible Voices* podcast

"This book reminds us that there is a subtle but critically important distinction between being a 'knight' and being an ally. In the healthcare industry, being an ally is more than just a moral imperative; it could quite literally be a matter of life and death."

— Dawn Haut, MD
Leader of a large federally qualified health center (FQHC)

"Karen Catlin's *Belonging in Healthcare* shows the importance of allyship in healthcare and then points the way for each of us. Being an ally is a continuous journey of learning and taking action for change, and this book shares practical ways to sponsor others in their careers, expand our networks, improve hiring, make the workplace more inclusive, and more."

— Philip Welkhoff, PhD
Director at a global philanthropic foundation

ALSO BY KAREN CATLIN

Better Allies®
Everyday Actions to Create Inclusive, Engaging Workplaces

The Better Allies® Approach to Hiring

Present! A Techie's Guide to Public Speaking
(with Poornima Vijayashanker)

Belonging in Healthcare

The *Better Allies*® Approach
to Creating More
Inclusive Workplaces

KAREN CATLIN

Better Allies Press

FIRST EDITION, November 2022

Paperback ISBN: 978-1-7327233-6-8

Editing: Sally McGraw
Cover design: Melissa Tenpas
Illustration in Chapter 12: Danielle Coke

Icons in Chapter 1: from the "Noun Project" by Adrien Coquet, Dinosoft Labs, unlimicon, Thomas' designs, ProSymbols, Ben Davis, and corpus delicti. Licensed under Creative Commons CC BY 3.0.

Author's website: www.karencatlin.com

CONTENTS

INTRODUCTION

I almost didn't write this book. After all, who am I to advise healthcare professionals on allyship or anything else? Although I've been a leadership coach and advocate for inclusive workplaces for many years, the bulk of my work experience is as a software engineer and tech executive. I love tech, and I understand how tech companies operate. My understanding of the healthcare industry pales in comparison.

But here's why I felt compelled to bring this book to life. It all started with an email I received a few years ago. Dr. Dawn Haut — who leads a large federally qualified health center (FQHC) in the American Midwest — read my book *Better Allies: Everyday Actions to Create Inclusive, Engaging Workplaces*, and told me:

> This book was recommended to me a while ago. I finally got around to reading it and WOW! The timing could not be more perfect. It was the right message at the right time. I work in a safety net hospital system in the midwest. Our mission is to provide services to under-resourced communities. We are constantly evaluating ways we can be more welcoming in the

neighborhood health centers where we are located. Your book really resonated - both professionally and personally. Thank you!

I connected with her soon after, and she admitted she didn't pick up my book for ages because she thought my background in tech would make the content irrelevant to her work in healthcare. (I get it!) Yet, once she started reading it, she couldn't put it down. She read it cover to cover in one sitting.

I was beyond honored to learn this. When I wrote *Better Allies*, I hoped to make a difference inside the walls of tech companies. Hearing that what I'd written was helping healthcare providers in their critically important and emotionally complex daily work surprised me.

And it planted a seed in my mind: I could do more.

Since then, I've been invited to speak about allyship at large healthcare organizations, medical schools, research institutions, and pharmaceutical companies. My message of simple, everyday actions people can take to become better allies and create more inclusive workplaces resonated with these audiences. I've also heard from healthcare leaders who incorporate ideas from my book into their weekly updates to inspire their staff. This positive reinforcement fueled me to reach more people working in this field, which I hope to do with this new book.

Before I even wrote an outline, I planned out my research. Since I'm not a healthcare professional myself, I knew I had my work cut out for me as an author. I started following thought leaders in healthcare equity on social media, attended webinars on inclusion in healthcare, and read the first (of many) articles published in medical journals. When I started conducting interviews for this book, the first person I reached out to was my childhood next-door neighbor, Dr. Resa E. Lewiss. She's now a professor of emergency medicine & radiology, and she's been instrumental in helping me understand the healthcare landscape.

From there, I interviewed dozens of other people who are underrepresented in medicine, nursing, physical therapy, long-term residential care, and hospital administration. I also spoke with allies who are working hard to use their privilege to create more inclusive spaces. You'll read about their experiences and many other cautionary tales I've collected in the coming chapters.

Along the way, I've also learned about the demographics of healthcare workers. Many of which are equally surprising and frustrating.

For example, the ethnic breakdown of healthcare work is extremely skewed. Of the 9.8 million workers employed as healthcare technicians and practitioners in the United States in 2021, the U.S. Census Bureau found that two-thirds were non-Hispanic white.[1] Another 6.4 million people worked in healthcare support roles[2] — such as nursing assistants, home health aides, and personal care aides — and Black and Hispanic people made up relatively larger shares of this workforce.[3] Basically, the best-paid healthcare jobs are held primarily by white people, while the lower paid roles are held by people of color.[4]

This is especially true among practicing MDs. A 2020 UCLA study found that the proportion of American physicians who are Black has increased by only 4 percent over the past 120 years, and the proportion of doctors who are Black men remains unchanged since 1940, at less than 3 percent.[5]

In addition to racial inequities, the industry is still grappling with gender pay gaps and uneven distribution of roles. Women make up more than 74 percent of full-time, year-round healthcare workers in the United States,[6] but the vast majority of doctors are still male,[7] as are the majority of hospital leaders.[8]

In February 2022, I listened to a Women in Medicine Twitter broadcast and learned that women hold relatively few roles in medical academia. Only 18 percent of deans are women, and about 25 percent of full professors are women. The speakers explained that while women are entering med school, they're not advancing into positions of leadership. Without career growth, some drop out of the field, which directly impacts patient care. Case in point: When women surgeons operate on women patients, there are fewer complications and lower re-admittance rates to the hospital. Patient care suffers because we're not seeing women stay in medicine.[9]

Frustrating disparities also exist in nursing. Less than 13 percent of registered nurses (RNs) working in the United States are men, and yet women nurses earn just 94 percent of what men nurses earn.[10] There's a similar breakdown among licensed practical nurses/licensed vocational nurses (LPNs/LVNs): almost 89 percent are women, while 11 percent are men. Women LPNs/LVNs earn 95 percent of what men earn.[11]

A diverse and equitable healthcare workforce isn't just important, it's critically necessary since these skilled professionals are caring for an increasingly diverse patient population. For instance, less than half of American children age 15 and under are single-race, non-Hispanic white.[12] This shift is expected to continue, with the population group of people who are two or more races steadily increasing through 2060.[13] Additionally there are about 1.2 million nonbinary LGBTQ adults in the United States,[14] and a Pew Research Center survey found that growing shares of US adults know someone who is transgender or who uses gender-neutral pronouns.[15] A diverse group of healthcare providers that reflects the varying cultures, races, genders, and identities of patients they serve will create a safer and more equitable experience for all.

As demographics stand right now, predominantly white and male healthcare professionals don't always deliver the same level of care to patients who are not white, male, or both. Here are two striking examples: Black, American Indian, and Alaska Native women are two to three times more likely to die from pregnancy-related causes than white women. These disparities have "persisted over time," despite the fact that most pregnancy-related deaths are preventable.[16] Racial disparities in treatment for the COVID-19 virus have been well documented, with disproportionately high rates of infection and death among Black, Native American, and Alaska Native populations.[17] The causes behind these poor health outcomes are complex, of course, but implicit bias is undoubtedly a factor. Bias also cuts both ways in the world of healthcare: It may cause doctors to fail to treat patients equitably and also cause patients who distrust healthcare workers of color to reject their guidance and care.

Yet the problem isn't just with the lack of diversity. It's more foundational.

Dr. Ashley McMullen, an assistant professor of medicine at the University of California, San Francisco and a primary care internist based at the San Francisco VA Hospital, encourages us to move beyond anchoring on representation in medicine. While diversity is essential and should be a priority, she shared, "The buck does not stop there. ... Everybody has a role to play to work towards the environments where people can come in and not only see themselves represented, but feel like there's space for them to be seen as an individual and be respected."[18]

This attitude around employee treatment is increasingly crucial as retention issues continue to rise. The aftermath of the pandemic has proven especially challenging; the healthcare sector lost millions of workers during the height of COVID-19, and job recovery has been slow, especially in long-term care. Health aides and assistants, workers from underrepresented racial and ethnic groups, and women with young children have also been slow to return to jobs in healthcare.[19] The field has experienced high turnover rates for several years running, and given the aging Baby Boomer population and probability of another global contagion, this exodus of skilled workers may become a true crisis.

Collectively, I hope we can drive change so that more healthcare workers stay in healthcare, thrive in their careers, create environments where patients feel comfortable and respected, and deliver the best patient outcomes possible.

This book is written as a guide for healthcare professionals everywhere, including those who work in academic settings, community health systems, long-term care facilities, and private practices. Whether you're providing direct patient care, teaching, doing research, or serving in a leadership role, it will help you spot situations where you can be a better ally to colleagues from under-represented groups and identify actionable steps to take that will make a difference.

As I wrote each chapter, I did my best to discuss the challenges facing members of all marginalized groups, with a particular focus on women, Black, Indigenous, people of color, people with disabilities, and LGBTQ+ people. My personal experience as a white, straight, cisgender woman who is not living with a disability is bound to influence my perspective, but I've leaned on research and stories that reflect the experiences of groups to which I do not belong.

Before you read on and dive into the first few chapters, I must emphasize that this book is not about tactics for offering more equitable patient care. While this is an important topic, I don't have the medical expertise to cover it adequately. Plus, as Dr. Deidra C. Crews, Dr. Chiquita A. Collins, and Dr. Lisa A. Cooper wrote in the JAMA Health Forum, separating workforce diversity initiatives from health equity efforts will lead to more effective approaches for both areas. They point out that addressing the two individually could lead to "incorporating the appropriate and distinct expertise, infrastructure, and leaders needed to tackle unique institutional and societal problems."[20]

As a further validation for my focus on workplaces, not health equity, I've learned about large organizations with a Chief Health

Equity Officer and a Chief Diversity and Inclusion Officer. While there's a significant amount of overlap, there is also recognition that the work should reside in different lanes, each with different approaches and governed separately.

Ultimately, I've come to believe that though allyship cannot rectify health equity issues, it can form a foundation to deliver more equitable patient care. As Dr. Haut told me:

> In a community health center, we need to create a respectful, trusting culture in every single part of our being, from our body language to the way we talk and interact with each other. A patient who walks through our front door picks up on our culture immediately. And if that culture doesn't come across as trusting and respectful, a patient won't trust us. They won't share their concerns with us, and they won't believe we'll be good stewards for them. Even if they decide to go through with their appointment, they'll change all their answers to, 'I'm good. No problems here.' While we can check the box that they came in for the appointment, we're not actually providing any value.
>
> So, while addressing inequities in healthcare is critically important, I don't think health disparities should be the focus of your book. Instead, start with the workforce, on every level. For example, our health centers are located in under-resourced neighborhoods and we have prioritized recruiting more people who live in the communities where we are located. But having a diverse workforce is not enough. We need to ensure that the team comes together, holding each other accountable, and not tolerating microaggressions and other forms of non-inclusive behavior. Once there is an inclusive culture, high quality patient care will follow. Healthcare professionals in general are well-trained and know what to do. It is a privilege to be invited into someone's life on such a personal level, but that doesn't mean that the trust can be taken for granted. Regardless of what letters are after your name, trust has to be earned. Our goal is to form a true partnership between patients and the health care team, which can happen in the context of an inclusive healthcare culture.

When she shared that perspective with me, I felt both an incredible responsibility and a call-to-action. I knew I had to write this book, and I'm honored that you're choosing to read it.

Although it's designed to be read cover to cover, I hope you'll also refer to this book whenever you want to level up your ally skills and sharpen your competitive advantage around attracting and retaining healthcare talent. Use it as a resource when you need to help others course-correct in everyday workplace interactions, in team huddles or administrative meetings, at grand rounds or conferences, when hiring employees or evaluating students for training programs, or during performance review time. I'd love to see this book on desks everywhere, serving as an accessible and supportive resource for aspiring allies and the underrepresented people they work with and for.

Being an ally is a journey, and it's a journey that I, myself, am on. I'm thrilled that you'll be joining me. Let's go.

PART ONE

STARTING THE JOURNEY

1

THE ALLY JOURNEY

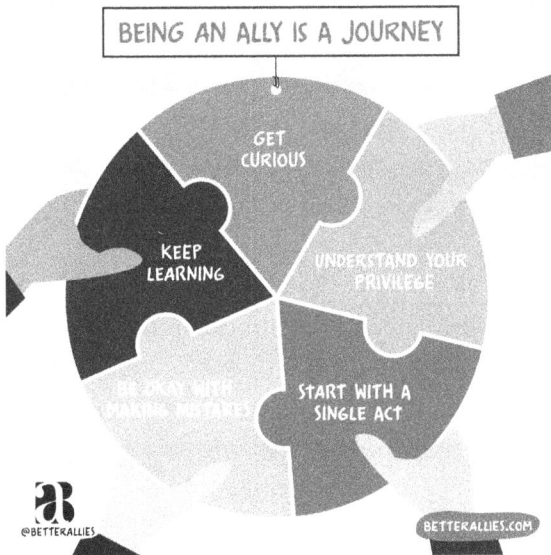

Allyship is a process. Even seasoned allies with wide-open minds are constantly learning and absorbing new information about how to leverage their privilege to support people who are different from them. I'm one of them! After all, we each have perspectives that are shaped by our own experiences, so we can't possibly imagine or understand all of the other viewpoints that exist in the world. We must learn about them as we encounter them and adjust our mindsets accordingly. So your first tip for being an ally is to **get curious**: Be open to learning, improving, and changing your opinion.

This may seem frustrating at first because it's an abstract, long-term goal with no definite end points. I get it. Many of us would like to earn an ally badge and consider ourselves lifetime members of the Genuinely Good Human Beings Club. So, I wrote this book to help everyone who sees allyship as a goal to reframe it as a journey. As you read these chapters, you'll move forward, and I guarantee you'll pick up actionable ideas to be a better ally.

Instead of feeling frustrated that you'll never reach some mythical, fully-fledged ally status, remember that we're all learning together. We all need to start by getting curious. The ally journey is an enlightening and worthwhile one, even though it's a perpetually ongoing one. And people with privilege who are *truly* dedicated to empowering all embrace the fact that doing so means being in a constant state of learning.

Speaking of which, the time has come to discuss privilege in both abstract and concrete terms. I promise to keep it non-judgmental and encouragement-focused.

Let's talk about the "p-word"

Understanding your privilege is key to becoming a better ally. At its core, privilege is a set of unearned benefits given to people who fit into a specific social group. Due to our race, class, gender, sexual orientation, language, geographic location, ability, religion, and more, we all have greater or lesser access to resources and social power.

People who are marginalized in multiple ways experience amplified marginalization and drastically reduced privilege. This is due to intersectionality, the fact that the combination of someone's identities creates an intersection of overlapping and compounded oppressions.[21] I appreciate this example by Kittu Pannu, who wrote about intersectionality in the LGBT community for Impakter:

> One could assume that a black, queer woman would, in essence, have a more difficult life experience than a heterosexual white male just by virtue of her experiences as a woman, compounded with her experience as a black person, and topping it off with her queer identity. Her life will be just a little harsher, her earning potential just short of the people around her, her ability to say with certainty that she gets everything she deserves not as strong as a white male's ability. She would have to work that much harder to be taken seriously in today's heteronormative, white, male-dominated world.[22]

The term *intersectionality* was originally coined by Kimberlé Crenshaw, who pointed out that in nearly all cases, being marginalized in multiple ways leads to diminished privilege and increased risk of discrimination and violence.[23]

Being a member of more than one underrepresented group can also make it hard to know why you might be experiencing discrimination. As Lorna Rodriguez, the vice chair of surgery at City of Hope in Southern California, told me, "If I'm not being treated well, I don't know if it's because I'm Puerto Rican, a woman, a lesbian, or a left-handed surgeon. It might be because of any one of these identities, all of them, or none at all."

But, regardless of our identities, all of us need to realize we have some privilege.

Now, here's where it gets tricky: Privilege is often invisible to those who have it. This means that many of us can get defensive when someone points out our privilege. It's tempting to think of privilege as being associated with extreme unearned advantages like having a massive family trust fund or being related to some influential person. Having your privilege pointed out might feel like the equivalent of being told that you're lazy, lucky, or undeserving of good things — or that your life has been easy. Many of us might be quick to respond that we've had our fair share of difficulties and faced down prejudices, too.

I have to admit I have fallen into this trap. Years ago, I remember my reaction when hearing someone say, "It's hard for me to get ahead in my career because I don't have a degree from a name-brand university." I found myself thinking, Well, sure, I went to an Ivy League school, but I did the work to get accepted, took out loans, and held a campus job to pay for it, and it wasn't exactly easy to graduate. I worked hard! And now I work just as hard to get ahead in my career as a woman in a male-dominated field. Fortunately, I didn't say any of that out loud. If I had, I'll bet the conversation would have ended right there.

Getting defensive means forgetting that privilege is simply a system of advantages granted to all people in a given group. It's a social structure that has become endemic to human cultures. It's not about who you are as an individual as much as it is about which groups you belong to and how society views and treats those groups. A person isn't privileged because of being a rotten, freeloading bum; they're privileged because they're white, middle-class, or cisgender.

Being privileged doesn't mean you've never worked hard, and it doesn't necessarily mean that your life has been easy. Here's a fabulous analogy from Sian Ferguson via the website Everyday Feminism:

> Let's say both you and your friend decide to go cycling. You decide to cycle for the same distance, but you take different routes. You take a route that is a bit bumpy. More often than not, you go down roads that are at a slight decline. It's very hot, but the wind is usually at your back. You eventually get to

your destination, but you're sunburnt, your legs are aching, you're out of breath, and you have a cramp.

When you eventually meet up with your friend, she says that the ride was awful for her. It was also bumpy. The road she took was at an incline the entire time. She was even more sunburnt than you because she had no sunscreen. At one point, a strong gust of wind blew her over and she hurt her foot. She ran out of water halfway through. When she hears about your route, she remarks that your experience seemed easier than hers.

Does that mean that you didn't cycle to the best of your ability? Does it mean that you didn't face obstacles? Does it mean that you didn't work hard? No. What it means is that you didn't face the obstacles she faced.

Privilege doesn't mean your life is easy or that you didn't work hard. It simply means that you don't have to face the obstacles others have to endure. It means that life is more difficult for those who don't have the systemic privilege you have.[24]

Look across the healthcare field, and you'll have no trouble finding people with more privilege than others. Many of them are older white, straight, male doctors or administrators. Perhaps they attended highly selective medical schools. They may have held leadership positions in professional organizations. They probably have strong networks of people in similar positions of privilege. They are the majority.

Yet privilege is not limited to straight, white guys.

I'm a white, straight, cisgender woman who's not living with a disability, which means I have a lot of privilege myself. I hold a degree from Brown University. I'm a published author and a TEDx speaker. Formerly, I was a vice president of engineering at a well-known tech company. Yup. That's a lot of privilege. And my experience is a reminder that people who are members of systematically oppressed groups (such as women working in tech) can still have privilege due to their membership in other groups (such as being white, straight, etc.).

Fifty potential privileges in healthcare workplaces

In my book *Better Allies*, I created a list of "50 Potential Privileges in the Workplace" to help people understand their privilege. It's been more effective than I ever could have imagined. I regularly hear from readers how it helped them realize that many things that come easy for them, things they take for granted, are not universally experienced by all of their coworkers. That realization helps them become more empathetic and provides a foundational awareness that all allies need.

The list of 50 potential privileges has also been incredibly popular. The free pdf version on my website is downloaded hundreds of times every day.

I knew I had to create a version of this list for healthcare settings. Many items would stay the same, but some would need updating to incorporate what I learned about privilege through my many interviews for this book. What you'll find below is this updated list.

As you read it, keep a tally. Then review it again, reflecting on the benefits or obstacles you face at work because of each privilege you have or don't have. Note any items that surprise you and make you wonder, Does anyone actually face this challenge?

1. I'm white (or I can pass as white).
2. I'm male.
3. I'm straight.
4. I am cisgender, identifying as the gender I was assigned at birth.
5. I'm not living with disabilities, visible or otherwise.
6. I have a degree and certification that are recognized by the country where I live.
7. I attended an elite university.
8. I have an impressive list of credentials after my name.
9. English is my first language (in English-speaking countries).

10. I don't receive comments about my accent or how I pronounce certain words.
11. My job doesn't require me to work nights or weekends.
12. I've never been passed over for a job (or fired from one) based on my gender, race or ethnicity, religion, age, body shape or size, disability, or sexual orientation.
13. I've never been bullied or harassed by patients because of my gender identity, race or ethnicity, religion, age, body shape or size, disability, or sexual orientation.
14. I am partnered and feel comfortable speaking openly about my significant other.
15. My partner takes on a large share of household and family responsibilities.
16. I don't have to worry about how having children will impact my career or how an unwanted pregnancy could derail my career.
17. I'm rarely, if ever, late to work or miss work because of a child's illness or family emergency.
18. I feel welcome at networking opportunities.
19. I'm not asked to do menial tasks that colleagues of another gender or race are asked to do.
20. Others don't routinely assume I'm at a lower seniority level than I am.
21. Others don't call me by my first name while using titles for my peers of a different gender, race, or professional role.
22. Others don't make up nicknames for me because my name is difficult for them to pronounce.
23. I feel comfortable actively and effectively contributing to team huddles, morning rounds, and other meetings I attend.
24. I'm rarely interrupted or ignored in conversations.
25. I'm confident that if I raise an idea, I'll be credited for that idea.
26. I recently received feedback about a job skill I need to learn to grow my career.
27. I can devote time to learning new job skills and can join professional development sessions offered at my workplace.

28. I can talk about political or identity-oriented extracurricular activities without fear of judgment or bias from colleagues.
29. I can observe the holy days in my religious tradition without using vacation days.
30. I'm provided with gloves, gowns, and other PPE that fit my body size (including during pregnancy).
31. I have access to scrubs or a uniform that meet my religious requirements.
32. I haven't been asked how I rigged the system to get into my medical training program.
33. I've never been called a "diversity hire."
34. When meeting people at professional events, they assume I'm attending in a professional role (versus being the partner of an attendee).
35. At events, people don't mistake me for a member of the support or catering staff.
36. I feel physically safe at work and professional events.
37. I feel safe leaving work late at night and going home after evening events.
38. I don't receive unwanted sexual advances at work.
39. I haven't had to change jobs because of harassment.
40. I have stable housing.
41. I'm confident that if I lost my job, I'd be able to land another one without worrying about paying bills.
42. I can afford to join out-of-office lunches or after-work social activities.
43. I can manage monthly payments on any debt I have, and I'm not anxious about the loans I took out to pay for my education.
44. I never have to decide which bills to pay or go without meals because I can't afford food.
45. I'm not financially supporting a parent, grandparent, sibling, or extended family member.
46. I don't have a long career gap on my résumé.
47. I've never been arrested, incarcerated, or charged with a criminal offense.

48. People never touch me or my hair without consent.
49. I don't receive abusive comments on social media.
50. I don't remember the last time someone was condescending or overly pedantic when explaining a topic to me.

Even if you happen to have all 50 of the above privileges, the intent here is not to make you feel guilty or ashamed. By contrast, the invitation is simply to be aware of your advantages and leverage them empathetically; beating yourself up about them is totally counterproductive, but **understanding your privilege** is a critical part of the allyship journey.

It's also worth noting that privilege is often a key ingredient in cultivating professional confidence — confidence that you can leverage your network to get a new job or a leadership role in a professional society. Confidence to pursue locum assignments without being concerned about your next full-time position. Confidence to submit articles or papers for publication, find a publisher for your book, or score a speaking engagement. Confidence that people will direct questions to you if you're the expert or the most senior person in the room. Confidence that you're getting paid equitably. Confidence that people believe you landed your current role because of experience and potential, not solely because you helped your organization meet a diversity goal. The list goes on.

Because of my privilege, I know I've received many benefits over my career, and those benefits have empowered me with confidence. I feel ready to use my standing to help foster confidence in others now, and if you are also in a position to do so, I hope you'll join me.

Roles allies can play

It's up to people who hold positions of privilege to be active allies to those with less access and take responsibility for making systemic changes that will help others be more successful. Active allies utilize their credibility to create more inclusive workplaces where everyone can thrive, and they find ways to make their privilege work for others.

Changing entire systems can feel daunting, but wielding privilege as an ally doesn't have to be complicated. **Start with a single act** and build from there. Try to make one aspect of your department's culture more inclusive, or speak up when you see bias crop up in workplace conversation. We all know the saying "a journey of a thousand miles begins with a single step," and allyship is the same. You've got to start somewhere, so choose a single act as your allyship launchpad.

If you'd like to make sure that your single act is part of a strategic plan, consider the type of allyship *role* you'd like to play at your hospital, clinic, lab, or office. For my book *Better Allies,* I came up with seven archetypes to help readers explore the many ways allies can make a difference. Like my list of 50 privileges, these roles have been a helpful tool for my readers to understand there is no single definition of what it means to support colleagues from underrepresented groups. I knew I needed to update them for healthcare, so I've added examples and ideas specific to the field.

Let's dive in.

The Sponsor

I once worked for a software company that was acquired by a larger company. In the first few months following the acquisition, I noticed something interesting. My new manager said things in meetings along the lines of "What I learned from Karen Catlin is the following ..."

By doing this, he helped me build credibility with my new colleagues. He took action as an ally, using his position of privilege to sponsor me. His shout-outs made a difference and definitely made me feel great.

Sponsors can also recommend someone for a leadership role on a committee or board of directors. When Dr. Matthew Chow was on the nominating committee for the board of Doctors of BC — an association of 14,000 physicians, residents, and medical students in British Columbia — he recommended and advocated for a woman from an underrepresented race to be a member of their board. Sometimes, sponsors don't even realize they're acting as allies. As he shared, "I don't know if I deserve to have this labeled as allyship; I just thought I was doing a good thing for someone."[25]

When an ally takes on the role of the Sponsor, they vocally support the work of colleagues from underrepresented groups in all contexts, specifically in situations that will help boost those colleagues' standing and reputations.

Other ways to act as a Sponsor:

- Talk about the expertise you see in others, especially during performance calibrations, nomination discussions, and promotion decisions.

- Recommend people for high-profile assignments, learning opportunities, and committee leadership roles.
- Write powerful letters of recommendation.
- Share colleagues' career goals with decision-makers.

(Much more on sponsorship in the coming chapters.)

The Champion

In March 2020, I saw this tweet from Dr. Renzo Guinto:[26]

> **Renzo Guinto**   ...
> @RenzoGuinto
>
> Just declined an invite to speak in a #COVID19 webinar when I learned that there is no single woman in a panel of 8 men (I will be 9th). Even in crisis time, & especially in this time, we must remain consistent with our convictions. #NoToManels #WomeninGlobalHealth #MaleAllyship

All-male panels (known as "manels") are so widespread in healthcare that an increasing number of individuals and organizations are pledging to eradicate them. In 2019, *The Lancet* adopted a No All-Male Panel Policy, acknowledging that the traditional predominance of male speakers excludes the full breadth of available expertise and opinion. Their editors will not serve as panelists at public conferences or events when there are no women on the panels, and they're committed to gender balance in events they sponsor or organize.[27]

Some male speakers, such as Michael Strübin, Director of Digital Health at MedTech Europe, have even added, "Won't speak on all-male panels" to their Twitter bios. White people of any gender can use a version that says, "Won't speak on all-white panels." (I've done this myself.)

When an ally takes on the role of the Champion, they act similarly to the Sponsor but do so in more public venues. They work in solidarity with initiatives designed to promote more inclusion, taking public stances. Champions also willingly defer to colleagues from underrepresented groups at morning rounds, noon conferences with residents, administrative meetings, and professional events, sending a meaningful message to large audiences.

Other ways to act as a Champion:

- Direct questions about specific topics to those with subject-matter expertise instead of answering them yourself.
- Advocate for more women, people of color, and members of other underrepresented groups as keynote speakers and panelists. (More on this in Chapter 6.)
- If you are asked to take a leadership role on a professional committee and know someone from an underrepresented group who'd be an equally good fit (or better), recommend that person (after asking them first if they'd like you to put them forward).
- Be vocal and genuine in supporting policies and initiatives to create more inclusive workplaces.

The Amplifier

In a webinar on allyship hosted by the American Association of Women in Radiology, Dr. Beth McFarland shared a fantastic example of amplifier allyship. She explained how Dr. Susan Asher, a woman more senior than she, would amplify her in meetings. She'd say, "I'd like to reinforce what Beth just said." Those words made McFarland feel what she just said was important, and they helped amplify her point.[28]

Here's another way to be an amplifier. Dr. Marina Del Rios Rivera, an associate professor in emergency medicine at the University of Iowa, remembers being a junior faculty member at a national committee meeting. They were discussing disparities in cardiac arrest outcomes for people of color. "Someone commented that it didn't make sense to consider the disparities given the overall low survival rates, and instead we should focus on a model system of care that would benefit everyone," Del Rios Rivera told me. She then pushed back, pointing out that within those so-called model systems, not everyone was benefiting equally. And that as you work toward equity, you might identify things that are not being done well for the overall population. She also underscored the importance of discussing this topic more frequently and openly, especially as the US population becomes more diverse. However, as she spoke, it became clear she was losing the battle. "But then this older white man stepped up and gave this beautiful speech about how the whole concept of public health is thinking about the health of everyone, including those that are the most vulnerable in society," Del Rios Rivera shared. "When he spoke, the room finally agreed that we needed to talk about it." She added, "I was grateful that this one white male in the room had the guts to speak up."

When an ally takes on the role of the Amplifier, they work to ensure that marginalized voices are both heard and respected. This type of allyship can take many forms, but it is focused on representation within communication.

Other ways to act as an Amplifier:

- When someone proposes a good idea, repeat it, and give them credit.
- Create a code of conduct for shift huddles, morning rounds, meetings, and any shared communication medium, including email, chat, and other discussion forums.
- Invite members of underrepresented groups within your organization to speak at meetings, write for institution-wide newsletters, or take on other highly visible roles.

The Advocate

Over her career, Dr. Del Rios Rivera has mentored many Black people, Latinx people, and others from underrepresented minority groups. She often tells them that, while she knows how valuable their work is, they need to realize that everyone will be looking at them under a magnifying glass. Her message? "You are going to have to be not just good, but great." She encourages her mentees to partner with her on research projects, create abstracts, and write papers to round out their CVs. She emphasizes, "It's not going to be enough to have the A grades and the good evaluations. I want to help ensure that their records are competitive enough so that they can get to whatever stage in their training they want."

Advocates might simply validate someone's work. After some negative experiences during her medical training, Dr. Jenna C. Lester admits that she lost some confidence in her original work and ideas. In an episode of *The Visible Voices* podcast, she shared, "It's scary having someone send you what feels like a professionally threatening email when you're trying to publish something." She credits her mentor, Dr. Meg Chren, who kept telling her the paper was too important not to be published. Chren pushed and advocated for her, which had an incredible impact on Lester. "Through that, I realized that I do actually have a very important message, and this person who is so accomplished has validated that for me. I'm so grateful."[29]

Here's one more way an Advocate might take action. A study of nearly 40 million surgical referrals found that male physicians had a strong preference for referring their patients to male surgeons.[30] Over time, this biased tendency disadvantages women surgeons, leading to lower volumes of referrals and contributing to pay disparity. I can only hope there are male physicians out there disrupting this norm and ensuring that they are referring patients to women and other surgeons from underrepresented groups.

When an ally takes on the role of the Advocate, they use their power and influence to bring peers from underrepresented groups into exclusive circles. The Advocate recognizes and addresses unjust omissions, holding themselves and their peers accountable for including qualified colleagues of all genders, races, abilities, ages, body shapes and sizes, religions, and sexual orientations.

Other ways to act as an Advocate:

- Look closely at the invite lists for events, strategic planning meetings, dinners with influential people, and other career-building opportunities. If you see that someone from a marginalized group is missing, advocate for them to be invited.

- If you're in a position to refer patients to specialists, ensure that your referral list is diverse.
- Offer to introduce colleagues from underrepresented groups to influential people in your network.
- Ask someone from an underrepresented group to be a co-author or collaborator on a proposal or conference submission.
- Encourage people from underrepresented groups to publish their work, and if they are unpublished, offer to help them through the process.

The Scholar

I spoke with my college friend Dr. Paul Haut, who most recently worked as the chief operating officer for a large children's hospital in the Midwest, overseeing a workforce of 5,000 people. When I asked why the topic of inclusion in healthcare workplaces was important to him, he emphasized that providing the best patient care requires you to have respect for people throughout your workplace. Haut admits he had a big awakening soon after George Floyd's murder in May 2020, when he realized, as he put it, "I can't provide equitable care to the patients unless I'm truly living that as an organization with our own teammates. Because if they don't feel respected, how are they going to translate respect to the ones they're caring for?"

Haut then embarked on a journey to learn about addressing racism in the workplace. "It was an intentional, intensive dive into trying to understand and educate myself to even begin to know how to act differently." He added, "This wasn't like continuing education where I was earning credits to maintain a certification; I needed to rethink my whole construct."

(As part of his scholarship, Haut read my book *Better Allies*. I'm forever grateful that he passed his copy to his wife, Dr. Dawn Haut. As I mentioned in the Introduction, she's the person who catalyzed me to write the book you're now reading.)

When an ally takes on the role of the Scholar, they seek to learn as much as possible about the challenges and prejudices faced by colleagues from marginalized groups. It's important to note that Scholars never insert their own opinions, experiences, or ideas, but instead simply listen and learn. They also don't expect marginalized people to provide links to research proving that bias exists or summaries of best practices. Scholars do their own research to seek out relevant information.

Other ways to act as a Scholar:

- Investigate publications, podcasts, or social media by and about underrepresented groups within your field.

- Ask coworkers from marginalized groups if they'd be comfortable talking with you about their experience working at your organization or institution.

- If your employer or professional association has specific discussion forums for underrepresented groups, ask if they'd be comfortable letting you join to observe. Asking is essential: Your presence may cause members to censor themselves, so be sure to check in before showing up.

The Upstander

In late 2021, Dr. Kelly Paradis, an associate professor of medical physics at Michigan Medicine, was surprised to learn that her institution wasn't sure if they would participate in the new Ann Arbor city ordinance requiring free menstrual and sanitary products in all public bathrooms. After all, the ordinance was designed to make menstrual products more accessible and reduce inequality. The university is located in the city, but operates outside of its jurisdiction and was not required to follow the ordinance. So, Paradis took action, purchasing tampons from Costco for the bathrooms in her department. She also emailed the DEI committee chairperson, sharing her surprise about the university's decision. Although she doesn't know if that email made an impact, the good news is that Michigan announced soon afterward that they would offer free feminine hygiene products in their buildings.

Here's another example of upstander allyship. On Twitter, Vidya Pundit-Dermody, head of nursing for Children's Services at Medway NHS Foundation Trust, posted, "For the first time in my 21 years in the NHS, a parent asked for a white doctor." When Pundit-Dermody heard this happened to a group of doctors who are members of ethnic minority groups, she accompanied them on the final consultation and spoke up. "I told [the patient] in no uncertain terms that this was not a reasonable request and that we would not be facilitating this request."[31]

The Upstander is someone who sees omissions or wrong-doing and acts to combat them. When an ally takes on the role of the Upstander, that ally acts as the *opposite* of a bystander. They push back on offensive comments or jokes, even if no one within earshot might be offended or hurt.

Other ways to act as an Upstander:

- Always speak up if you witness behavior or speech that is non-inclusive, degrading, or offensive. Explain your stance so everyone knows why you are raising the issue.
- During rounds, shift huddles, and other meetings, shut down off-topic questions that are asked only to test the person speaking.
- Take action if you see anyone being bullied or harassed. Simply insert yourself into a conversation with a comment like, "Hi! What are you folks discussing?" and then check in with the victim privately. Ask if they are okay and if they want you to say something to the harassers or a supervisor.

The Confidant

During the 12 years Dr. John Jones (not his real name) spent as chief of an emergency department (ED), he frequently would hear from medical specialists that they were being consulted too frequently. For example, after being called at 3 a.m. for input on a fracture, an orthopedist might complain to Jones that the ED doctor on duty should have been able to handle it on their own. For Jones, receiving and monitoring these issues was simply part of the job. However, at one point, he told me he started receiving a disproportionate number of complaints about one Black ED doctor asking for input from specialists. So Jones sat down with this doctor to ask about his threshold for calling a consult and his comfort level with managing patient needs himself.

Jones was surprised by the Black doctor's response, so much so that he remembers it clearly to this day. That doctor said he felt he needed to consult more often because he was Black. If he were to make a mistake or a wrong decision without consulting, he would be subject to more criticism because of his race. At that point, a light came on for Jones. He got some insight into this doctor's experience growing up, going through the educational system and medical training, constantly feeling like he needed to perform at a higher level or make fewer mistakes. Because of his race, he chose that practice style. Jones, who is white, would never have known or been able to support him if he hadn't taken the time to talk to him.

When an ally takes on the role of the Confidant, that ally creates a safe space for members of underrepresented groups to express their concerns, frustrations, and needs. Simply listening to their stories and trusting that they're being truthful creates a protective layer of support.

Other ways to act as a Confidant:

- Believe others' experiences. Don't assume something couldn't happen just because you haven't personally experienced it.
- Listen and ask questions when someone describes an experience you haven't had. Don't jump in with your personal stories.
- If you are a supervisor, hold regular "office hours" and encourage all of your team members to speak with you about issues troubling them.

The perfectly imperfect ally

In this chapter, I've shared just a few examples of how people with privilege have acted as allies in specific roles. It's important to note that, while these people all choose to use their power to support others, they're humans and, therefore, not perfect. And they don't need to be. They simply need to **be okay with making mistakes**.

It can be hard to have conversations about race, especially if you haven't experienced the racial inequity and systemic oppression other people face. Or to discuss gender inequity as a man in a male-dominated setting. Or, if you're cisgender, to know how to support a coworker who is going through a gender transition. You may be concerned you'll make a mistake and say the wrong thing. Or act in a way that's not helpful and possibly even hurtful. It can be much easier to pull back from these conversations and become simply bystanders.

But here's the thing. The world needs more Upstanders. We need more people who see wrongdoing and take action. People who push for change. People who aren't comfortable with the status quo, even though they may have benefited from it.

We also need people who are okay with making mistakes along the way. I appreciate what David Leonhardt, editor of "The Morning" newsletter from the *New York Times*, shared when he encouraged journalists to perform a yearly pundit accountability exercise:

> There is no shame in being wrong at times. Everybody is, including knowledgeable experts. The world is a messy, uncertain place. The only way to be right all the time is to be silent or say nothing interesting.[32]

Let that sink in: The only way to be right all the time is to be silent.

Yet staying silent when we see biased, offensive, or inappropriate behavior doesn't make us neutral, it makes us complicit. It means we're okay with the status quo. It means the opposite of allyship.

In an article titled "Get it wrong for me: What I need from allies," Megan Carpenter of Microsoft wrote:

> I want a bunch of people who are interested in becoming allies to me to get it wrong. Because I promise, you will get it wrong, likely more than once. But please get it wrong, for me. Be wrong on my behalf. Try stuff, learn stuff, make attempts, and fail. Embrace the discomfort of not knowing, of not being certain, of not understanding, and then be motivated enough to learn and get better. I will give you grace if you give me effort.[33]

Let's all put in the effort and be okay with making mistakes. Because the best allies are willing to make mistakes and keep trying. They acknowledge when they're wrong or could do better and correct their course. They resist getting defensive and insisting that they're already doing enough. They listen. They iterate. They accept their mistakes and **keep learning**.

By the way, I make mistakes, too. More than I care to admit. With each mistake I make, I have an opportunity to learn and do things differently. I also share them in my weekly "5 Ally Actions" newsletter so others can learn with me. If you'd like to be one of them, head to *www.betterallies.com* and subscribe to receive it every Friday.

Being an ally is an active choice and a brave one. It's normal and natural to fear making a social faux pas or to worry about insulting someone whose life experiences differ vastly from yours. But working toward allyship requires us to be courageous about making mistakes, knowing that any brief discomfort we experience is inconsequential compared to the good we may do as active allies.

Fortunately, there are many opportunities in every healthcare workplace to listen, learn, and take action as allies. It's something anyone can do. In the coming chapters, we'll explore how to spot situations where you can be a better ally and everyday actions that will make a difference.

Actions for Better Allies:
Understand Your Privilege and Use It for Good

An essential part of allyship is being open to learning, improving, and taking action.

- Review the list of 50 potential privileges in this chapter. How many apply to you? What benefits or obstacles do you face at work because of each privilege you have or don't have?
- Identify at least one way you can be a better ally, using the archetypes in this chapter.
- Understand that being an ally is a journey. We all make mistakes. Don't let that hold you back from taking action. Don't opt out.

2

KNIGHTS VERSUS ALLIES

My own allyship journey began when I noticed some alarming trends in behavior all around me. People who seemed to care about diversity and inclusion in their workplaces, but made insensitive remarks in meetings. Or they wrote quick messages, using non-inclusive gendered language by mistake. Or they laughed at jokes without stopping to think about who they would offend. I knew I'd done all of those things myself, too, and wanted to find ways to change.

I may have been naive, but I thought I could foster more inclusive workplaces everywhere by helping people spot non-inclusive situations and take everyday actions to disrupt them. I wanted to help everyone act as better allies. (Myself included.) And what's the first thing anyone does when they want to change the world? They start a Twitter handle, of course.

I named mine @BetterAllies and launched it in 2014. Back in those early days, I did what I hoped would organically grow my followers. I tweeted frequently, sometimes with images that might attract more attention, and I followed other people tweeting about inclusion and diversity, hoping they would follow me back. I also wrote some articles about why I started @BetterAllies.

In one of these articles,[34] I described my mission and shared some examples of my posts on Twitter. In publishing it, I hoped it would help increase awareness of my initiative. I also had a feeling it might generate some criticism. As Jason van Gumster, a coder and author, says, "Haters are an inevitable part of sharing your work."[35]

I mentally prepared myself on publication day, hoping for support yet ready to handle any backlash. When I checked Twitter early in the morning, I saw many great comments and retweets of the article. Phew!

Next came responses from some folks who disagreed, saying things like, "I'm here to earn my paycheck, not take care of other people." (Expletives removed. Several of these folks needed to both vent *and* swear.) And there were a handful of pointed jabs calling me a creep and instructing me to eff off — nothing I couldn't handle.

But then — a surprise. I saw a few critical tweets that made me think deeply about my work on Better Allies and how it might be perceived. These tweets were from women who completely dismissed the need for allies. Women who didn't want to be placed in a homogeneous group that couldn't speak for themselves. Women who bristled at the implied need for knights to ride in on white horses and save them from toxic workplace cultures.

I'd expected to hear from some haters, but to learn from them? That caught me off guard.

It also got me thinking about how actions that were meant to be supportive could feel patronizing. I then realized that good intentions were never going to be enough. Real allies also needed to consider the repercussions of their actions carefully. Those tweets also helped me refine my own goals: I don't want to be a knight riding in to save the day. I don't want to view anyone who is underrepresented as a virtual damsel in distress. I don't want to serve as anyone's protector. No. Never. Instead, I want to transform current workplace cultures into ones where everyone can thrive. I want to question the norms that have allowed folks like me to get ahead, encourage productive conversation around prejudices, and take everyday actions to support members of marginalized groups. And I want to bring others along on this journey.

Tech policy expert and community organizer Corey Ponder wrote about coming to the same realization in an article titled "Allyship is Not the Hero's Journey."

> Underserved and underrepresented communities aren't looking for — nor do they need — heroes or last-minute miracles. Allyship isn't about being a savior. Allyship is the journey of the trusted sidekick. And that is because sidekicks do three things very well —
> 1. They show up for everyday moments.
> 2. They are willing to confront ugly truths, especially about themselves.
> 3. They use their special abilities to help the protagonist achieve their goals.
> … When we show up as trusted sidekicks, we create a permissive environment that allows people to be their most authentic and productive selves. We empower people to fight for and build the world they want to see. And that is the true journey of an ally.[36]

Like Ponder, I know that part of that journey will involve teaching myself and others how to translate our heartfelt intentions into meaningful, constructive actions — and avoid being inadvertently condescending or patronizing. We also need to be sure to avoid making it all about ourselves.

How to tell a knight from an ally

So, what are the differences between ally actions and knight actions? I believe it comes down to two things: mindset and systemic change. Allies take action to *empower* individuals, not to rescue them. Allies also seek to create systemic changes instead of making one-off savior moves. Here are some examples.

Scenario 1

Dr. Chang (not her real name) noticed one of her colleagues was looking especially tired after an overnight shift, and she asked him, "If you don't mind, may I ask how old you are?" He answered, "Sixty-six." She told him that many emergency departments have policies where physicians over a certain age don't have to work overnight shifts and offered to check to see if they had such a policy. When Chang asked about it, their scheduler told her, "Yes, we have a policy, but they need to ask to be taken off night shifts."

Chang was floored and immediately told her colleague he could request not to be assigned overnight shifts. She also told another older colleague about it. These one-off moves helped them both.

But that's not all. When a new scheduler was hired, Chang asked him to share the policy with all the faculty. He agreed and sent out a global email to everyone. As a result, not only did everyone now know that faculty over 55 didn't have to take overnight shifts, but they also learned about another aspect of the policy: pregnant people in their third trimester were also excused from these shifts. By encouraging the scheduler to proactively share the policy, Chang empowered many of her colleagues to request a more reasonable schedule.

Scenario 2

Dr. Eileen Barrett is an associate professor of medicine and the director of continuing medical education at the University of New Mexico. In a blog post for Women in Medicine, she described meeting two students whose first languages were not English. One was raised in a Spanish-speaking home, and the other in a Navajo- and English-speaking home. Barrett had heard of a medical school that planned to say the Hippocratic Oath in several languages during graduation, and she asked if these students would want that to happen at theirs. They both said yes.[37]

That interaction led Barrett to investigate which languages the World Medical Association (WMA) maintained for the Physician's Pledge, and she petitioned to include Navajo. (Spanish was already available.)

Acting as a knight, Barrett could have worked with a translator to create a Navajo version and requested that her university read both Navajo and Spanish along with the English version at their upcoming graduation. This would have resulted in a more inclusive experience for at least two students and their families, but it wouldn't help others who speak Navajo at other medical schools.

To have an even more significant impact, Barrett not only got the translation done and read at her students' graduation ceremony, she also asked the WMA to accept the Navajo version as an official translation of the Physician's Pledge. Which they did.

By the way, Barrett didn't stop there. She collaborated with a former resident to get the Pledge translated into Arabic, and she's also working with a leader in Zuni Pueblo on another Indigenous language translation.

The importance of Barrett's allyship may be understated, but it's impactful. Remember that student who was raised in a

Spanish-speaking home? She told Barrett that the only part of any of her graduations her mother ever understood was when the Pledge was said in Spanish at her medical school graduation.[38]

Scenario 3

Dr. Benito Nieves (not his real name) is Puerto Rican and was one of only a few Latinx medical students in his program in med school. He told me, "I went into medicine, wanting to serve my community, knowing that there are disparities that exist not just for Puerto Ricans, but for the broader Latinx community as well." I wasn't surprised when he mentioned that, in medical school, when he came across patients who spoke only Spanish or had limited English language skills, he would translate for them and get involved with their care. There weren't many others who could speak Spanish, and he felt a responsibility to help them get equitable care.

But Nieves faced a problem. He soon realized that by focusing on only Spanish-speaking patients, he couldn't get enough clinical experience in diagnosing and treating a wide variety of conditions, whether chronic liver disease, COPD, or something else. While other students would jump at opportunities to learn about new conditions when patients came into their clinic, he continued to focus on helping Spanish-speaking individuals. After all, they needed his advocacy. But he was limiting his learning by working so often with the Spanish-speaking population; they came in with whatever they came in with.

He felt judged by others who couldn't see why he missed the mark or wasn't exposed to particular diagnoses. Even though he was helping the team overall and centering on patient care, he didn't feel as valued as his peers.

Could a knight have spoken up and ensured that Nieves could help diagnose the next patient presenting with COPD symptoms? Sure, but better would be to seek systemic changes that would remove his burden of having to translate for every Spanish-speaking patient. For example, the hospital could invest in adequate translation services. An ally could also advocate that the hospital track the changing demographics of their community to ensure that the translation services would meet its needs.

Scenario 4

Cynthia Walsh, who has 45 years of experience in acute care and nursing home administration, told me about a time when she helped a talented nurse on her staff become certified in wound care and infection control by covering the cost of the program. Yet, Walsh's boss had recently retired, and her replacement started questioning the department's support of this nurse's professional development. Eventually, she blurted out, "You know, we can barely understand her. I don't know why we are investing so much in her." (The nurse was from Vietnam, and, while fluent in English, had a strong accent.)

Walsh had the perfect response. "Our not being able to understand her is just as much our problem. That's not a reason not to invest in her. And I can work with her on that." As a knight, Walsh set up this nurse for success, who became a valuable wound care nurse for that facility through the COVID-19 pandemic.

I asked Walsh if she acted more systemically, not just advocating for this nurse but also for the career development of all the nurses. Her answer? "Definitely." Working with their administrator and the HR director, Walsh helped to set up career ladders, offered lots of training, and changed the criteria on performance evaluations to recognize and reward staff. She followed up on her knight actions with broader-impact ally actions.

Scenario 5

Say a member of your staff is a nonbinary individual, and you've had several conversations about the restroom signage in your clinic. You both agree that it's time to update the labels, and since your department takes up the whole floor, you have the power to spearhead some changes.

A knight might tape "All Gender" signs to the restroom doors and proudly make an announcement to the department via email.

In addition to getting temporary signs up ASAP, an ally would open a conversation with the administration team about restroom policies, recommending a review of the clinic's facilities to determine a longer-term solution. (Many thanks to my friend Jeannie Gainsburg and her book *The Savvy Ally: A Guide for Becoming a Skilled LGBTQ+ Advocate* for this example.)

As you can see, knight actions aren't inherently bad — but they are often stopgap measures. They may address inequity or discrimination for a single person or group but miss the opportunity to push for systemic or long-term change. Knight actions also have a built-in pitfall: They tempt the people who take them to do a little bragging on the side.

Forgo bragging rights

In April 2022, Dr. Ijeoma Opara, an assistant professor at Yale, tweeted:[39]

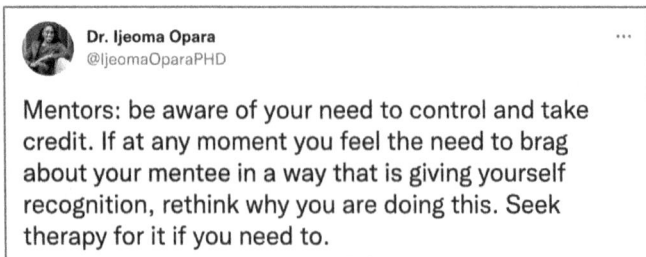

> **Dr. Ijeoma Opara**   ...
> @IjeomaOparaPHD
>
> Mentors: be aware of your need to control and take credit. If at any moment you feel the need to brag about your mentee in a way that is giving yourself recognition, rethink why you are doing this. Seek therapy for it if you need to.

This tweet was part of a longer thread about something that happened earlier in her career when a white faculty member told people that she "made" Opara. That person also asked Opara to tell anyone who congratulated her for awards and grants that she, the faculty member, had mentored her. That faculty member wanted to receive some of the credit and kudos herself.

As allies, let's learn from Opara's cautionary tale. If we ever want bragging rights for the work someone did after we used our position of privilege to help them, we can remember that knights may brag, but allies don't demand acknowledgment. Instead of putting ourselves in the spotlight, let's shine that light on their accomplishments.

Let's also not claim any sort of ally badge.

While I was scrolling through LinkedIn posts a while back, one person's job title caught my attention. He's a vice president at a large tech company and appended "Ally" to his professional title. For example, "VP of Sales | Ally."

Making this claim doesn't sit right with me. It feels performative. It also goes against my slogan, "Being an ally is a journey." We shouldn't ever claim we're done. We shouldn't ever reward ourselves with a proverbial ally badge or cookie. Instead, we should continue listening, learning, and taking action.

When I posted about this on Twitter, someone asked, "But is there a way he could communicate that he will help others??"

I replied, "Maybe 'Aspiring Ally' or 'Ally-in-Training'?" To me, these options convey that a person is engaged in learning about equity and allyship but also knows that their learning will be continuous. It also feels more honest and approachable, something any ally should want to broadcast.

How to screen your actions

Worried that your good intentions may lead to knight-like behaviors? Use this rubric to screen your actions and responses for savior-style thinking:

- What do I hope to accomplish by doing this?
- How many people will this help?
- How will my action/response change ingrained behaviors within my organization?
- If I do/say this, will it matter to anyone a year from now? Five years from now?
- Do I expect recognition in return?

There will be times when catalyzing large-scale change will feel impossible, and that's just fine. Take action in the moment, for a single person, yet strive to have a lasting impact. The goal is to do more and do better as often as you can without making it all about yourself. Perfection may be impossible, but improvement is well within reach. And on that note ...

Allies do what's right, not what's easy

Often, the knight move is the simplest and the easiest course. It can be tempting to take action quickly so you can feel like you're having a real, measurable impact right away. Let's face it: The working world is fast-paced, especially in healthcare, and days are often filled with competing priorities. Plus, there never enough hours in the day. Why bother taking on a big initiative to drive systemic change when we can get something done, check it off our list, and know we helped at least one person?

Because it matters. Because the larger, systemic changes will help shift the ratios in favor of all those who are marginalized under the current systems. Because doing what's right instead of what's easy will lead to a more inclusive workplace where everyone can thrive — and ultimately that will result in better patient outcomes.

In healthcare, we don't need knights in shining armor, but we do need allies to take action and be ambassadors for change. How will you make sure you're acting as an ally, not a knight? What systemic changes can you institute to create more inclusive workplace cultures — not just for a marginalized individual or two, but for all?

Actions for Better Allies:
Be an Ambassador for Change

Helping individuals is laudable, but the larger responsibility of allies is to take actions that will have lasting, beneficial effects on systems (as often as possible).

- When lending a hand to a single person, step back to look for systemic changes that will benefit many.
- Suggest new processes to shift ingrained behaviors and create a more inclusive culture.
- Pay attention to your motivations: Focus on what will authentically support marginalized people over the long term, rather than actions that will make you feel or look good in the moment.

3

EVERYDAY DISCRIMINATION

When Dr. Zaiba Jetpuri was an 18-year-old considering studying pre-med in college and wanted to get experience working alongside a physician, she applied to be a scribe. After a successful phone interview with one physician, Jetpuri stopped by their office for a tour and to sign some paperwork. That's when the physician told her something shocking: that she couldn't wear her hijab, stating, "We don't allow any accessories here — no hats, no jewelry, no religious affiliations. People aren't allowed to wear necklaces with crosses." The physician went on to explain, "Wearing your headscarf here would make my patients scared."[40]

Jetpuri's story is just one of the examples of non-inclusive behavior that I learned about in doing research for this book. This chapter includes many more. Some are frustrating, and many are heartbreaking. Unfortunately, I don't think any are one-off incidents.

While Jetpuri's experience illustrates overt workplace discrimination, some of the behaviors we'll explore in the coming pages fall under the heading of microaggressions; they're more "death by a thousand cuts" than a single painful blow.

Now, if you've never heard the term "microaggressions" before, you're not alone. It describes a phenomenon that has existed for hundreds of years but has only carried this particular label since the 1970s. Columbia University psychology professor Derald Wing Sue, PhD, defines the term as follows:

> Microaggressions are the everyday verbal, nonverbal, and environmental slights, snubs, or insults, whether intentional or unintentional, which communicate hostile, derogatory, or negative messages to target persons based solely upon their marginalized group membership. In many cases, these hidden messages may invalidate the group identity or experiential reality of target persons, demean them on a personal or group level, communicate they are lesser human beings, suggest they do not belong with the majority group, threaten and intimidate, or relegate them to inferior status and treatment.[41]

Sounds pretty awful, right? Anyone who's been on the receiving end can confirm that *it is*. In fact, for some people, microaggressions are harder to bear than more overt bigotry because they're subtle but ever-present, small but ongoing. They wear a person down slowly over time, like dripping water on a stone, gradually convincing them that they're less-than, through barely noticeable social cues and offhand remarks.

On the journey to be better allies, we need to be curious about microaggressions. We need to seek out and pay attention to the experiences others have in our workplaces because, chances are, there's non-inclusive behavior happening around us.

Here's what those behaviors might look like in your healthcare workplace, along with everyday actions to respond with when you witness them.

When you don't look the part

On Twitter, doctors frequently share examples of the everyday discrimination they face, many of which have to do with physical appearance. If someone "doesn't look like a doctor" by arbitrary social standards, they may face near-constant questioning of their credentials. Here's just one example of this bias in action from Dr. Uché Blackstock.[42]

> **uché blackstock, md** ✅
> @uche_blackstock   ...
>
> For the umpteenth time, I was asked again today by a parking garage attendant (**looking at my MD license plate for hospital parking), "Are you the doctor or is your husband?".

I love Blackstock's response when this happens. "At this point, I smile and ask them, 'Why would you ask me that question?' and then they start stammering."[43]

In my interviews, I heard even more stories about appearance-based bias. Dr. Marina Del Rios Rivera, the associate professor in emergency medicine you heard from in Chapter 1, is often the only person of color in the room. She told me that if she's working with a white male resident, she often sees EMTs, nurses, and the security guard approach the resident first before asking her about her patients. Or, if she's working with a resident who is a woman or person of color, they both get ignored, and the workers go to the white male attending physician.

In another interview, I heard about a nurse who told a burqa-wearing third-year resident they couldn't accept an order from her and needed to ask a doctor. The person who witnessed this incident emphasized to me, "Residents are doctors!"

I spoke to Dr. Ally Flessel when she was a first-year OB-GYN resident at St Joseph Mercy Hospital in Ann Arbor, Michigan. She shared an all-too-common situation for women doctors: the assumption that she must be a nurse. It happens when she walks into a room, and a patient says into their phone, "I have to hang up now. The nurse just came in." It also happens in ride shares with her friends. When a driver asks, "What do you do?" and they answer, "Oh, we're in medical school," the response is always some form of, "Oh, that's so great. You want to be a nurse?" It even happened to her mother when shopping for Christmas gifts. She stopped by a sock store at the mall, mentioned that her daughter was in medicine, and the salesman brought her over to see the nurse-themed socks.

While these situations may seem harmless, they create a real cumulative impact. In an article in the *Harvard Business Review* titled "When People Assume You're Not In Charge Because You're a Woman," researchers Amy Diehl, PhD, and Leanne M. Dzubinski, PhD, wrote,

> Role incredulity is a form of gender bias where women are mistakenly assumed to be in a support or stereotypically female role — secretary, administrative assistant, court reporter, nurse, wife, girlfriend — rather than a leadership or stereotypically male role, such as CEO, professor, lawyer, doctor, or engineer. In these instances, women must expend extra energy and time to assert and sometimes prove their role. Their words may lack the credibility and authority inherent in their position.[44]

Let's take a closer look at the energy required to address role incredulity for women and others who are underrepresented in their fields. Doing this will help us understand how it can impact patient care and careers.

Imagine walking into an exam room and finding a patient who looks disappointed because you're not who they want to see or expect to see.

On an episode of *The Visible Voices* podcast, Dr. Resa E. Lewiss shared just such a story. As a fourth-year resident in emergency medicine, Lewiss remembers walking into an examination room where a father was holding his 5-year-old son. The father's face just dropped. Was it because she was young, a woman, or both?

Her guest on the show was Dr. Ashley McMullen. (You may remember her from the Introduction of this book.) McMullen, who is Black, explained, "It's easy to bring that back onto yourself, to say that I'm not enough. You can become insecure, start to second guess yourself. ... And, when you put energy into those types of things, or you allow somebody else's negativity to influence how you present, it creates a vise around your mind and your ability to think creatively, especially in situations where you really need to think outside the box [to treat the patient]."[45]

Dr. Del Rios Rivera gave me further insight into how role incredulity microaggressions might affect patient care. "Recently, a white nurse disagreed with me about the management of one of my patients. When I tried to explain why a different management was indicated, she turned her back on me and walked away." The situation worsened when Del Rios Rivera saw the nurse talking to a white male resident about the patient. "While that resident was involved in the management of the patient, ultimately, the patient was my responsibility. The license is mine. If something goes wrong, it's me who they're naming in a malpractice suit." Del Rios Rivera interjected, explaining why she had chosen the particular course of action. The nurse was disrespectful, saying it was a private conversation and had nothing to do with her. When Del Rios Rivera pointed out that it did because she was responsible for the patient's management, the nurse once again turned her back and just walked away.

We can only hope that the patient's care wasn't negatively impacted.

Here's one more. Daytheon Sturges, PhD, PA-C, shared a thread on Twitter that started with:[46]

> **Daytheon Sturges, PhD, PA-C, CHES®**   ...
> @daytheon
>
> A ▊ - So yesterday on my flight there was a medical
> emergency involving a passenger in the seat right in
> front of me. I immediately jump up (I'm a family
> medicine PA) as did the woman behind me (internal
> medicine physician) and sprang into action. 1/6

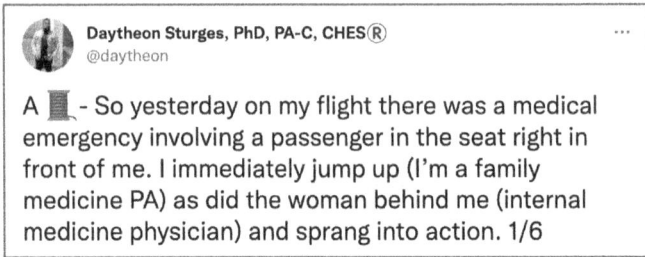

Sturges went on to explain how a man rushed from the back of the plane, literally shoved him out of the way, and announced that he was a surgeon. (Note that Sturges is a Black man.) He wrote, "There was reference to [the woman from the seat behind me] as a nurse (not MD) and to me that help had arrived."

The flight crew spoke up in the moment, letting the surgeon know that the pair had the situation under control. The surgeon returned to his seat, and Sturges and the woman continued to treat the patient. (Good news: The patient result was great.)

They may not have realized it, but those flight attendants spoke up against role incredulity. Just as we all should in healthcare workplaces.

Not sure how to get started? Speaking up to ensure that everyone is addressed using their titles or consulted appropriately for input is essential, but combatting role incredulity isn't always about verbal confrontation. Here's a creative approach that a group of women surgeons in the UK took to stop being mistaken for nonsurgical staff. They ordered personalized operating room scrub caps with their names and specialties. The idea came from Dr. Gillian Cribb, whose cap reads, "Hello, my name is Gill Cribb Orthopaedic Surgeon."[47]

Introducing Dr. Fauci and Deb

At a press conference during the early days of the COVID-19 pandemic, then-President Trump deferred a question about mortality rates, saying, "I'd like Dr. Fauci or Deb to come up" to answer it.[48] "Deb" is Dr. Deborah Birx, a physician who should have been referred to with the same respect as her colleague Dr. Fauci.

Similarly, in a study of how people were introduced during grand rounds, researchers found distinct gendered differences. When men introduced women, they used their formal titles 49 percent of the time. When introducing other men, this jumped to 72 percent. By contrast, women introduced speakers of any gender by formal titles almost all of the time (96 percent).[49]

In other words, men showed more professional respect to other men. Not so much for the women. (It's important to note that one of the authors of that study acknowledged a lack of research beyond the male-female binary. They wrote, "We urgently need to find out how gender bias, in language and elsewhere, affects medical professionals who identify as nonbinary, genderqueer, and transgender."[50] I couldn't agree more.)

This microaggression also happens to women speakers at medical conferences. Several studies have found that women are less likely to be introduced by their formal doctoral titles when compared to men.[51]

Women physicians often head to Twitter to share personal examples of the "Dr. Fauci and Deb" phenomenon. Here are a few:

- Dr. Sophia Kogan posted, "Just received group work email. Men physicians were 'Dr' & women physicians were 'first name'."[52]
- Dr. Oni Blackstock shared a screenshot of an email addressed to three people: "Dear Oni" and two people referred to as Dr. along with their last names."[53]

- Dr. Arghavan Salles tweeted, "Just last week was in a mtg where other people were introduced as Dr A, Dr B, Dr C, Dr D. I was Arghavan."[54]
- Dr. Nancy Yen-Shipley tweeted a photo of two almost-identical hand-written notes from a medical equipment sales rep. The letter to a woman doctor started with a salutation of "Hi [first name redacted]." By contrast, the salesperson wrote "Dr. [last name redacted]" to a male doctor.[55]

I've also heard this happens on call schedules and during hospital rounds. It's so pervasive that the medical satire site Gomerblog posted a fictional story about a woman surgeon who was fed up with being called by her first name for years when her male colleagues were called by their title. Out of frustration, she decided she would take matters into her own hands and legally changed her first name to "Doctor."[56]

Kidding aside, it's important to note that this differential treatment may not be caused only by gender bias.

Some people attribute this behavior to familiarity and camaraderie. Dr. Shikha Jain is an associate professor of medicine in hematology and oncology at the University of Illinois Chicago and the founder of the nonprofit Women in Medicine. After she published a paper about gender disparities in introductions at oncology conferences, a former boss reached out. Jain told me, "She admitted that she didn't realize she had been doing this, explaining that she introduced women she knew by their first names and others by their titles because she didn't know them. Yet, because of my paper, she changed her approach."

Others justify their actions by insisting they use titles for more junior people to elevate them and first names for more established doctors. When the host of the *Docs With Disabilities* podcast introduced his first guest, a woman doctor, as Diane, followed by his male guest as Dr. Bullock, he was called on it. He went on to explain that he uses the Dr. title for residents, fellows, and junior faculty, and first names for colleagues. For him, it had nothing to do with gender but instead reflected their level of training.[57]

Regardless of the intent or reasoning, the bottom line is impactful. Not using someone's title can undermine their perceived authority and expertise, especially when their peers receive different treatment. It can make them appear less qualified than their colleagues.

When introducing people or referring to people in emails or call schedules, let's use their formal titles. Regardless of their gender, how well you know them, or their level of training. This is an allyship practice rooted in equity and, hopefully, an easy one to employ.

Extra scrutiny

In "Nursing while Black," Dr. Calvin Moorley, a professor of nursing at London South Bank University, wrote, "An ethnic minority nurse in charge of a shift or clinical area is more likely to be questioned or challenged for their decision taken."[58]

Unsurprisingly, this extra scrutiny is not limited to the field of nursing.

According to a study of the overall labor market by Costas Cavounidis and Kevin Lang of Boston University, Black workers receive extra scrutiny from their supervisors, which can lead to less favorable or constructive performance reviews, lower wages, and even job loss. With increased surveillance comes increased employee nervousness. Small mistakes are more likely to be caught, leading to negative feedback and reduced pay over time. This research demonstrates how discrimination creates a feedback loop that results in ever-increasing racial gaps in the labor force.[59] It's a harmful cycle, and one that can seem difficult to break.

I've also read stories from women surgeons who were judged by different criteria than their male counterparts. For example, they were told to smile more. They were also expected to be empathetic with patients and "sufficiently likable" in ways that were totally different from what was expected of male surgeons.[60]

Here's one quick way to check for extra scrutiny and biased feedback: Ask yourself, Would I make the same comments about someone of a different identity or background? Kristen Pressner, a global HR executive, gave a TEDx talk on bias and recommended the "flip it to test it" experiment, saying,

> Maybe you are a superhuman person who manages to intercept those brain shortcuts at exactly the right moment to ensure you're behaving bias-free and consistently with your values, and beliefs, and all of your actions. It could very well be. But what have you got to lose to double-check yourself? If we all started to flip it to test it, we might just be surprised at how often we would choose to behave differently. Because what if you're missing an opportunity to see the world differently?[61]

Try it the next time you're about to give feedback to someone who's a member of an underrepresented group.

Bullying

In a letter published in *Nature Human Behaviour*, Dr. Susanne Täuber and Dr. Morteza Mahmoudi summarized their concerns about bullying in academia, sharing numerous anonymized examples. They also explained:

> An emerging body of research suggests that mediocre academics in particular resort to bullying, to remove their competition. Experimental research has shown that when male hierarchies are disrupted by women, this incites hostile

behaviour specifically from poorly performing men, because they stand to lose the most.[62]

Täuber and Mahmoudi described some of the systemic behaviors that support bullying. For example, an organization that allows ever-changing performance criteria for promotions or tenure. Or a culture that encourages competition between employees. Bullying can also take the form of questioning someone's credentials.

A Black doctor, who'd been tasked with improving some hospital procedures, heard that a semiretired former department chair was angry that she hadn't sought his approval before making her recommendations. It turns out that there was an implicit understanding that no major changes would happen without his consent, but no one had told her. When she met with the former chair to discuss his concerns, he invited a colleague to support his position. The two of them ganged up on her, asking about her education, her class ranking, and even "where did you come from."[63]

Of course, some bullying happens simply because some people are jerks. In surgery, there can be an aggressive and often hostile culture that contributes to bullying of surgical residents and fellows. As Dr. Peter Angelos wrote in a closing commentary for a collection of #MeToo stories for *Narrative Inquiry in Bioethics*: "Why is it acceptable to behave this way in surgery? Without question, being on the receiving end of verbal abuse and angry tirades can take the joy out of surgical training, and there is certainly no evidence that it results in better surgeons."[64] In that same collection, Dr. Anji Wall implored, "As surgeons, we must create a culture of zero-tolerance for abusive behavior in and outside of the operating room. We cannot continue to value the aggressive, arrogant alpha-male. We cannot treat technical excellence as a hall pass. No one is too good to be kind." (Many thanks to Dr. Pringl Miller who spearheaded and edited this collection.)

This behavior can have an immediate copycat effect, trickling down from surgeons to residents. Dr. Dawn Haut told me about one such example. "I was on my general surgery rotation, and as students, we had to be there at 5 a.m., ready in the operating room. Each day, we gathered for rounds by a big whiteboard that listed the names of the patients and the reason for the surgery." She went on to explain, "One day, when I arrived, everyone started snickering. When I looked up at the board, someone had written my name up there and added that the procedure I was having was breast augmentation. I happen to be flat chested, which I'm comfortable with, but it was awful having it called out like that."

Personally, I don't know how someone goes on with their day after such bullying, staying present in the work that needs to get done for the patients who need care. I wish someone had spoken up with a simple, "We don't do that here," and erased Haut's name from the whiteboard before she even arrived.

Standing up against bullies may not be easy, but it is essential for allies to do so. When witnessing a bully in action, each of us has a simple choice: Call it out or be complicit. If doing so means stepping outside of your comfort zone, here are some responses to consider to enforce more inclusive cultural norms:

- **"We don't do that here."** (My personal favorite, as you can tell from the above example)
- **"We're better than that."**
- **"Not cool."**
- **"That's against our code of conduct."** (Assuming your workplace has anti-bullying policies)

Offensive jokes and slurs

When Dr. Shikha Jain (who you heard from earlier) was in training, her attending would make sexually explicit jokes about her in front of the patients and in front of the team. She admits laughing it off to just get through her rounds. Eventually, it got to the point where it was uncomfortable for the entire team. Yet, no one spoke up. Jain told me, "I think it's because people figured if it wasn't bothering me, then they didn't need to say anything."

But here's the thing. As allies, we should say something. If we don't, we become complicit in allowing the joking to continue. We send a message that we're fine with the behavior.

And it's not limited to offensive jokes. We should also speak up when we hear someone using a degrading slur. Perhaps it's the N-word, as someone at Seattle Children's Hospital used to describe Dr. Ben Danielson.[65] Or calling a woman surgeon a "bitch" for giving orders under the pressure of time, as happened to Dr. Sabha Ganai during her surgical residency.[66]

So how do you go about speaking up? The easiest way is simply to have some scripted responses in your back pocket. In the moment, you might freeze up and doubt yourself, so memorizing a few stock callouts is a great way to prepare yourself to confront inappropriate jokes and comments. Here are a few suggestions:

- **"I don't get it. Can you explain the joke to me?"**
  This forces the speaker to dig into their reasoning aloud, which brings bigotry to light.
- **"That wasn't funny."**
- **"Wow, that was awkward."**
- **"Did you really just say that?"**
- **"Ouch."**

Racial microaggressions

In my interviews, I heard about a Black man training to be a surgeon. He was considering applying for a surgery rotation in a rural area of the United States that would provide training on many different surgical skills. Yet, he was leaning against it because of the racism he expected to receive from the predominantly white staff. While he could handle racism from patients, he didn't want to deal with it from the people he'd see day after day. As a result, he said no to this otherwise fantastic training opportunity.

As you likely know, this surgeon-in-training is not alone. Frustrating stories about the racism that healthcare professionals face are extremely common, and pop up regardless of position or discipline. Here are just a few more.

Dr. Kimbell Kornu, an Asian American physician, wrote, "As a medical student, I enjoyed rotating at the VA hospital because of the veteran population. However, immediately after I walked into a patient's room, a veteran told me, 'Go away. I don't want a Jap doctor.'"[67]

When I spoke with Kara Shafer, a registered nurse in Seattle, she shared, "Just last week, a Black nurse asked me to administer a shot for a patient who refused to let her do it." When Shafer (who is white) walked into the room, the patient asked, "Are you from here?" Shafer told me that she works in the same city she was born in, so she said, "Yeah." The patient's response? "That's good. Not that it matters or anything." But, as Shafer told me, it actually does. In Shafer's words, "The patient's just racist."

Such racism is shocking to Dr. Alaettin Carikci, the former head of diversity and inclusion at the Great Ormond Street Hospital for Children in London. In our interview, he explained that most nurses in the United Kingdom are from ethnic minority backgrounds because the National Health System outsources nurses from the Philippines, Africa, India, and

Southeast Asian countries. When he sees white patients not treating nurses very well, he thinks, When you're at your lowest, how is it possible that you still think that you can be racist? Those nurses are there to help you and provide you with the best patient care possible.

But racism doesn't just come from patients. As a fourth-year medical student, Dr. Benito Nieves (who you heard from in Chapter 2) remembers talking to a friend about their upcoming rotations. In their program, some second-year students joined the fourth-year rotations. After Nieves joked, "It will be fine as long as they stay in their lane," his friend replied, laughing, "Yeah, otherwise you'll shank them." Nieves was caught off guard, hearing his friend conflate a rough prison culture rife with makeshift knives to his Puerto Rican heritage. As he told me, "When I heard that, it reminded me of a feeling that I had always had in medical school: I'm not sure if I belong here. I don't know if this is a place for me."

Racism also pops up in the form of diminishing someone's success by tying it to a diversity goal. In an episode of *The Visible Voices* podcast, Dr. Matifadza (Mati) Hlatshwayo Davis, director of health for the City of St. Louis, Missouri, described some of the comments she's received over her career. They included, "Well, you know, they made you the associate program director because they needed a Black face." Also, "Well, you know, it makes them look good to have you in a position of leadership."[68]

When hearing any kind of racist comment, an ally can speak up with, "What makes you say that?" Similar to asking someone to explain an offensive joke, this approach gets the person to confront their bias. They may decide it's not worth explaining and drop the topic quickly.

You're so articulate

Dr. Courtney Gilliam, a Black woman, has had people tell her, "You are so articulate." This familiar phrase reminds her "that I am not welcome and that I am an outlier in the workforce and in leadership."[69]

Wondering why Gilliam and many other Black people I've spoken to think being called articulate is not a compliment? Because of the underlying assumption that they couldn't possibly be well-educated, well-spoken, or articulate. It's a lousy stereotype.

For allies who might hear someone saying, "You're so articulate" to a Black colleague, I recommend the seek-common-ground-and-educate approach. For example, "I used to think calling someone articulate was a compliment, but I have since learned many Black people don't think so ..." Then summarize the underlying negative stereotyping.

To pay a true compliment, allies can make it meaningful while reducing negative stereotyping by providing context. It's as simple as explaining the baseline of our comparison. For example, "You have a unique ability to simplify any problem." Or, "I watch a lot of webinars, and you are the best at engaging a remote audience."

Can I touch your hair?

Lisa Proctor, a Black registered nurse, wrote about her experience working in a primarily white hospital. "Over the years, my coworkers felt safe to query me about Black culture. Since nursing remains a mainly female profession, most questions centered on hair. And because my hairstyles varied, I received many questions, including the request, 'Can I touch your hair?'." Some would just touch it without asking.[70] Proctor added, "I tried to brush it off as 'no big deal,' but I could not shake the feeling of now being the animal in the cage at the zoo."

Someone's hair or any part of their body is not ours to touch. It's disrespectful to think that we have the right to do so, whether we ask first or not. If you see someone doing this, consider making the universal "time out" sign with your hands while saying, "Not cool."

Here's another example of something that's not cool: men who feel entitled to comment on a woman's appearance. It's the workplace equivalent of catcalling and impacts women of all races.

I spoke with a doctor who shared that, twice in one day, a man said that her butt looked good in the dress she was wearing. Later, that same man asked her, "You've never been sexually harassed, have you? That doesn't really happen?"

File that story in the "Can't make this stuff up" folder.

Mispronunciations and nicknames

I have to admit I tend to mispronounce names that I'm not familiar with. While this may not seem like a big deal in the moment, I realize it can have a cumulative effect, and I'm working to get better. After all, if someone has a name that their colleagues struggle with, that can be one more reminder that they are different from the norm. It might make them feel they don't belong or that they're less important than others.

In a *Harvard Business Review* article titled "If You Don't Know How to Say Someone's Name, Just Ask," inclusion strategist and author Ruchika Tulshyan wrote,

> Learning to pronounce a colleague's name correctly is not just a common courtesy but it's an important effort in creating an inclusive workplace, one that emphasizes psychological safety and belonging.[71]

Tulshyan cited a study that reported when students of color had their names mispronounced in the classroom, it affected their social-emotional well-being and, by extension, harmed their ability to learn. The study also concluded that mispronouncing the names of students of color constituted a racial micro-aggression because it created shame and dissociation from their culture.

While it may be tempting to get around this problem by giving someone a nickname that's easier to pronounce, please don't. Steer clear of any temptation to say, "I'll just call you Sue" or something similar to their name, but not of their choosing. Doing this would prioritize your comfort level and convenience over their agency and identity. That's some deep-seated disrespect.

It's also not okay to ask someone to select a different moniker for themselves because you might be having trouble saying their name. Yes, this happens. During an inspection of a hospital in the United Kingdom, employees raised a concern: Line managers had told them to adopt a "Western work name" since their name was too difficult to pronounce.[72]

To learn how to say someone's name, here's a simple, inclusive idea from author Nneka M. Okona:[73]

Nneka M. Okona ▮▮ ✓
@afrosypaella   ···

A tip: if you have no idea how to pronounce someone's name don't make it weird or corny or xenophobic by implying that their name is hard to say or that you're puzzled or even laugh about it.

Just say, "Can you say your name for me? I don't want to mispronounce it."

See? Easy.

Last but not least, I'm a fan of a website called NameDrop.io, which allows you to record a short audio clip of how to say your name. You can then add a link to it from your email signature. For example, my signature now includes "Click to hear my name," which links to *www.namedrop.io/karencatlin.* (If you're curious, go listen to it.)

I've also recorded my name on my LinkedIn profile page; people can listen to it by tapping the speaker icon after my name.

Even if you think your name is easy to pronounce, take a moment to record yours and help normalize doing so.

When you're viewed as a token

Even though she's an associate professor, Dr. Marina Del Rios Rivera (who you heard from above) told me, "I still feel that I have to justify my presence. There's sort of this assumption that somehow you got to where you are because you're a minority, and they were just trying to diversify the environment. Or that somehow you had an easier time when in fact, it's not true." When Del Rios Rivera and I spoke in April 2022, then-Judge Ketanji Brown Jackson was in confirmation hearings for the U.S. Supreme Court, and Del Rios Rivera pointed out, "Judge KBJ is a good example of this, of having to be overqualified to get a role."

She went on to share some poignant examples from her own career.

When Del Rios Rivera was interviewing for an academic position, a faculty member announced in her group interview: "It is refreshing to meet someone of your background with your credentials. You show that we don't have to compromise on quality." While meant as a compliment, she took it as an insult. "What that told me is that they assumed my credentials weren't going to be good enough, and that they had called me in just because I had a Spanish surname."

At another point in her career, Del Rios Rivera had resigned from her position, and when she offered to help find her replacement, her boss asked, "Can you help me find another Latina?" While his intention may have been good (to keep the department diverse), that's not how it landed. Del Rios Rivera felt dejected, that she had been in that department only because of her demographic and not because of the dozens of papers she published or the grant money she brought in.

I've come across many other examples, too. One of my coaching clients, a Black woman, heard that a white executive at her company had disparagingly called her "a token." For context, she is a talented leader with decades of industry experience. I fumed when she told me.

If you're not familiar with tokenism, it's about making only symbolic efforts to be inclusive, such as hiring people from underrepresented groups to give the appearance of racial or gender equality. It also happens when a single person from an underrepresented group is included to meet a "quota." That person becomes the "token."

By calling someone a "token" or a "diversity hire," we undermine them. We send a message that they're not qualified to do their job and that we're not expecting them to perform at the same level as their peers.

If you witness someone being tokenized (or are being tokenized yourself), consider speaking up with these phrases:

- "What makes you say/think that?"
- "I'm pretty sure everyone we hire has to pass the same rigorous interview process." For emphasis, add, "My interviews were really thorough. How about yours?"

One size doesn't fit all

In an article for the Association of American Medical Colleges (AAMC), I read about medical equipment that's hard to use by women, who typically have smaller hands than their male counterparts. At 5'3" tall, one trainee explained that "her hands were too small to drive the endoscope into the colon and easily adjust it because of the position of the buttons."[74]

Another woman explained that "during her five years of residency, surgical gloves were rarely ordered in her size and she was rebuked for not having the grip strength to operate the surgical stapler with one hand."

There can also be a problem with lead gowns worn during procedures: The standard sleeveless radiation-blocking gowns fail to protect the breast tissue near the armpits. The impact? A 2016 study pointed out that women orthopedic surgeons get breast cancer at a higher rate than the general population of women in the United States.[75] By the way, the gowns also often don't fit bodies in the later stages of pregnancy.

My hope is that allies speak up when they notice protective gear not being available in suitable sizes, and that there is a process to give feedback to medical equipment manufacturers.

How to respond when there's a power imbalance

While I've shared some examples of how to speak up throughout this chapter, I also want to acknowledge it can be hard to say something in the moment, especially when there is a power dynamic at play.

When Dr. Marina Del Rios Rivera (who you heard from earlier) was a medical student and a resident, she remembers hearing people make fun of Latinos' accents and joke about them being dramatic with their pain. "I wondered if I should say something, and maybe risk getting a poor evaluation. Or should

I just let the comment slide and do the best that I can to advocate for my patient on an individual level?"

While it happened all the time, Del Rios Rivera told me about one specific incident during her trauma rotation. "We were in the operating room. The patient, a young Latino, had been in a motor vehicle accident. He had been drunk and caused the accident, but he was very sick and needed surgery." She went on to share, "I remember hearing a barrage of bad words and complaints from the white male attending, who said that this was a waste of hospital resources. And that this person's life wasn't worth saving because it was just an added cost to the healthcare system. And that his taxes would end up paying for this." This patient could have been Del Rios Rivera's cousin or her brother. She just stood there, hoping tears wouldn't drop from her eyes as she held the retractors. To this day, she reflects on that surgery, still unsure if she should have said anything. Given the power dynamics, she might have been kicked out of the room if she did speak up. And that might have negatively impacted the patient's outcome.

I get it. And focusing on patient safety may help.

Dr. Dawn Haut, who you heard from earlier, told me about a game-changing approach she learned from the Agency for Healthcare Research and Quality (AHRQ). It's about having conversations across the healthcare hierarchy in the day-to-day course of work to create a culture of safety. The approach uses the acronym "CUS," which reminds someone to say,

- "I am concerned!"
- "I am uncomfortable!"
- "This is a safety issue!"

Haut emphasized, "As a physician, if the nurse or medical assistant I'm working with doesn't feel comfortable calling out the fact that I'm about to make a mistake, we've got a safety issue."

I also think CUS can be used to call out discriminatory behavior, especially when an ally wants to speak up to someone with more power and privilege. Christopher Phung, a nurse practitioner in the emergency department at Jefferson Health in Philadelphia, told me about a shift he had a few years ago. The ER was pretty quiet, and he and his colleagues had a couple of vacancies. "Then the charge nurse gave me three or four new patients within 30-40 minutes, which was nuts." When I asked Phung why he thought the charge nurse did that, he said he couldn't say for sure, but some of her friends were also working that day, and perhaps she didn't want to upset them by giving them the assignments. As a result, Phung wrote up the charge nurse. While he felt the support of colleagues who agreed it was uncalled for and unfair, I wonder if those colleagues would have been more empowered to act as allies by telling the charge nurse they were concerned about patient safety given Phung's unreasonable load.

Here's one more idea that Dr. Shikha Jain (who you heard from above) teaches her students: Use your body language to stand up to someone more senior than you. By moving closer to the person being attacked, you can make it feel like they're going after two people instead of just one.

Discrimination isn't limited to overtly malicious and intentional acts. It's often embedded in our everyday interactions and decisions, even in the systems that govern our workplaces. As allies, it's our responsibility to recognize and combat everyday discrimination in every way we can. I hope this chapter has given you some ideas and motivation to get started.

Actions for Better Allies:
Speak Up Against Microaggressions

Microaggressions are all around us, and they have a powerful cumulative effect. Speaking out against them at first can be uncomfortable, but it becomes less so with practice. Having a few simple strategies in your back pocket helps, too. Here are seven from this chapter to get you started.

- Use people's titles or refer to their expertise when introducing them.
- Stand up to bullies with "We don't do that here," "We're better than that," or "Not cool."
- In response to a racist or sexist comment, say, "I don't get it. What makes you say that?"
- Use the seek-common-ground-and-educate approach. For example, "I used to think that, too, but I have since learned ..."
- Learn to pronounce people's names.
- Say, "I am concerned. I am uncomfortable. This is a safety issue." (CUS)
- Move closer to someone who's being discriminated against.

4

LISTENING, BELIEVING, AND LEARNING

In the previous chapter, I shared many examples of everyday discrimination faced by healthcare workers. Yet, this peek into the experiences of people from underrepresented groups was just that: a peek. It was far from comprehensive, nor was it meant to be. Instead of cataloging every non-inclusive behavior that might happen in a workplace, which is simply not possible, my goal was to help you immerse yourself in perspectives other than your own.

Hopefully, you're now in the right mindset to accept a challenge — a challenge to be curious, to listen and be open-minded, to believe what others tell you even though you may never have experienced something similar, and to iterate as you learn. On the journey to be better allies, we need to be open to constant learning and be willing to reevaluate "the way things are done around here."

What does that mean in action? For starters, it means learning how to discuss discrimination that you have never experienced with someone who experiences it on a regular basis.

How to open the door to learning

There are no two ways about it: Broaching subjects like sexism, racism, harassment, and discrimination in the workplace is hard. These are tough and touchy topics, and many potential allies worry that simply bringing them up may cause rifts. Or impact their careers negatively. Or that they may say the wrong thing and make the situation worse. This is understandable and worth acknowledging.

However, it is *not* an acceptable excuse for inaction. The ally mindset means taking responsibility for learning to do what's right instead of falling back on what's easy or safe. Sparking meaningful change requires pushing past our own fears and being willing to get vulnerable. And even make a few mistakes.

Dr. Shikha Jain, the associate professor and founder of Women in Medicine you heard from in Chapter 3, told me, "When it comes to this type of work, there's so much fear about how to handle the situation. People need to know that doing something, even if it's not the right something or the perfect something, is better than doing nothing at all."

Sometimes, doing something starts with asking a colleague how you can best support them.

When I asked my friend Dr. Paul Haut (the former hospital COO you heard from in Chapter 1) if there was a time, in hindsight, when he wished he had been a better ally, he shared a powerful story. Here's the context. He had a fabulous staff member on his team, a Black woman with an impressive résumé. When new senior leadership joined the organization, things started to go sideways. This new leader, a white man, ignored the existing strategy she had developed and made some demeaning, disrespectful comments to her. Haut noticed this happening yet didn't speak up. Given the power dynamics, he admitted, "How was I supposed to push back in a respectful way, especially when my job was on the line?"

Haut is not proud that he stayed silent. He has since left that organization, and on his way out, apologized to his staff member, saying, "I feel like I didn't do enough for you." Her response? While she appreciated that he wanted to help her, she told him that she was an adult and could handle it. If things didn't work out for her with the new leader, she'd leave and find a better environment.

In other words, his first action to support her could have been simply checking in. Instead of guessing what she might need and speaking up based on conjecture, or not saying anything at all, he could have listened and learned.

This approach is key to effective allyship. We shouldn't assume that we know what's best for a colleague, and we need to realize that it's potentially harmful to take action on our assumptions. (In Haut's case, he might have undermined his staff member even further by giving his boss the impression that she couldn't speak up for herself.) It's far better for those in positions of power or privilege to open productive discussions with people from underrepresented groups about how they'd like to be supported by allies. If this is you, here are some best practices.

Ask to ask. You'd like to talk with a colleague about their challenges or how you can be a better ally, and that's great! But as someone in a position of privilege, you should ask if your colleague is comfortable and willing to discuss their experiences. Don't assume that they're just waiting to be plied with questions. Ask if they'd be open to a dialogue around discrimination or bias, and *then* dig into your specific questions. This is especially important when it comes to issues of race. Many well-meaning white people ask their Black friends and colleagues to explain cultural and historical contexts or make them feel like they must speak on behalf of all Black people. This is draining and exhausting. So, before you dive into your questions, ask to ask.

Acknowledge your fears. Consider opening a dialogue by owning up to your worries about the topic. When you approach a discussion about discrimination by saying, "I'm hoping to get your insights, but am a little concerned about putting my foot in my mouth," you pave the way for honesty. In fact, if you're a leader (by title or informally) and choose to be sincere about your imperfections, doubts, and mistakes, you automatically make it safer for others to voice their own feelings and fears.[76]

Be open and respectful. This may seem obvious, but in the context of discrimination discussions, "being open and respectful" may take on some less-than-obvious implications. If you're approaching a member of a marginalized group with questions about their experiences, you must be prepared to acknowledge and accept any information they impart. Broadcasting respect means trusting the speaker to share their truth.

For instance, if a Black nurse tells you, "The charge nurse watches over me a lot more than my white colleagues," and you say, "Oh, that can't be true. She's fair with everyone," you are invalidating and dismissing their perspective. Similarly, as you hear about biased behavior, you may be tempted to respond with a positive spin, such as, "I don't think they meant to offend you." Even if your own experience runs counter to what they're telling you, it's your job as an ally to listen to and respect their viewpoint. Approaching dialogue from a respectful place helps diffuse tension and create space for meaningful sharing.[77]

Don't get defensive. As you hear about someone else's experience, you may identify things you could have, or should have, done differently to support them directly or to create a more inclusive culture. You may also find yourself getting defensive, which is understandable. Focus on why you are having this conversation (to listen and learn) instead of making excuses for your behavior. (More on this in the next section.)

Apologize. If you realize you made a mistake, don't double down on your stance. Instead, share a heartfelt apology and discuss how you can do better.

Steer clear of "I'm sorry if I offended anyone" statements. Instead, own it. Thank the person, take responsibility for what you did, and explain what you can commit to doing or learning moving forward.

Work up your courage for a redo. You might hear about times when you could have been a better upstander in the moment. Perhaps you didn't know what to say or didn't want to disrupt the conversation. Maybe you didn't feel safe calling something out. I get it. Regardless of the reason, you can always circle back and revisit the situation. In her book *The Wake Up: Closing the Gap Between Good Intentions and Real Change*, Michelle MiJung Kim implores us to "work up your courage for a redo."[78]

She shares some suggested phrases we can use to revisit a situation:

- "Hey, can we check in about something that happened last week?"
- "I'm sorry I didn't address this earlier, but I've given it some thought and want to share this."
- "I've not been able to get this off my mind, can we have a quick chat?"

Which one can you imagine using?

How to learn without getting defensive

In 2021, I had the opportunity to attend a virtual conference where Dr. Bernice King, CEO of the King Center and daughter of civil rights leaders Dr. Martin Luther King, Jr. and Coretta Scott King, was interviewed. One of the topics she addressed was how people could take action to address bias in the workplace. As you might imagine, I was paying close attention.

Dr. King emphasized the importance of getting out of our silos and connecting with coworkers in a real way. She encouraged us to be curious and understand their world. Learn where they are. Give them space and place to have genuine and honest conversations.

As an example, she told us about a woman who wanted to remove the Confederate flag from a government building. Instead of getting angry and defensive when a man pushed back, she asked why the flag was important to him. Not to trick him, but to understand him. In turn, he then asked her why it was important to her to remove the flag. They were able to have a genuine, honest, and productive conversation.

While listening to Dr. King, I remembered a zinger of a phrase: **Be curious, not furious.** I first heard this from Kat Gordon, an advocate for inclusion in the creative industry. (I believe she learned it from a therapist.) It's a perfect mindset for those times when someone disagrees with us or points out when we've made a mistake on the journey to be a better ally. Give it a try.

Another helpful approach is to **focus on action and improvement.** Hearing that you are doing something wrong is never fun, but without constructive feedback, we can never improve. If a colleague from an underrepresented group says you undermine them in front of patients, try to set your feelings aside and focus on the action you can take to rectify the situation. What's important here is making changes that will create positive ripples into the future.

In my book *Better Allies,* I wrote about how critical it is for allies to accept and absorb criticism and feedback. I quoted Robin DiAngelo, author of *White Fragility: Why It's So Hard for*

White People to Talk about Racism, and her anecdote is so powerful, I'm including it here, too:

> In my workshops, I often ask people of color, "How often have you given white people feedback on our unaware yet inevitable racism? How often has that gone well for you?" Eye rolling, head shaking, and outright laughter follow, along with the consensus of rarely, if ever. I then ask, "What would it be like if you could simply give us feedback, have us graciously receive it, reflect, and work to change the behavior?" Recently, a man of color sighed and said, "It would be revolutionary." I ask my fellow whites to consider the profundity of that response. It would be revolutionary if we could receive, reflect, and work to change the behavior.[79]

It's easy to get defensive. Especially if we are white because — as DiAngelo points out in her book — white people have been conditioned to believe that being white is the equivalent to being "neutral." When someone points out that whiteness or the embedded mechanisms of white supremacy are the sources of widespread racial injustice and suffering, a common white response is to feel personally affronted. Having never thought of "whiteness" as a concept at all, white people are caught off guard and resist the idea that they're part of a large and harmful racial force. This is classic white fragility: discomfort and defensiveness on the part of a white person when confronted by information about racial inequality and injustice.

It can be hard to do in the moment, but it becomes easier when allies remain actively open to difficult feedback. It's our job to listen, believe, and learn, even when it feels uncomfortable. Only after that can we move ourselves toward meaningful action.

As Maya Angelou wisely said, "Do the best you can until you know better. Then when you know better, do better."[80]

A guide to red-flag language

Being an ally requires learning about your own ingrained prejudices, but it also requires helping those around us acknowledge theirs. At the risk of entering broken-record territory, *none of us is bias-free,* yet many of us have no idea which biases we exhibit. Furthermore, many people have no idea that certain phrases or assertions reflect personal prejudices.

The following is an abbreviated list of phrases that should raise red flags for allies. In other words, when you hear any of them, pay attention and be ready to take action.

Red-Flag Phrases

The candidate wouldn't be a culture fit. (More on this one in Chapter 10.)

The candidate doesn't have that qualification (when discussing criteria omitted from a description for a job or training program, but that more privileged candidates have).

They wouldn't want this role because of the travel, long hours, or overnight shifts.

I'd like to see them prove they're capable before promoting them (when discussing some responsibility they've previously had).

I don't want to lower the bar.

I don't believe they did this research on their own.

There's not enough pipeline to hire more people from that underrepresented demographic.

They rigged the system to get into med school.

Annie, can you take notes? (More on this one in Chapter 8.)

I'm not racist/sexist/homophobic, but …

I don't see color (or gender).

I've never seen the kind of harassment they reported, so I don't think it could happen here.

I'm sure they didn't mean to offend anyone.

That last one is a doozy. It can be hard for allies to accept that intentions aren't enough and that words can still be harmful even when spoken in good faith. Let's dive a little deeper into that concept.

How "assuming positive intent" behaves in the wild

It's fairly common for organizations to embrace the maxim of "assume good intent." This approach can shift a negative mindset to a positive one[81] and help people avoid negative biases they may hold toward colleagues or patients.[82] In fact, it's my go-to stance when I find myself starting to get annoyed by someone speeding by me on a highway, weaving in and out of traffic. Instead of getting angry, I force myself to think, Maybe there's a family emergency they're rushing to. Always assuming the worst about everyone under all circumstances is a recipe for an unhappy life, and assuming positive intent is a way to remind ourselves that we never know the full story of others' lives. It has become a shortcut for "Think beyond your own experiences." That can be valuable.

Yet, in our workplaces, "assuming positive intent" sometimes gives careless or ignorant employees a get-out-of-jail-free card; they can say racist or sexist or otherwise inappropriate and harmful things and just claim that they "didn't mean to be offensive" — that their intent was to give an innocuous compliment, make a joke, or point out something that *seemed* harmless.

This approach also puts people from marginalized groups in the position of "breaking the rules" if they see discriminatory behavior and choose to call it out. They're not "assuming positive intent" when they object; they're seen as being "disruptive," "angry," or "overly negative." And when Black people or other people of color "break the rules," they face much harsher social repercussions than their white counterparts.

Imagine a white male physician who works closely with a Latina nurse. They have a solid relationship overall, but he comments on her appearance nearly every day. His remarks are generally positive, like "You look fantastic today!" or "You look great in that turquoise scrub. Latinas aren't afraid of bright colors, are they?" His intent may be to build a connection with her or boost her confidence in her appearance, but the net effect is that she feels objectified. If his comments include references to her hair, curves, or how her choices reflect her culture, she may also feel ethnically pigeonholed.

Now imagine her choices. She can go to human resources and say that this physician's daily compliments make her uncomfortable, but she risks being scolded for failing to "assume positive intent." Lodging her complaint may ruin her relationship with that physician and others who hear about it. Her other option is to grit her teeth and endure his observations, gradually becoming more frustrated with his well-meaning behavior. She remains miserable, and the physician continues behaving in inappropriate and offensive ways without knowing he's doing anything wrong.

Intent is not valueless, especially because plenty of people do racist and sexist things with full knowledge of how their actions will be received. That said, positive intent is not a justification for discrimination or ignorance. Insisting that colleagues "assume positive intent" can create damaging conditions in the workplace. So instead, let's work to set expectations around *demonstrating* positive intent through respectful action.

Let's also be sure not to claim, "that's not what I intended" ourselves when we're told something we did or said is not inclusive. As my friend Melinda Briana Epler wrote in her book *How to Be an Ally,*

> The worst harm from a microaggression can come from denying someone else's harmful experience by centering it on your own intent. Trust people's unique experiences. Use your curiosity to build compassionate empathy. Really work to understand what they are going through — not what you are going through, or what you imagine you would go through in a similar situation. What matters is what they are going through and what you will do about it as an ally.[83]

Combating the bystander effect as an ally

Although this chapter is all about listening, believing, and learning, these actions are not enough when we see biased, offensive, or inappropriate behavior. We also need to speak up.

Does coming forward and objecting feel uncomfortable? For many of us, the answer is a resounding "Heck yes." But this discomfort is nothing compared to how it feels for the person whose racial group is being joked about. Or the colleague who is forced to endure constant commentary about her appearance. Or the coworker who is being excluded due to a disability. The discomfort of allies pales in comparison to what people from marginalized groups are forced to live through on a daily basis for the entire duration of their lives.

Let's explore a few situations where allies could have moved from *bystanders* to *upstanders.*

Situation 1

Dr. Avital O'Glasser, an associate professor of medicine and the medical director of a clinic at Oregon Health & Science University, told me about some challenges she faced as a parent with young children. Her son, who was premature, developed asthma as a baby. When he would come home from daycare with a cough, she'd worry about whether she'd make it to work the next day. "I'd lose sleep, wondering if I'd be able to send him to daycare." Her group didn't have a backup plan for people calling in sick, and some of her colleagues weren't supportive or sympathetic.

What happened: O'Glasser's colleagues often didn't do anything to support her during these caregiving emergencies. She persevered, but it could have caused her to drop out of medicine entirely.

What should have happened: O'Glasser told me that her experience, combined with more recent pandemic-related shifts in sick call thresholds, shaped how she now shows up as a leader. When someone contacts her saying they can't work because their child is ill and how sorry they are, she insists they stop apologizing. She tells them, "I want you to disconnect from worrying about patients. We've got that; the leadership has that. You focus on yourself and your family."

Situation 2

Dr. Goldstein (not her real name) told me that it's common for the overnight shift emergency team to go to breakfast together. Sometimes they head to the hospital cafeteria, and sometimes they go somewhere nearby. After all, shared meals help build camaraderie and morale. She was shocked when she discovered it was common practice at one teaching hospital for attendings to bring their team to a local strip club for the "Legs and Eggs" breakfast special. She asked a faculty colleague who told her about the breakfast ritual, "Wait. You did what? Were there any women on the overnight team?" He replied that yes, there was a woman junior resident and that she loved it.

Goldstein paused and pushed back a bit. She said, "First, how do you know she loved it? Second, what is she going to say? There's a clear hierarchy: You're the attending making the decision and inviting the team out. There's a power dynamic, and of course she wants to be a part of the team."

What happened: Goldstein's colleague didn't realize that not everyone feels comfortable going to a strip club. Some might feel it's unprofessional and unethical. Moreover, some people might not feel empowered to say anything because they want to fit in with the team.

What should have happened: Her colleague could have recommended a few other breakfast spots where the entire team would be comfortable.

Situation 3

Dr. VK Gadi is now the director of medical oncology at the University of Illinois Chicago. When he was in his mid-career, he witnessed an emotionally abusive relationship between a male faculty member and a junior woman. He told me that, even with the power imbalance he faced, "I spoke up and defended the junior person, and immediately the senior people, who were mostly white men, closed ranks around the faculty member."

When I asked if those senior men were acting out of allegiance or disbelief, Gadi responded, "Actually, I think it was something far worse. That they didn't want the drama. After all, you can't punch something that's shapeless and formless."

What happened: The senior men formed a seemingly impenetrable wall of support around their colleague to minimize and obscure the abuse.

What should have happened: Any one of them could have used their position of power and privilege to ask a question or two about what had happened, validating the experience while learning more about it. (More on this in the next section.)

Gadi admits it was a vulnerable time in his career, and he's always wondered if he should have been more aggressive in his support. Fortunately, it all worked out well in the end. Other senior men and women faculty members stood up against the abusive behavior.

Being an Upstander

As an ally, how can you equip yourself to confront discrimination and inappropriate behavior when you see it? Here are some ideas from the Teaching Tolerance website.[84]

Be ready. Start to think of yourself as an Upstander who can and does speak up. Visualize yourself seeing injustice and taking action. Consider queuing up some open-ended responses like "What makes you feel that way?" or "What makes you say that?" Both will help you to be curious, not furious, as I mentioned earlier in this chapter. Another idea is to practice responding to inappropriate behaviors with a simple "We don't do that here."

Verbalize what you're seeing. Because many people have no idea they're biased, sometimes just reflecting back at them jars them into understanding. Point out behavior or language bluntly, but avoid accusations. Try this: "Andy, what I hear you saying is that all Latinx people are overly dramatic about their pain." Or "Susan, you're classifying an entire gender/ethnicity/group in a derogatory way. Is that what you mean to say?"

Compare to past behavior. Letting someone know they're doing something out of character is a great way to alert them to inappropriate behavior. Try appealing to their better instincts with something like, "Jonathan, I've always known you to be a fair-minded person. I'm surprised to hear you say something that sounds so biased."

Set boundaries. You may not be able to change someone's mind, but you can set limits to their behavior when they're around you. Try "Don't tell racist jokes in my presence anymore." Or "I don't think homophobic remarks belong in the clinic. Please respect my wishes."

Now for an important "don't": Don't just call someone a racist or sexist or homophobe to their face. "If your goal is to communicate, loaded terms get you nowhere," says Dr. K.E. Supriya, an expert on the role of gender and cultural identity in communication. "If you simply call someone a racist, a wall goes up."[85]

Consider your current tendencies when you witness biased behaviors. When you see something, do you say something? Do you push back? Do you say, "Not cool," or ask, "What makes you say that?" If not, now's the time to start.

It can happen anywhere

No one wants to believe that their own workplace is oppressive, racist, or overflowing with sexist behavior. In fact, "That doesn't happen here" is often the default response when leaders are informed about bias within their organization's walls.

Yet again, defensiveness serves no purpose. In fact, it can work against the inclusive workplace you're striving to foster. Case in point: In June 2022, the British Medical Association reported that the National Health Service (NHS) could see a mass exodus of Black, Asian, and minority ethnic doctors due to persistent racism. This report was especially concerning given the COVID-19 pandemic and the fact that the NHS was already short of thousands of doctors. One of the issues raised? Many of the doctors surveyed did not report the racism they experienced at work, either out of fear of recrimination or being labeled a troublemaker, or not believing their concerns would be properly investigated.[86]

When people refuse to believe that bad behavior is happening under their own roofs, they do their organizations a disservice. Their denial prevents them from learning, growing, and addressing issues that negatively affect women, Black people, LGBTQ+ people, Latinx people, and others from marginalized groups working so hard for the communal success of their organizations. If leaders fall into patterns of denial, their organizations may garner reputations as workplaces that are unfriendly to workers from underrepresented groups and will have increasing difficulty hiring a diverse workforce. It's a domino effect that leads to a nasty cascade of repercussions.

So regardless of your position within your organization, resist the urge to say, "That doesn't happen here." Especially if employees or colleagues come forward and tell you that *it does*. Instead of steadfastly and stubbornly insisting that your workplace is already as equitable as it can be, work hard to make it even better.

Want some tips to kick-start that process? Here are three:

- **Listen.** Spend an entire day attempting to ask questions of your colleagues instead of making statements (as often as possible). What did you learn? How did it feel?
- **Believe.** The next time someone tells you a story or piece of information that makes you balk, pause. Count to five and evaluate *why* you have doubts.
- **Learn.** If you have a close relationship with a member of an underrepresented group in your organization, ask if they'd be comfortable discussing inequities in your shared workplace. If they agree, ask, "How can I change my own behaviors to be more inclusive?"

Organization-wide learning

After George Floyd was murdered in May 2020, organizations across the US had a wake-up call to address inequities in their workplaces, including many healthcare provider networks.

Kessie Davis (not her real name) is the chief human resources officer for a Midwestern urban safety net health system. She told me about the listening tours they organized for their CEO and other leaders to learn about the experiences of their Black employees. "The voice of the employee is a very powerful voice. Our workforce is changing rapidly, and some of the processes and procedures that we've had in place for a long time may not necessarily fit at this time." She went on to emphasize that, because inclusion can look different from what leaders might expect, they had to practice accepting and believing what Black employees told them. Their leaders needed to understand their employees' values, what made them uncomfortable, and what conditions would allow them to work at their absolute best and care for the patients. Through these listening tours, Davis's team uncovered multiple insights and took action by changing policies, procedures, and practices to create a better workplace for all.

While listening tours are one way to hear the voice of the employee, Davis pointed to two additional approaches they use: a Diversity and Inclusion Council and employee resource groups, each of which has an executive sponsor who shares concerns and ideas raised by these groups with the senior leadership team. Davis said, "We're always looking for ways to bring ideas to the table and improve our workforce overall, which will improve innovation and patient care." (You'll find more about employee resource groups in the next chapter.)

Here's another idea to foster organization-wide learning: Host a storytelling series to get to know the individuals you work with and be curious about their experiences. Dr. Kelly Paradis, the associate professor of medical physics you heard from in Chapter

1, told me about their "Becoming Series." It's a facilitated conversation where an employee tells the story of who they are and how their life experiences influence how they see the world. Overall, the goal is to help employees get to know each other better, which in turn helps create more understanding and inclusivity.

The series originated in 2019 at the Michigan Institute for Clinical & Health Research (MICHR). Since then, it has become one of their most popular Diversity, Equity, and Inclusion offerings. Because of its success, other departments across Michigan Medicine now host these conversations, too.

Consider creating a similar storytelling series for your team or organization. Start with one person who is willing to share their story. Meet ahead of time to identify the flow of the interview, using prompts such as the following, inspired by what MICHR and Paradis shared with me:

- When did you first realize your personal identities, such as racial/cultural/ethnic background, gender identity, sexual orientation, religion, or nationality?
- Are there experiences that have shaped your identities, such as caregiving, immigration, work/life integration, power dynamics, societal stereotypes, mental health, infertility/loss, or abilities and disabilities?
- What is a place of belonging for you?
- What does inclusion mean to you?
- Do you have challenges or personal growth areas in your own DEI journey?

Allies never stop learning

When it comes to spotting other allies, here's your biggest tip-off: They're the ones humbly and eagerly asking the tough questions. They're the ones who are quick to hold themselves accountable when they screw up. They're the ones who listen compassionately and learn constantly. Those are the people you want to seek out, the people you want to observe and emulate.

Allyship involves lots of advocacy and action, but it's all built on a foundation of listening, believing, and learning. When aspiring allies charge ahead, making changes and revising policies, it isn't long before they lose sight of the real goals. If we truly want to help shift the balance of power and fully support people from marginalized groups, it is absolutely crucial to continually solicit and incorporate *their* feedback about the issues that *they* want addressed. Skip that key step, and allyship is hollow and meaningless. Listen. Learn. Do. Repeat. Doing this will imbue your actions with meaning and value, now and into the future.

Actions for Better Allies:
Listen, Believe, Learn

Being an effective ally includes the less forceful but equally important activities of listening to alternative perspectives, believing the information that people from underrepresented groups share, and learning from their stories and our own mistakes.

- Be vulnerable and honest when you open discussions with colleagues who have less power and privilege than you.
- Resist the urge to get defensive.
- Review the list of red-flag phrases in this chapter, and speak out when you hear them.
- Take action when you see or hear about bigotry, harassment, or discrimination. Be an upstander, not a bystander.
- Recommend organization-wide learning opportunities.
- Accept that, yes, prejudice does exist in your workplace.

PART TWO

SHIFTING YOUR BEHAVIOR

5

DIVERSIFYING YOUR NETWORK

I can only imagine how surprised Dr. Sarah Temkin was when she noticed the editor and deputy editors of the prestigious *Obstetrics & Gynecology* journal were all men, despite the fact that 60 percent of OB/GYN doctors are women.[87]

This frustrating staffing decision could have been made for a variety of reasons. For starters, women are underrepresented in leadership positions across all professions,[88] including virtually all medical specialties.[89] Given this, a medical journal led entirely by male editors is somewhat predictable.

Then there are the gender disparity issues in the field of journalism. Although 64 percent of all US magazine editors are women,[90] most are in non-leadership positions. (In fact, Reuters found that every major news market has a majority of men among the top editors, including countries where women outnumber men among working journalists.[91]) This gap is particularly pronounced in medical journals, with women holding just 21 percent of editor-in-chief positions, including for journals covering women's health issues.[92]

These and other gender discrimination-fueled reasons could all be at play, but here's a less obvious one to consider: the "just like me" network phenomenon. Homogeneous networks form because of how we create professional connections: by spending time with people with whom we have something in common. Herminia Ibarra, PhD, a professor of organizational behavior at the London Business School, describes this phenomenon by saying, "Left to our own devices … we produce networks that are 'just like me'."[93] Since our networks are the pools from which we draw professional referrals, we tend to nominate, recommend, and advocate for people "just like us" for jobs, editorial boards (like the OB/GYN journal), and leadership roles in professional societies.

Naturally, the "just like me" network phenomenon isn't limited to gender issues, nor is it something that affects male networkers exclusively. In her TEDx talk, Dr. Shikha Jain described forming the steering committee for the Women in Medicine Summit. She invited people from a variety of institutions and specialties to include a diverse set of perspectives. Yet, someone called her and said, "Have you noticed your entire steering committee is made up of Indian women?" She quickly replied, "No, that's not possible. I don't even know that many Indian women." But when she reviewed her committee, she saw she had indeed tapped people just like her. Armed with this realization, she then reached out to people she wouldn't normally think of asking, ending up with a more diverse steering committee.[94]

As you can see, network bias is both prevalent and unconscious. We gravitate toward colleagues we find relatable, and those colleagues often overlap with us demographically. Is it possible that you've built your own "just like me" network without realizing it? Reflect on the makeup of your professional network. If it's homogeneous, you've got work to do.

Wondering where to start? Keep reading.

How to spot a truly effective network (hint: it's diverse)

One of the dangers of indulging "just like me" networks is excluding people who *aren't* just like you from important professional and personal connections. Colleagues who socialize together share ideas, recommend resources, and hatch plans. Colleagues left out in the cold never get the chance to contribute to those outside-of-work conversations, and that exclusion can negatively impact their professional trajectory in various ways.

I spoke with a retired radiologist who remembers taking her young children to a golf club after a long day's work. As she gazed out the window, she saw four male colleagues teeing off for a round of golf. "I realized right then that I would never be included. I'd never be able to really fit in with the boys." She also missed out on a canoeing trip these men took to northern Canada. When they returned, all four talked about ideas for papers they had brainstormed together during their getaway.

Another radiologist shared a similar story with me. "As the first woman to join my department, I felt like the Lone Ranger for the longest time. I remember how the boys would go off on these fishing and camping trips. And one time I was jokingly invited to come along as the cook. It was an old boys' club, and they were reluctant to have any women come along and join their ranks."

Old boys' clubs can also form at professional conferences. When she attended national Emergency Medicine meetings early in her career, Dr. Resa E. Lewiss (who you heard from in Chapter 2) knew that there was a group of people — mostly cisgender, heterosexual, married men — who would head together to a strip club after the day wrapped up. She told me, "I was never invited. Nor did I wish to be. However, I always wondered what professional relationships or academic opportunities I was missing out on because I wasn't a part of that group."

Of course, not all men gravitate to these professionally inappropriate, exclusionary groups. In my interviews, many people emphasized that they've worked with men who consistently treat everyone respectfully and fairly.

Regardless, research shows that, outside of work, men tend to hang out with their male coworkers, perhaps grabbing a beer after work, joining a virtual poker game, going to a ball game, or heading to the golf course. By contrast, women are more likely to spend time with nonwork friends, such as book club members, fellow volunteers for a nonprofit, members of a religious organization, or, if we have kids, other parents from playgroups and school.[95] For women who handle the lion's share of housework and childcare, squeezing in time for networking can be extra challenging. Home responsibilities can make it tough to pull off attending evening events or out-of-town conferences.

There's also plenty of research exploring how diverse our networks are (or aren't) regarding race. As I learned from a report from the Kapor Center for Social Impact, 75 percent of white people don't have any people of color in their social networks.[96] This isn't just upsetting because it reflects overall racial divisions in our society; it's also disappointing since diverse networks are truly valuable to both individuals and organizations. As Anthemis founder Amy Nauiokas wrote in *Harvard Business Review*, "Diverse networks can foster new ways of thinking by connecting you to people whose viewpoints, insights, resources, and lived experiences differ from your own."[97] In other words, when we self-separate by race, we miss out on the opportunity to become more innovative through collaborating with people who bring a wider variety of insights to the table.

Nevertheless, men network with men, women with women. White people network with other white people, Black people network with other Black people, and Latinx people network with other Latinx people. People network with others in their professional circles and not so much with those in non-professional roles. We want to be around people who understand us, and instinctively know that people who are similar to us are likely to relate to our challenges and triumphs. It's human nature.

It's also counterproductive. Talking among ourselves creates an echo chamber effect. Networking with people in our own fields and/or people who share our same gender identities, ethnicities, educational backgrounds, and income brackets, for example, allows us to vent and swap stories, but it doesn't encourage us to learn about wildly different experiences. And it certainly doesn't open our minds to the struggles that people with different and more marginalized experiences than us face in their lives and careers. Lacking this breadth of understanding makes us less empathetic, less creative, and less able to collaborate effectively with people who aren't "just like us."

Our personal networks benefit from diversity, too. In another *Harvard Business Review* article, by Paul Gompers and Silpa Kovvali, I read about the importance of building diverse friend networks. It turns out that friendships across lines of ethnicity and sexual orientation reduce implicit bias. And these benefits carry over to work, where expanded networks and mindsets can improve individual and organizational performance.[98]

So how do we step outside our comfort zones to connect with a wider variety of colleagues? What's the best way to start growing our networks as allies? We can simply get to know *all* the individuals we work with and be actively curious about their experiences.

Here's how one physician, Dr. David Brown, puts this into practice. He told me, "When I walk down the hall and see people changing over the beds for the next surgical case, I say hello. When someone comes in to restock the instruments, I thank them and ask how they're doing." Brown firmly believes that once we get to know people, it's easier to step in when we notice non-inclusive behavior.

I also love this tip from Singapore-based performance coach Jedidiah Alex Koh. He says, "Diversity promotes the cross-pollination effect. The ability to cross-pollinate will allow for a new exchange of ideas and concepts from across industries and cultures. I will look at networking events across sectors and industries and take part in some of those to create deeper connections."[99] Healthcare professionals shouldn't feel limited to networking within their field.

Here's one last practice that will help you build a varied and robust network: Seek out people who disagree with you. It will be challenging, yes, but also a fantastic way to learn, practice listening, and expand your understanding of how viewpoints are formed. Leadership strategist April Armstrong recommends this practice, saying,

> Ask questions from a place of curiosity, with the sincere intent to learn, expand your awareness and discover perspectives foreign to you. People who see the world differently have often had very different experiences in their lives or families and think fundamentally differently than you do. Rather than make them wrong, make a new friend.[100]

I'll share even more strategies for diversifying networks later in the chapter.

Disrupting inequitable access

Dr. David Brown, who you met above, is particularly interested in encouraging healthcare professionals to diversify their networks because he wears multiple hats. In addition to being an associate professor of otolaryngology at Michigan Medicine, he serves as the associate dean and associate vice president for health equity and inclusion. Brown is intent on deconstructing an old view of medicine, with mostly white straight male doctors, and rebuilding it so that everyone can bring their authentic selves to work, feel valued, and effectively contribute to the care of others.

While Brown is seeing more people of color enter medicine, he's concerned they aren't getting the same teaching, attention, or access to opportunities as white students. Here's just one example. "I have students of color who come up to me within their first three months of medical school, telling me that their white classmates have research projects and are doing great things. They let me know that they had no idea that these things even existed or that they should be doing them."

I heard a similar concern from Dr. Diane Cejas on an episode of the *Docs With Disabilities* podcast: "People don't recognize how many doors are closed to Black physicians and disabled physicians just because we might not even know that those doors exist."[101]

Brown pointed out that opportunities can get hidden in the curriculum, and students learn about them via social connections. Perhaps from their parents, connections from their college, or even people they meet when they change into their hospital gear. He also shared this disturbing truth bomb: Opportunities are more likely to present themselves in the men's locker room than in the women's since most surgeons, leaders, and chairs are men.

To address this disparity in access to resources, Brown recommends being mindful of whom you mentor and sponsor. Jot down their names, and consider if they're representative of the demographics in the department. If they aren't, reach out to students and residents from underrepresented groups, ask if they'd like to connect, get to know their goals, and ask if there's anything they need or that you can offer them.

And if you're connecting with students of your same gender in the locker room, Brown recommends being intentional about overcoming that geographic barrier. Start conversations by the coffee machine, in the operating room, in the hallway, and at social events where everyone is invited.

As allies, it's our duty to improve access to information, opportunities, resources, and connections within our networks. And outside of them, too. In her book *How to Talk to Your Boss About Race: Speaking Up Without Getting Shut Down*, Y-Vonne Hutchinson points out that "bias thrives in ambiguity." She then implores us:

> Give away all of the inside knowledge you can. Make things as transparent as possible for your colleagues of color. Talk about the unwritten rules. Share your salary and negotiation tips. Share advancement opportunities. Help people find the resources they need to do their jobs better.[102]

Consider how you might start doing this right now. What information will you share to help others, especially those from underrepresented groups, thrive in your workplace? How will you spread access to opportunities and resources so everyone you know has more equitable access?

Building respect and trust

Although expanding our networks to include people who are different from us is critical, it's equally important to steward the professional relationships we already have. This includes our current coworkers and direct reports: people who deserve our attention, support, and respect as much as colleagues at other hospitals or our old medical school professors.

Marva Serotkin is acutely aware that fostering respect among current coworkers is essential in the healthcare industry. For 20 years, she was the CEO of The Boston Home, a long-term residential facility specializing in caring for adults with advanced progressive neurological disorders. Before that, she ran a state hospital. Today, she is a consultant, a speaker, and involved with nonprofits in the Boston area.

When I spoke to Serotkin, she mentioned a recent committee meeting where they discussed why people are leaving the long-term healthcare workforce. One of the key issues raised was a lack of trust, which was exacerbated by the COVID-19 pandemic. She explained, "There were no gowns, there were no masks [for anyone in long-term care facilities]. We prioritized resources for our hospitals at the expense of the most vulnerable population: the elderly living in congregate settings. For those who worked during that time, they'll remember it."

Yet, this issue existed well before COVID-19. What she frequently heard as CEO, particularly from Black and Brown employees, was a feeling of a lack of respect. And that continues to this day. Her call to action? "We have to find a way to address the perceived lack of respect that people feel in the workplace."

To build trust at The Boston Home, Serotkin did small things to let employees know she cared about them. She'd approach someone and say something personal. She would write a note after a death in the family. She urged other leaders and first-line supervisors to do so as well.

"If you understand what makes employees tick as individuals, what they really want, people will perform. But if you ignore them, or people feel that you really don't understand the needs that they have, or the demands that they have with their jobs and their families, you'll have a problem," Serotkin told me. She went on to add, "There has to be that feeling of commitment from the organization. And I think a lot of people just miss that. To me, it's so simple."

I heard a similar story from Dr. Paul Haut, who you met in earlier chapters. As COO of a large children's hospital, he focused on being a hands-on leader, getting to know all the team members by walking around and asking how they were doing. (Haut is a personal friend, and, knowing him as I do, I'll bet he also knew all of their children and dogs by name.) The familiarity he built over time helped Haut show up as an ally, especially early in the COVID-19 pandemic.

In the spring of 2020, the hospital's foundation raised funds to support their healthcare heroes working at the hospital. The hospital decided to use the money to fund a food pantry for team members. "What was shocking to all of us was how many of our team members needed it and were served by it," Haut explained. "It cut across all functions of the workforce."

Yet, some leaders pushed back, questioning why even entry-level workers might need such a resource. After all, they had been raising their minimum wage every year to get it to a living wage. Haut spoke up, pointing out, "You have no idea what's happening in their house." He was able to share stories about team members and their dependent family members. Haut admits being shocked by how many of his work colleagues didn't always think beyond the individual employees at the hospital, not considering it was their responsibility to support the well-being of employees' families, too.

Along with the food pantry, the hospital also opened a free snack closet for team members who needed to grab something quickly to eat on their breaks. That initiative also received some initial pushback. Haut heard concerns that it would be abused, that employees would steal from it or take more than their fair share of the snacks. When some of that did happen, Haut spoke up again. He encouraged people to look beyond any bad behavior they observed and think about what was underlying it. He told them, "Clearly, there's a motivator, most likely poverty and hunger." Which Haut knew was true because he had spent time getting to know people and diversifying his network across the organization.

Building respect and trust among colleagues and coworkers is work that often falls to the bottom of our networking priority lists — but it shouldn't. Whether we're in formal leadership roles, seen as informal leaders who set the tone in a clinical setting, or hanging out at the bottom of the org chart, we can help create a safer, more equitable, and healthier work environment by ensuring that everyone feels valued and trusted.

Tapping into employee resource groups

Dr. Benito Nieves, who you've heard from in previous chapters, is a native Spanish speaker. He told me that whenever he met hospital staff who were Latinx, he would have a conversation with them in Spanish. Nieves explained, "As a result, I felt connected to them, felt cared for by them, and wanted to care for them."

He underscored the importance of this connection: "The alignment that comes from a shared identity could help address the power dynamics that are so strong in hospitals and other healthcare institutions."

Nieves believes employee resource groups (ERGs) can be leveraged to help forge connections and build community across professional and nonprofessional roles within a healthcare workplace. ERGs are voluntary, employee-led groups of individuals who join together based on shared interests, backgrounds, or demographic factors such as gender, race, or disability. According to the Institute for Corporate Productivity, roughly 90 percent of major US employers currently have ERGs, and they are becoming more important to work culture with each passing year.[103] These groups provide a space for under-represented employees to connect with one another, reduce feelings of isolation, and experience some relief from any daily aggressions they've endured at work. But they also benefit the organizations in which they reside. Some consult ERGs to identify gaps in their business strategies, rely on ERGs to help new employees get comfortable during the onboarding process, and collaborate with ERGs to decrease attrition and increase engagement. It's encouraging to see these groups gain visibility and importance across industries.

Here's an example of how ERGs can champion the needs of the groups they represent in the healthcare field. Medical-device maker Medtronic has a women's ERG with more than 20,000 members, and the group catalyzed some significant company-wide changes during the COVID-19 pandemic. In 2020, the ERG serving women focused on easing burdens for its members who were suddenly facing acute childcare challenges while working from home. They presented a formal flexible-work initiative to top executives at the company, and their insights created a springboard for the evolution of a global Medtronic policy. The company soon sanctioned shortened schedules, compressed workweeks, and flexible start and stop times.[104]

As allies, let's join ERGs that match our identities and actively participate. Let's diversify our networks across the positional authority and job responsibilities in our institutions. And let's encourage our organizations to value the voices of underrepresented groups by consulting with ERGs and responding to their feedback.

Of course, if there's an ERG for allies, join that one, too. Or consider forming one if your organization doesn't already have a dedicated space for people to discuss how to be better allies.

Can allies attend identity-specific networking events?

I've made the case for diversifying our networks above. But if we naturally segregate by gender or race, this can prove challenging. Suppose a man is actively seeking to increase the number of women in his professional network. Is it okay for him to attend a Women in Medicine summit or another event for women? Similarly, is it all right for a white person to attend an event for Black or Latinx people?

The answer is, "It depends."

If the event is designed to create a safe space for marginalized group members to discuss the challenges they face and support each other, allies who aren't part of that marginalized group shouldn't show up. Period.

However, I believe that allies have a lot to gain from attending events for underrepresented groups that include open discussions where allies can learn about experiences they don't face themselves, expand their networks, and get involved in supportive ways. I also believe that there are three boxes that should be checked if you're a person with substantial privilege and you'd like to attend a gathering that's been specifically organized for people who are marginalized in a way that you are not. Make sure:

- You'll be welcome (Not sure? Check the website, or ask the organizer and respect their response.)
- You want to attend to become a better ally.
- You're prepared to listen and learn.

Simple as that.

And here's a story from my own experience that highlights how easy it is to join networking events when they're held virtually (for COVID-19 safety or other reasons).

On June 19, 2020, I dialed into the keynote for the Juneteenth Conference, an event made for and featuring Black people in technology. It started with 8+ minutes of silence in honor of George Floyd, followed by an outstanding talk by Danny Thompson about his professional journey, inspired by a rapper who wanted to learn to code. Thompson spoke about going from frying chicken to helping 44 people land their first jobs in tech. His focus on helping bring positive change to his city (and his personal life) was inspiring and left me wanting to do more to help my community. In fact, hearing his keynote made me say yes to a meeting invitation I received just days later to consider serving on a board of directors of Digital NEST, a nonprofit focused on teaching digital skills to youth in rural agricultural areas of California. If I hadn't attended Thompson's talk, I might've passed on that meeting. Attending as an ally shaped my choices, for the better.

Leveraging your network

I loved learning how Dr. Avital O'Glasser, the associate professor of medicine you heard from in the previous chapter, shifted her mindset from being comfortable with just a couple of close professional friends to embracing a wide, diverse network. When she was younger, she thought, Why do I need a network? Why can't my professional pathway sail on the momentum of my own strengths and passions? But, O'Glasser realized that to grow her career, she needed to build connections with others in her specialty internationally, and she found them out on Twitter. Next, she stumbled into a vibrant women in medicine community online. "It was transformative," she told me. Colleagues she met on social media have opened career doors for her. "I know that I have gotten positions on national committees and invitations to work on projects because someone [in my network] recommended me. I've also been contacted by my connections because they're serving as a guest editor for a special edition of a journal, and they want me to write for it."

Then there's job hunting.

When I asked Dr. Resa E. Lewiss, the emergency medicine professor you've heard from a few times already, about how she has found new roles over her career, she shared, "There are headhunters, recruiters, and online job postings." She went on to explain, "But, as you are promoted and advance in your career, those opportunities are more difficult to access except by word of mouth and by having allies or sponsors. The power of networks can't be overestimated." When seeking a new role, she reaches out to people in her network, telling them, "By the way, I'm looking. Please keep me in mind if you hear of something."

People with diverse networks also benefit because a variety of people know and trust them and can speak up on their behalf, even if they aren't in the room.

Dr. Lorna Rodriguez, the vice chair of surgery you heard from in Chapter 1, knows someone did this for her. She remembers having to make a decision for her team in the moment, without being able to discuss it with them first. Knowing it would be controversial, she arranged a meeting for a few days later. But, in the meantime, people started hearing about the decision and complaining to each other. Rodriguez later found out that someone spoke up, defending her. She explained, "A white woman heard the complaints and said, 'I know Lorna very well, and she's always very fair.'" Rodriguez told me how that small act of allyship helped people be more receptive to understanding and supporting her decision.

By the way, knowing how much her online community supports her, O'Glasser also pays it forward. She does this with intention, leveraging the diverse network she's created. "If I'm recruiting speakers, I make sure not to have manels. If I'm assembling an ad-hoc work team, I slow down and ask if I have gender diversity? Racial diversity? Diversity of time in the profession?"

O'Glasser emphasizes the importance of being intentional about building a diverse network and then utilizing it as you have opportunities to offer. As allies, we need to realize that neither will happen organically. We have to be mindful and hold ourselves accountable.

Intentionally diversifying your network

"Just like me" networks can have a negative impact on creating diverse, inclusive workplaces. Those involved in hiring new staff or recommending people for professional opportunities naturally look to people who are part of their professional networks because they know and trust them, but when those networks are homogenous, this translates to favoring and advocating for folks like themselves. Depending on referrals is standard, and if those referrals come from a homogeneous network, it results in just hiring more homogeneity. (This is one possible reason for the male-led editorial team at the OB/GYN journal you learned about earlier in the chapter.)

It's also common for leaders to favor their network members when assigning career-advancing stretch goals, reviewing candidates for promotions and key spots during reorganizations, and creating succession plans. We instinctively bolster the people we know and trust, who are almost always, without fail, people just like us.

In other words, if you only open doors to people in your network, chances are they'll be for people similar to you. If you've read this far, you'll undoubtedly recognize that to be problematic (or so I hope). Luckily, diversifying your network isn't the onerous task you may fear it to be. In addition to the three strategies I shared earlier in this chapter, there are plenty of other simple, easy actions you can take to widen your professional circle outside your comfort zone. For example:

- The next time you're grabbing coffee at work or attending an event or conference, reach out to people who aren't like you. Introduce yourself to someone of a different gender, race, age, or other visible difference. Get to know them and stay in touch with them. Perhaps you'll be able to learn from them or introduce them to a career opportunity down the road.

- Attend industry events for people who are different from you. Each is an opportunity to listen and learn about their experiences and, of course, to expand your network. Not sure if you'd be welcome? Check the event information or ask the organizer. Many such groups and gatherings are open to allies.

- Try a conference on a topic that isn't your exact area of expertise. Attend any panels that feature a diversity of speakers, and follow them afterward on social media. Take the time to connect with other attendees.

- Volunteer for an organization that serves a diverse populace.

- At every workplace event, networking opportunity, and party hosted by professional associations, force yourself to talk to one total stranger who is different from you. Just walk up, introduce yourself, and ask them what they're working on right now that excites them.

Of course, there are many ways to expand and diversify your connections online. You can:

- Join online discussion forums for underrepresented groups (after asking first if you'd be welcome).

- Listen to a variety of podcasts by or featuring people from marginalized communities.
- Follow people of different genders, ethnic backgrounds, sexual orientations and identities, ages, abilities, and so forth on social media.
- Positively acknowledge what people from under-represented groups post online to help build their reputations and prevent others with more privilege from claiming credit for their work.[105]

If you're ready to make an even bigger move to diversify your network, offer to be a mentor for someone who is underrepresented and is seeking a mentoring relationship. Informally or formally, it can make a difference. Respond to that next email seeking your advice. Volunteer through a formal mentoring program.

By the way, mentoring is a two-way street. When we share our experiences and advice with others, we have the opportunity to help them grow in their careers. At the same time, we can learn from them and grow in our own careers.

Networking in the #MeToo era

A note for straight men: As you read this chapter, you may have found yourself thinking, How on earth do I network with women in this climate? One wrong word, joke, or choice, and I'll get thrown into the penalty box! You might be scared you'll get fired, be sued, or ruin your career.

This is a *somewhat* understandable reaction. Research by LeanIn.Org found that men in senior leadership roles are 3.5 times more likely to feel uncertain about scheduling a work dinner with a junior-level woman than with a junior-level man.[106] And according to the Pew Research Center, 51 percent of Americans believe the #MeToo movement has made it harder for men to know how to interact with women in the workplace.[107] This dynamic feels new to many men, and many men are unsure how to navigate it without feeling fearful and vulnerable.

Some have even adopted something called "the Billy Graham rule" or "the Mike Pence rule." This is a practice where a male leader avoids spending time alone with any woman who isn't his wife. Regardless of the motivation behind it, this rule is a real thing, and it has real consequences for women and their ability to advance under male supervisors. There are both corporations and individuals who have adopted it.[108]

I've met some of these men. A business unit leader once announced during a workshop I was facilitating, "My wife gets jealous when I have a work dinner with a woman coworker," and then asked, "How should I handle that?" My snarky side wanted to scream at him to go to couples' therapy. Instead, I simply recommended, "You could always bring along another coworker. Or only meet coworkers of any gender over breakfast." I'm hoping that the discussion had an impact — if not on him, then at least on his employees who were in the room that day.

I'm disturbed by this mindset. No one should be excluded from out-of-office activities where colleagues get to know each other, share ideas, and learn from each other. Whether it's a work dinner, a round of golf, a camping trip, or something else.

While avoiding women altogether may make some men feel more comfortable, it also has the toxic side effect of further isolating and ostracizing women in the workplace. The #MeToo movement is not meant to drive a giant wedge between people of different genders when it comes to professional networking and mentoring, but if men take a giant step back, it will.

If you are a male leader, first of all, don't become part of this trend. As my friends David Smith, PhD, and Brad Johnson, PhD, emphasize in their book *Good Guys: How Men Can Be Better Allies for Women in the Workplace*, "If you are a man in any sort of leadership role, intentional interaction with women is a nonnegotiable job requirement."[109] So, check yourself often. Reflect on your week and ask yourself if you avoided being alone with a coworker because of concerns that they, or others, might think it was more than a professional interaction. If the answer is "yup" or "well, maybe," there's work to do.

Next, be open and honest about your concerns. If you want to chat with a woman colleague over coffee instead of in a meeting room but worry she might take it the wrong way, say so. Try this: "How would you feel about going to an outdoor café for this meeting? If you'd be more comfortable talking at the hospital, that's fine, too. I just thought a change of scenery might be nice." Offer choices, offer an out, and you'll show the other person that their input is welcome and they're not powerless.

Actions for Better Allies:
Diversify Your Network

Most of us have largely homogeneous networks. Here are some tips for ensuring that your network is diverse and more effective:

- Do a network inventory. List out the people you feel are your top ten contacts. Are any of them marginalized in ways that you are not? If not, start in your own backyard: Who within your organization could be a great addition to your current network?
- Seek out people who disagree with you and engage them in respectful conversation. Listen and learn.
- The next time you attend an event of any kind, introduce yourself to someone who doesn't look like you.
- Seek out media, including podcasts and blogs, by people who are different from you.
- Remember to network with your current coworkers and colleagues as a way to foster respect and trust. Be mindful of doing this across functions, racial boundaries, and power differentials.
- As you diversify your network, be generous with your inside knowledge and talk about the unwritten rules for growth and success.

6

RESHAPING REPRESENTATION

A few years ago, TV news host Rachel Maddow made a zinger of a comment when visiting a university to hand out a prize for a prominent female scientist: "What is up with the dude wall?"[110]

We've all seen them. Walls covered with portraits of men who have made significant contributions to their fields or institutions. It's one way to honor them. Speaking from personal experience, it can be a lovely tribute for family members. My grandfather, Clifford Smith Sr., is memorialized posthumously in a wonderful portrait in a hall of the Westerly Hospital in my home town in Rhode Island. He served on the hospital's board of directors for almost 30 years and was their president for two years. He was also an older white man.

While I'm incredibly proud of my grandfather and his service to the community, I know he was one of many white men who held leadership roles at the hospital. Men who were respected because they looked the part. Men who leveraged their networks to give back but also to get ahead.

So, let's consider the message that "dude walls" broadcast about who is valued, who belongs, and who looks like success.

In a study of the impact of such portraits at Yale School of Medicine (YSM), students described the portraits as "a visual demonstration of YSM's values, which they identified as whiteness, elitism, maleness, and power." Some students said that the portraits "exacerbated feelings of being judged and unwelcome at the institution."[111]

Stepping back, let's realize that "dude walls" aren't limited to framed oil paintings or grids of leadership photos. They can be embodied in awards granted and promotions given. They show up in the imagery used in presentations, brochures, websites, and textbooks. They're present in homogeneous all-male speaker lineups at conferences and grand rounds, leadership roles in professional associations, and authors of journal articles. They're reinforced by the pronouns we use. And allies can use our position and privilege to take action to improve diversity in all of these situations.

In awards and honors

The Alpha Omega Alpha Honor Medical Society (AΩA) membership is one of the highest honors, maybe *the* highest, for a medical student in the United States. It can significantly impact a student's professional success, increasing the likelihood of securing interviews at the most competitive residency programs. Membership can also be a game-changer for physicians, introducing them to an elite network of physician leaders.

Under "How Members Are Chosen" on the society's website, you'll find the following statement: "AΩA is committed to national leadership in advancing diversity and inclusion in the profession of medicine ... Chapters are expected to embrace and respect differences and foster creativity in how they celebrate students who contribute in these important ways. AΩA expects an unbiased, inclusive nomination and election process." Yet, a 2017 study found that the student selection process was imbued with bias. Specifically, white students were six times more likely than Black students and twice as likely as Asian students to be accepted as members of AΩA.[112]

So the organization clearly states that it values diversity, yet fails to reflect it in its membership population. Given the advantages that AΩA membership imparts, this is a rift that desperately needs addressing.

As you might expect, AΩA is not the only organization whose stated goals around representation fail to match its actions. In March 2022, the Australian biomedical research foundation Snow Medical announced they made the difficult decision to suspend the University of Melbourne from its prestigious Snow Fellowship program. Why? The University granted their honorary doctorate to six white men. In fact, during the previous three years, none of their honorary doctorates went to women or people of non-white descent. (Snow Medical explained that, before making their decision, they reached out to the University and found that while policies on gender equality and diversity are in place, the award outcomes do not align with the University's stated goals.)[113]

Here's one more example. Each year, the UK's Royal Society selects fellows for their outstanding contributions to science. After the 2022 recipients were announced, Cambridge University proudly issued a news release about their faculty receiving this recognition: nine scientists, all of whom were men.[114]

If your organization grants awards to researchers, employees, students, or other members of your community, review the lists of recent recipients. Does the representation match the diversity of your institution or community? Does it align with your stated diversity goals? If you have the equivalent of a homogeneous "dude wall," reach out to the award coordinator, point out what you're seeing, and encourage them to revisit their process.

In imagery

After the publication of our book, *Present! A Techie's Guide to Public Speaking*, my co-author, Poornima Vijayashanker, and I created a presentation to share its key messages and drive awareness (and hopefully sales). After we outlined our talk, I dove into designing a slide deck, using stock photography and other images to reinforce our speaking points. And I purposefully chose photos of women, taking the opportunity to showcase diversity — or so I thought.

I believed I'd done a good job with our slides, until we delivered that talk at the Palo Alto Lean In Circle meeting in 2016. My daughter Emma, who was in the audience, gave me feedback afterward. She pointed out that all of the stock photography was of white women, most of whom had blond ponytails. Jeepers. I hadn't even noticed. (As you might have guessed, I immediately changed the slide deck to reflect more diversity.)

By contrast, I remember being happily surprised as I watched the recording of a talk for the Women in Medicine Summit in 2020. Dr. Seth Trueger shared how he acts as an ally, including steering away from stock photos that pattern-match a doctor as a guy with white hair.

Then there's the beautiful illustration of a Black fetus which went viral in late 2021.[115] It was drawn by Chidiebere Ibe, a self-taught illustrator and medical school student who had noticed the absence of Black skin in his textbooks. Another medical illustrator, Ni-ka Ford, commented:[116]

> **Ni-ka** ...
> @NikaFord_
>
> Amazing to see so much awareness being brought to the need for more inclusivity and diversity in medical illustration. Bias towards able-bodied whiteness in medical education materials is very harmful, it contributes to inequality and disparities in healthcare.

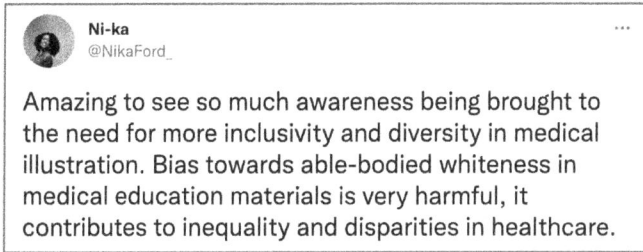

Others agree. As a first-year medical student at Harvard, LaShyra Nolen realized they were being taught how to diagnose Lyme disease on white skin but not on darker skin. In an article for the *New England Journal of Medicine,* she explored how the images used in textbooks can affect medical education, pointing out that "the United States may be in danger of graduating large numbers of physicians who are unable to serve the needs of our ever-diversifying patient population."[117]

According to research, fewer than 5 percent of images in medical textbooks show dark skin.[118] This may be why almost half of graduating dermatology residents in the United States report feeling uncomfortable diagnosing skin disease in patients with dark skin, as reported by Dr. Jenna C. Lester, a dermatologist and founder of the Skin of Color program at University of California, San Francisco.[119]

Beyond patient care, diversity in medical illustrations can also bring more diversity to the field. Someone left this telling comment on Ibe's Instagram post of his drawing of the Black fetus: "Seeing more textbooks like this would make me want to become a medical student."

Think about the subtle — or not-so-subtle — messages you send wherever you use images. Not only in presentations and textbooks, but also in scholarly articles, social media posts, marketing brochures and posters, and websites. If you're showing only white people, men, or people with no visible disabilities, for example, what stereotypes are you reinforcing?

It may be understated, but the simple act of using stock photos and illustrations of people from underrepresented groups makes a difference. And there are many resources (some of which are free) to make it easy for you. I've listed several of my favorites on my website at *www.betterallies.com/resources*. Make them your go-to libraries for finding stock images.

Don't deceive with images

After I encouraged subscribers of my "5 Ally Actions" weekly newsletter to feature diversity in their slide decks and websites, someone emailed me, asking an important question: "I recognize that representation matters and makes a huge difference…but when does inclusive representation cross the line into false advertising?"

They pointed out an all-too-real scenario. Imagine an organization where all the media, training, publicity, slideshows, videos, etc. depict a beautiful and wide diversity of people, but it is grossly misrepresentative of those who actually work there.

Allies, we need to be genuine and authentic with our use of photos. Let's not try to deceive anyone by showcasing more diversity than we have in our student body or workforce or implying we have a more inclusive culture than we do.

Avoid negative stereotypes

Of course, images can also convey negative stereotypes. For example, dermatology textbooks use dark skin tones more frequently to show sexually transmitted diseases than common diagnoses such as acne.[120]

I appreciate the usage guidelines provided by The Gender Spectrum Collection. While written specifically for their stock photos of transgender and nonbinary models, it can be applied to any situation:

> Understanding the stereotypes and tropes that have accompanied transgender media representation — such as trans subjects being cast only as sex workers, portrayed solely in states of apparent victimhood or crisis, and being characterized as deceptive and mentally unstable — can help you to avoid them. If your usage of one of these photos could feed into a stereotype or negative stigma, you probably shouldn't use it.[121]

Make imagery accessible

Once we have great representation in our imagery, we want to make sure blind people and others with vision impairments can take them in.

I learned about apps that simulate color vision deficiencies from Kathy, who subscribes to my weekly newsletter. One is called Chromatic Vision Simulator, and it uses your camera phone to let you see how presentations, websites, graphs, and other visuals appear to someone who is colorblind.

As Kathy pointed out, "Since eight percent of men and half a percent of women have some type of colorblindness, they could be a substantial part of your audience."

I immediately downloaded the app[122] (which is free) and used it to review my keynote slides. It's an easy-to-use tool to add to our ally toolbox.

For imagery we are posting online, keep in mind that people may use assistive technology such as screen readers. To help them understand what your images depict, add descriptions with HTML alt tags or in captions underneath the photos.

Last but not least, if you are delivering a talk and have imagery in your slide deck, consider this tip from the Digital Library Federation's Guide to Creating Accessible Presentations:

Describe any images, charts, and other visuals in your presentation as though you were delivering your presentation on the radio.[123] I need to work on doing this myself. It may take some practice and finesse to do it effectively, but I'm going to make it happen. Who's with me?

On stage

In the not-so-distant past, some clever person coined the term "manel" to describe a panel consisting only of men. A panel that subconsciously reinforces that men are the subject matter experts; that women don't belong. And then there are "manferences" — conferences that feature all-male speaker lineups. Across healthcare fields, these exclusionary events are not hard to find.

In a 2020 study, researchers found that men outnumber women as invited lecturers and panelists in most academic medical conferences by a ratio of 2:1. And that more than one-third of the panels were made up of all men.[124]

Another huge and ever-growing problem is the all-white panel, or "wanel." Here's an example I came across while writing this chapter: the 6th European Nursing Conference, scheduled for October 2022. Even with its theme of "Future Proof Nursing," not a single speaker of color was shown on their conference welcoming announcement.[125] Considering that the future will include a global population dominated by people of color, this is shockingly short-sighted. (The UN predicts that half of the population growth between now and 2050 is expected to come from just nine countries: India, Nigeria, Pakistan, the Democratic Republic of the Congo, Ethiopia, Tanzania, Indonesia, Egypt, and the United States.[126] All but the US are populated mainly by people of color.)

As a panel organizer myself, I can see how easy it is to select a homogeneous group. Most organizers reach out to their network to find people who can speak on the topic. If they lack diversity in their network (which most people do, as we learned in Chapter 5), chances are they will lack diversity at the event. However, ensuring that speakers represent a variety of viewpoints and experiences should be a goal for allies. It might be challenging, but it's important enough that we all should be willing to move outside our comfort zones to make it happen.

Speakers also play an important role in diversifying panels and conference lineups. Allies who are called upon as featured experts can further contribute to equitable representation by boycotting events that fail to assemble inclusive panel and speaker lineups.

In 2019, Dr. Francis Collins, Director of the National Institutes of Health, did this by proclaiming that he would no longer participate in conferences with all-male speaking panels:

> I want to send a clear message of concern: it is time to end the tradition in science of all-male speaking panels, sometimes wryly referred to as "manels." Too often, women and members of other groups underrepresented in science are conspicuously missing in the marquee speaking slots at scientific meetings and other high-level conferences. Starting now, when I consider speaking invitations, I will expect a level playing field, where scientists of all backgrounds are evaluated fairly for speaking opportunities. If that attention to inclusiveness is not evident in the agenda, I will decline to take part. I challenge other scientific leaders across the biomedical enterprise to do the same.[127]

Collins is not alone. As I shared in Chapter 1, *The Lancet* has a No All-Male Panel Policy, where their editors will not serve as panelists at a public conference or event when there are no women on the panel. There are many other examples as well.

As the Twitter handle "ManelWatchUS" patently pointed out: "#manels end when men refuse to serve on them."[128]

I encourage all who are reading this book to follow these examples. Before accepting a speaking engagement or panel slot, ask, "Will you have a diverse speaker lineup?" If you're a frequent public speaker, add "Won't speak on all-male panels" or "Won't speak on all-white panels" to your online bio.

That said, there will be times you'll forget to ask. I get it. If you inadvertently end up on a homogenous panel and get called out for it, here's a pro tip: Don't get defensive, and don't claim you're the victim. Here's a cautionary tale about someone who did.

Large professional societies typically have local, regional chapters. These smaller local chapters run programs for members and students who can't necessarily travel to national meetings, giving them the chance to still network and learn together. Sounds great, right? Except when it's not. I spoke to a woman I'll refer to as Dr. Smith (not her real name), who said the local chapter of her society has an old boys' club vibe. The leadership has been all men for a while, their speakers tend to be men, and those who are recognized as important for whatever reason are also all men. Smith is especially concerned about the message this lack of diversity sends to students and how their chapter may be, as a result, unwittingly limiting diversity in their field.

For example, this local chapter hosted a symposium to help early career professionals. When Smith noticed that all the judges were going to be men, she brought up the importance of diversity. Their response? "Yes, it's important to us." But later in the same year, when Smith saw the speaker lineup for their upcoming annual meeting, she got upset. Looking at the photos, she saw that every single one was a man. At this point, Smith turned to social media. She shared the story of her experience, along with the words "representation matters." Well, one of her colleagues who was scheduled to speak wasn't happy about getting called out. He told their supervisor that he had been publicly attacked by Smith. (Before posting, she had reached out to him directly about the lack of diversity, and he seemed supportive. But clearly, that support didn't extend to a social media share.) His male fragility put a wedge between himself and Smith, tainting a professional relationship that otherwise might benefit their institution and overall field.

By the way, this story is a shining example of DARVO — a situation where someone **denies** accusations, **attacks** their accuser, and **reverses** the roles of **victim** and **offender** so they're seen as the victim. It's a powerful form of gaslighting that uses hierarchical structures and power to maintain inequality.

DARVO was coined by Dr. Jennifer Joy Freyd, who studies it alongside her work on institutional betrayal and courage. In an episode of *The Visible Voices* podcast, Freyd explained that when an offender brings DARVO into play, the true victim may start to blame themselves, third parties tend to doubt the victim's credibility, and the perpetrator obtains a favorable outcome.[129]

Now for some uplifting news. Freyd's research shows that teaching people about DARVO reduces its power to destroy the victim's credibility.[130]

So, now that you know about DARVO, look for it. It might show up as a statement like, "I didn't mean any harm; they're making a big deal out of nothing. In fact, if they were more of a team player, I'd be able to get more of my work done on time." Or someone who's been accused of sexual harassment strategically maneuvering themselves to be seen as the victim, responding with outrage and attacking the person who filed a complaint about them.[131]

If you spot it, call it out. As I shared in Chapter 4, be an upstander, not a bystander.

In journals

If you're familiar with academic settings, you know that publishing research papers is necessary for career growth, getting tenure, and landing jobs. But are you aware that the process of getting published in journals is one that's riddled with privilege?

As Alan Weil, the editor of *Health Affairs*, explained in an article on racism in medical journals:

> If you're published, you're asked to review. If you're cited, you get tenure. If you get tenure, you get more resources to publish. The problem is the people who are outside of the circle, who don't have a track record of publication, who don't get funded or mentored, or have a heavy teaching load. Opportunities are not equally distributed.[132]

You know what else is a problem? A male and pale editorial board. As I learned from Dr. Melissa Simon, "Women and people of color are often shut out from the inner circles of editors who reach out to researchers they know to solicit submissions."[133] This concern is reflected in a study of two prestigious US medical journals, which found that women and people of color rarely served as lead or senior authors of research articles published during the past three decades. Even as the representation of these demographics increased within the field of medicine.[134]

To improve representation in scholarly publishing, there needs to be better diversity on editorial boards.

Remember the tweet at the beginning of the previous chapter about the all-male editor and deputy editor lineup of the *Obstetrics & Gynecology* journal? After I retweeted it, Dr. Alan McElligott, a professor of veterinary medicine, recommended:

It would be great if everyone could have a look at their fav[orite] journals + check the composition of the editorial boards! I have found several recently in which all the editors (or senior editors) are men - this is unacceptable in 2022! Please advocate for change.[135]

Allies, you know what to do.

With pronouns

For a long time, "he" was considered the default pronoun in the English language to refer to a single person. It took decades of effort for feminists to shift this standard by advocating for the use of "he or she" and "her or his," but many people still use "he" on occasion even if they don't know the gender of the person to whom they're referring. Doing so perpetuates bias. For example, imagine attending a hiring committee meeting for a nurse and hearing someone say, "When the candidate arrives, she should first meet with ___." The person is probably thinking about the demographic of nursing and reinforcing this stereotype by using the pronoun "she."

To circumvent this implicit gender bias and the awkwardness of saying "he or she," it's fine to use "them" and "they," even when talking about an individual person. The grammatically minded among us (including me) might find this awkward initially, but over time it becomes more familiar and natural. I'm now fine hearing (or saying), "When the candidate arrives, they should first meet with ___." In fact, I've even intentionally written this book using "they" and "them" in this way. (If your inner grammarian continues to resist, remember that revered writers, including William Shakespeare and Jane Austen, used "they" as a singular pronoun.[136])

In addition to employing "they" when a person's gender identity is uncertain, it's helpful to make yourself aware of the language people use to refer to themselves. Many nonbinary people use "them" and "they." There are plenty of people, whether cisgender, trans, or nonbinary, for whom it is impossible to know what pronouns to use just by looking at them. Even some cisgender people forsake the traditional "he" or "she" pronouns for "they" or something else. It's presumptive to assign someone a pronoun based on their physical appearance.

Not sure what pronouns to use? As I learned from Jeannie Gainsburg, author of *The Savvy Ally*, simply ask, perhaps making the situation more comfortable by sharing the pronouns you use first.[137] For example, introduce yourself and add, "I use 'she' and 'her' pronouns. How may I refer to you?" This approach is respectful, and their answer gives us clear guidance. It also gives the person an out if they don't want to share their pronouns. They can simply reply, "You can call me Jay."

Warning: You may get some pushback. As Dr. Alaettin Carikci, a diversity and inclusion leader you heard from in Chapter 3, told me, "In clinical settings, people may be dealing with a matter that's life and death, and they don't want to introduce themselves with their pronouns." Even though Carikci believes this practice is absolutely fundamental and should be done consistently for trans/nonbinary inclusion, he admits that you might be blamed for being "woke" when you do it.

Of course, if you don't want to ask a patient or a colleague about their pronouns, you can always just use "they" or their name until you learn more.

Now, for an important "don't." Please don't ask someone for their "preferred" pronouns on a form or in conversation. That makes it sound like using their pronouns is optional, which it's not.

And remember that if you are a cisgender ally, clarifying your pronouns is a simple but powerful act of support. Whether you do this verbally or in an email signature, as part of your video conference profile, or with a pin you wear on your lanyard, you are helping to normalize the practice of sharing pronouns. This is helpful to genderfluid, transgender, and other nonbinary folks, who get loads of pushback on the pronoun issue overall. (Coincidentally, on the same day that I was working on this chapter, I had an appointment with my physician. At her office, the receptionist just happened to be wearing a button that read "she/her.")

What's cool is that sharing your pronouns also provides an opportunity to let others know if you are bilingual. For example, a woman who speaks both English and Spanish could list their pronouns as "she/ella."

I haven't (yet) come across institutional guidelines for white coats that specify embroidering someone's pronouns under their name and advanced degrees, but I'm hopeful. Alternatively, if a workplace provides laminated name tags or badges, I'd love to see pronouns on them. As Carikci told me, some of the NHS hospitals in the UK have adopted this practice, though it's not yet common at all hospitals.

What about she/they?

During a recent virtual keynote that I gave on *Better Allies*, an audience member typed this question into the chat box: "What does it mean when someone specifies their pronouns as she/they?"

At the time, I didn't know the answer, and I have to admit I was relieved that the moderator didn't ask me to address it. Phew! There were plenty of other questions and not enough time to get to them all.

However, if I get the same question at a future talk, I'm now prepared, thanks to National Public Radio reporter Laurel Wamsley. They wrote:

What does it mean if a person uses the pronouns "he/they" or "she/they"? That means that the person uses both pronouns, and you can alternate between those when referring to them. So either pronoun would be fine — and ideally mix it up, use both.[138]

Apologize without making it all about yourself

In an article titled "I Am Neither," Kathia Ramos wrote about their experience of letting people know that their pronouns were now they/them. Their manager at the time was very understanding, yet mistakenly used their old pronouns. The first time wasn't a big deal. She apologized and moved on. Then it happened again.

As Ramos shared, "I didn't expect the apologizing to escalate to an explanation of how she was trying to use the correct pronoun. Time stood still while she apologized, and I could feel everyone's eyes on me. What appeared to be an effort to make herself feel better, actually made me feel worse."[139]

Allies, if we use the wrong pronouns for a coworker, let's briefly apologize and correct ourselves. Without launching into an explanation of how we're trying to use the right pronouns or making it all about us.

For role models

When I interviewed Dr. Dawn Haut (who you heard from in previous chapters), she told me, "There's a chance that I chose pediatrics because I saw more women role models in pediatrics." Haut added, "While I love kids, it was not the only factor in my career choice. I felt like I had 'found my people' amongst the pediatricians."

She's not alone. One study found that women are more likely to enter surgery programs with women faculty.[140] Another found the same results for people who are members of racial minority groups.[141]

Dr. Paula Magee described the lack of role models as one of the many "drips" that contribute to the leaky pipeline that keeps potential medical students from succeeding in medical school and beyond.[142]

And in an article for *STAT*, Dr. Charles Day, a professor at Henry Ford Health Systems in Detroit, emphasized the importance of better representation in faculty role models. Day explained, "The current leadership in academic medicine across the board continues to lack representation. That's one of the key variables if we are going to affect systematic change."[143]

While increasing the diversity in role models across healthcare may seem like a tall order, allies can do a few simple things to help. For starters, we can elevate and amplify all role models from underrepresented groups as often as possible. Know of a Black woman surgeon or a transgender professor of pharmacology? Let's retweet them and share their work as broadly as we can. Endorse them publicly by crediting them by name in presentations or during meetings. Point out what we've learned from them or what we admire about their work.

Let's take an active role in patching the leaky pipeline. (Much more on this in Chapter 10.)

For patients

When I asked Dr. VK Gadi (the medical oncology director you heard from in Chapter 4) why he cared about diversity and inclusion in healthcare, he emphasized, "The lived experiences of our patients and who they are contributes greatly to our understanding of their disease, but also how they're going to respond to our treatments. One thing that's been very clear to me is that having a diverse workforce that appreciates and comes from these environments is absolutely critical to meet the needs of those patients." It's not just diversity for diversity's sake. Gadi told me, "At the end of the day, it's not just about the workforce being diverse. It's that the most diverse workforce is capable and able to deliver the best healthcare."

Gadi grew up in small communities in the Deep South of the United States. He shared that his upbringing helps him "understand the dynamic of rurality," which in turn helps him be a better physician, especially for Black patients. Gadi, who is Indian, explained, "Being able to have shared cultural experiences builds trust. And even though I don't always look like the people I'm taking care of, those shared experiences help me make that bridge." He might introduce a Southern drawl into the conversation or make a connection to sports or favorite foods. "Whatever connection I can make at that visceral level allows somebody to see me as one of them and not one of some other."

Such connections lead to trust, which helps patients feel more comfortable talking to their healthcare providers. I spoke with a client who confided, "As a gay man, I feel comfortable going to a specific STD health clinic in Soho, which is known as a gay neighborhood of London. I feel at ease because everyone working there visibly identifies as LGBT. So I don't have to hide anything or feel ashamed about any kind of sexual interaction I might have had."

Let's also acknowledge that lived experiences can be critical to providing the right patient care. Here's just one example that will stick with me forever. In a video posted on Instagram, a person explained that they were the only Black nurse on a mom and baby unit when an outgoing nurse said that she'd requested a psychiatric consultation for a patient repeatedly hitting herself on her head. The Black nurse asked, "Is she Black?" The other nurse said, "Yes, how did you know?" The Black nurse then tapped the side of her own head and asked if that's what it looked like. The response? "Yeah, how did you know?" The Black nurse went on to explain that if someone has a weave in their hair and has an itchy scalp, they'll tap their head instead of scratching it. As you might imagine, the other nurse then canceled the unnecessary psych consult.[144]

The role of professional associations

There are hundreds of healthcare-focused professional associations, some with a global membership, others working at the national level, and many smaller local organizations and chapters. Generally speaking, they exist to support professionals in a certain field, informing their members of practice guidelines and new research while offering education to further their skills and stay accredited. Some have career centers with job boards and résumé writing advice. Larger groups also publish journals.

Regardless of the specific offerings, I think of professional associations as providing the equivalent of rocket booster fuel for their members' careers. Specifically, they offer activities that increase their members' visibility and credibility, such as publishing op-eds, thought pieces, and research papers. They also give out résumé-building awards, offer leadership positions on committees, and provide speaking opportunities on both small and large stages.

As a result, these organizations can play an important role in diversifying their field, if they make it a priority. By examining the demographics of who gets nominated for awards and committee roles, they can take steps to improve representation. They can work to ensure that their events feature diverse speaker lineups. They can insist that their editorial boards and the authors published in their journals represent the demographics of their membership base. They can change their bylaws to specify when a member will be dismissed for discriminatory or harassing behavior. (More on codes of conduct in the next chapter.)

I encourage allies to hold their professional associations accountable for reshaping representation. Here are some specific ideas:

- Advocate for a Diversity, Equity, and Inclusion (DEI) policy, if your association doesn't already have one.
- Volunteer to serve on search committees for leadership roles and create a strategy for identifying candidates from underrepresented groups.
- Vote in elections to increase the representation of people from underrepresented groups for leadership roles.
- Review the speaker lineup for every grand rounds, webinar hosted by a professional society, or other kinds of meeting, large or small. If you spot a lineup that's overwhelmingly homogeneous, contact the organizers and ask about it. Suggest people from your own network who could be swapped in or contacted for future speaking opportunities (after first asking if they'd like you to recommend them).
- If a professional association publishes a journal, review its editorial board. If it's homogeneous or lacking representation of your member base, speak up. (Like Dr. Alan McElligott recommended earlier.)
- Make sure the processes for recommending candidates for leadership and editorial board roles, offering to speak at meetings, and submitting articles to a journal are transparent and widely available to all members, not just to those "in the know" and highly connected to the editors.

- Request regular reporting on the association's board of directors, leadership, and staff demographics. (The American Nursing Association, for example, committed to providing such transparency in their 2022 Racial Reckoning Statement.[145])

Representation is a multifaceted concept that encompasses what we see, how we interpret it, and how we believe it reflects on us. It has been proven again and again to be a powerful force in human culture. In her book *Worldmaking: Race, Performance, and the Work of Creativity*, Dorinne Kondo insists that we all need to be "mirrored" in the public sphere (popular culture, media, leadership, etc.) to be considered fully human, fully social beings.[146] When people sense that the groups they belong to and the identities they hold aren't valued, they feel disenfranchised and invalidated. When they see themselves represented — in leadership roles, in imagery, as authors of books and papers, as honorees — they feel optimistic.

Marian Wright Edelman, founder and president of the Children's Defense Fund, has said, "You can't be what you can't see." Some critics call this statement hyperbole, but I agree with Edelman. Just as seeing people who look like us achieve and succeed can inspire us to follow in their footsteps, *never* seeing people like us achieve and succeed can hold us back. Representation isn't just "identity politics," and it isn't a minor issue. By insisting that people from a wide variety of backgrounds are represented across all of healthcare, we send the message that they are valued, needed, and welcomed in our field.

Actions for Better Allies:
Ensure Equitable Representation

Representation matters. We can and should take steps to ensure that people from underrepresented groups are represented in the awards we give, the content we create, the journals and educational material we consume, and the caregiving teams we're on.

- If you're in a position to select imagery for your hospital or organization's website or publications, make sure photos reflect the diversity of your employee and patient populations.
- Refuse to participate in "manels" or "wanels." When you see them, call them out.
- Share your pronouns. If you use the wrong pronoun for someone, apologize without making it all about yourself.
- Hold up role models from underrepresented groups every chance you get.
- Hold your professional associations accountable for reshaping representation.

7

TRANSFORMING MEETINGS

When I worked as a tech executive, I spent most of my days in meetings. Weekly one-on-ones with my staff to review progress against our objectives and discuss career growth. Quarterly departmental meetings to celebrate our successes and share strategic priorities. Engineering leadership councils to connect across our many teams. Large conferences hosted by professional organizations. The list goes on.

Throughout them all, I saw my fair share of non-inclusive meeting behavior. And unfortunately, I know those behaviors are not limited to tech.

In my research for this book, I heard and read about many examples of healthcare workers who were excluded from conversations, interrupted or ignored, or, at times, harassed. This type of conduct seems to be everywhere. In administrative meetings, morning rounds, and huddles at the start of shifts. At events hosted by professional associations. During noon conferences for residents and in other training settings.

In this chapter, I cover how to spot situations where you can take action, along with suggested steps to make the meetings you attend more balanced and equitable. I also address the role of professional associations in making their annual meetings and conferences more inclusive.

Idea hijacking

Cynthia Walsh, the acute care nurse and administrator you heard from in Chapter 2, remembers working closely with her boss on a renovation project. Together, they developed a plan to shut down a section of their hospital in Boston, moving all of the furniture and equipment so the renovation could take place. Her boss, who didn't have a medical background, also brought in a physician to add credibility to their plans. Walsh told me, "This physician, who had no expertise in my area, was obnoxious, patronizing, made rude comments all the time, and had no problem putting me down." Sadly, her boss never spoke up about it. Instead, he just laughed it off.

But that's not all. After Walsh completed the plan, that doctor presented it to the administrative team as his project and subsequently gave her orders about how to execute it. Walsh told me it was awful. She thought to herself, I created this plan. I should be telling him what to do.

As I heard her story, I found myself wondering, Why didn't her boss stand up and act as an ally? Why didn't he make sure she got credit for her plan?

Here's another infuriating example of idea hijacking. Dr. Shikha Jain (who you heard from in previous chapters) described attending a meeting about an initiative that, in her words, "I spearheaded, founded, and worked my behind off on." Someone told her that she could not be the representative for the initiative, explaining, "Well, Dr. Jain, we just don't want another pretty face out there."[147]

When I interviewed Jain, I asked her how an ally could have (and should have) acted in the moment. She told me that she wished someone had spoken up, saying, "Hey, didn't Shikha create this entire plan? Wasn't this her idea? Why are we concerned with her leading and being the face of this?" She added that, in that moment, there was definitely an opportunity for someone to do that. But because everyone was so taken aback, nobody did a thing.

Here's one more. I spoke with a radiologist who told me, "I can't tell you the number of meetings I went to where a woman would come up with a good suggestion. There'd be silence. And then, five minutes later, some man would say the same thing. And everybody would 'ooh and ahh' about how brilliant he was." When I asked her a specific example, she shared this scenario: Six or seven radiologists would sit down to discuss an x-ray. A woman would mention something that was clearly a good idea, and then a man would point out the same thing and get all the credit.

This scenario is all too common, and the frustration it creates is understandable. When allies encounter it, we can borrow a page from a group of women who figured out how to stop idea hijacking in its tracks.

In staff meetings during Barack Obama's first term as president of the United States, women adopted a strategy they called "amplification." When one of the women staffers made a key point, other women would repeat it and give credit to its author. This approach forced everyone in the room to recognize the contribution — and denied them the ability to claim it as their own.[148]

Women aren't the only ones who can amplify the voices of other women. Anyone can do it for someone who is less likely to be heard. I try to do it myself in meetings I attend. Of course, there are times when I'm not quite on the ball, and I miss the opportunity to amplify an idea contributed by someone from an underrepresented group. If someone else repeats it later in the meeting, I remind everyone who originated it, saying something like, "Great idea. Thanks to Alia for surfacing it earlier."

And that's not all. I strive to give people credit for saying the same brilliant idea, even if they did so in a previous conversation. Here's what that might look like: "I like that idea a lot. In fact, when Ana brought that up last week, I learned the following ..."

Not only do I want to amplify Ana's idea, I also hope to show her respect and help her build credibility by saying that I learned from her.

Allies can use their positions of privilege to discourage, if not eliminate, idea hijacking. Let's amplify and showcase the ideas of marginalized people around us. Give credit to the person who knows the patient better than anyone else, created the plan, or spearheaded the initiative, even if they aren't in the room. Let's make this happen.

Dismissing expertise

I spoke to a leader I'll refer to as Kayla Cook (not her real name), who oversees hundreds of nurses, medical assistants, and other healthcare professionals. She has spent her entire career working at a large public medical system and, as a Black woman, has noticed that the higher her title gets and the farther away from patient care she works, the more her voice is silenced. Others in their primarily white leadership meetings frequently disregard her recommendations, even though she might have the most experience with or insight into the topic. For example, during a recent discussion on employee retention and how pay increases might help, one of her colleagues commented on providing staff with additional money as an incentive for retention. Cook spoke up, sharing that financial compensation was not the only incentive to consider and that they should also focus on professional growth. No one listened to her. They didn't even acknowledge what she said.

As she shared with me, "I don't always have to be right, but I always have to be heard."

By contrast, when her colleagues reiterate what Cook has previously said, giving her credit, not only does it make her feel good but it also teaches everyone else how to treat her as a leader.

As allies, let's look for opportunities to acknowledge people who are members of underrepresented groups for their expertise and perspectives. It might mean simply stating, "I agree with so-and-so," to endorse what they've brought up. Or asking a follow-up question to ensure that their idea isn't dismissed outright.

"Manterruptions"

In a study published in the *Journal of General Internal Medicine*, researchers analyzed the initial few minutes of consultations between patients and physicians. After a doctor asked a question like, "What can I do for you today?" or "Tell me what brings you in today," they spent just 11 seconds on average listening to the patient before interrupting them.[149]

Let's face it. Doctors and other healthcare workers face a lot of pressure to be efficient. Yet, when interruptions happen in conversations with patients or colleagues, the results can impact care and discourage people from even bothering to speak up.

I'm not talking about the interruptions that are commonplace in clinical settings, such as monitor alarms, pages, and questions from other healthcare providers or patient families. Instead, I'm referring to what happens when you are mid-sentence, and someone interrupts you simply because they've become impatient. Such interruptions occur so often in meetings everywhere, and more frequently with men doing the interrupting[150] that many people refer to them as "manterruptions."

There are a host of reasons why guys may be more comfortable or skilled at interrupting others. It may be that it's culturally acceptable. Or that cisgender men's vocal cords are longer, resulting in deeper voices that project well and help them break into conversations. Or it could be that women have been socialized to say, "Excuse me ..." or "May I ask ..." when beginning to speak, making it easier to be interrupted.

According to Deborah Tannen, PhD, a professor of linguistics at Georgetown University, women may also be easy targets for interruption because they are already fearful of appearing too talkative. In an article for *Time*, she wrote:

> One reason women tend to speak less at meetings, in my view, is that they don't want to come across as talking too much. It's a verbal analogue to taking up physical space. ... When they talk in a formal setting, many women try to take up less verbal space by being more succinct, speaking in a lower voice and speaking in a more tentative way. Women have good reason for such caution — what I've described as the double bind. If they talk in ways associated with authority, they can be seen as too aggressive, and subject to the damning labels so readily applied to them. But if they don't — if they hold back in these and other ways — they risk being underestimated.[151]

Tannen also pointed out that even when women are specifically asked to weigh in, they might get interrupted. For instance, at the 2017 World Science Festival, a lone woman panelist was ignored for a full hour before the male moderator asked for her input. When she started to speak, he almost immediately began speaking himself, giving his interpretations of her theories.[152]

There's even research showing that patients are twice as likely to interrupt women physicians compared to men physicians.[153]

Regardless of the reasons — and the gender identity of the person being interrupted — allies have a role to play. When you work to minimize interruptions, you create a more equitable workplace, with the added bonus of helping everyone know that they're valued members of the team. When you allow patients to share their concerns fully, you contribute to better patient care. Here are some everyday actions to consider taking to help ensure that all voices are heard:

- When someone is interrupted, interject and say you'd like to hear the original speaker finish.
- If you see someone struggling to break into the conversation, say you'd like to hear other points of view.
- If you see a "repeat offender" who frequently interrupts, pull them aside and point it out.
- Maintain eye contact and stay focused on the person who was interrupted. Not only does it demonstrate your support for that person, but your body language also helps direct the conversation back to them.

Splaining

A few years ago, Dr. Tasha Stanton, an associate professor of clinical pain neuroscience at the University of South Australia, posted a tweet that caught my attention:[154]

> **A/Prof Tasha Stanton** ⋯
> @Tash_Stanton
>
> Friends at conferences - please do not assume that the people that you talk to do not know anything. I just got told that I should read what Stanton et al found about pain.
>
> I. Am. Stanton.

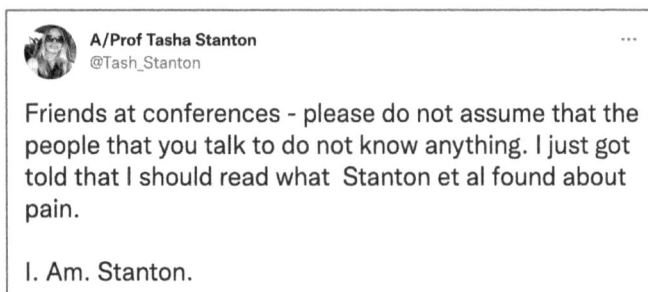

This was a classic example of "mansplaining." It's when a man explains something, typically to a woman, uninvited and about a topic she is either equally qualified or more qualified to comment upon. Here's one more. On Twitter, a man tried to explain the difference between a "vulva" and a "vagina" to a woman gynecologist.[155] This behavior feels condescending and patronizing in the moment, but it has considerably more insidious long-term outcomes. Mansplaining discounts a woman's knowledge when she voices her ideas or experiences and centers the conversation on the mansplainer. At its core, it's a form of verbal oppression through dismissal and silencing.

And unfortunately, this behavior is not limited to men.

Because of this, I prefer the term "splaining," which I first encountered in the book *How to Be an Inclusive Leader* by Jennifer Brown. She expands the traditional definition of mansplaining to any conversation where one person holds more power or privilege and assumes they have the intellectual upper hand. Brown's list includes whitesplaining, straightsplaining, able(-bodied)splaining, wealthysplaining, thinsplaining, and so on. As she writes, "Those who splain may have the intent of helping the situation, but the actual impact of their actions can feel condescending or insulting."[156]

How can allies spot splaining in action and avoid doing it ourselves? In an article for the BBC's Worklife website, product designer Kim Goodwin offered these three key considerations:

Do they want the explanation? If someone asks you a question, explain away! Unsolicited explanations may be fine (within reason) if you're someone's teacher or manager. Explaining after they've declined your help is almost always disrespectful. Conversation is a good place to start building the habit of consent.

Are you making bad assumptions about competence? Explaining things to knowledgeable people isn't just wasting everyone's time. You may, regardless of your intent, undermine them by implying you don't trust their competence or intelligence.

How does bias affect your interpretation of the above? Both questions are complicated by sexism and other kinds of bias. … We all like to think we treat people fairly, but men often assume women are less competent, and white people are likely to assume darker skin equals lower intelligence.[157]

Allies, let's keep our eyes open for any form of splaining. If we spot it, we can consider responding with a simple, "Let's hear from the resident who just spent all night with the patient." Or, "Do you know so-and-so has expertise in that topic? Let's ask them." And if we realize we're doing it ourselves or get called out, let's apologize and do better next time.

Off-topic questions and showboating

Dr. Shikha Jain, who you heard from above, told me, "When I was a medical student, I presented at my first national surgical conference. A surgeon in the audience was being a bit pushy." Her father, who's also a physician, was in the audience and grew frustrated with the showboating taking place. I love what happened next: "My dad stood up, and in a show of support, he simply said, 'Hey, let's keep things civil.'"

Not only did her father help in the moment, but he may also have been role-modeling how Jain could be a better ally herself in the future.

Jain told me about a tumor board where she witnessed a man attacking a woman's opinions. Jain spoke up, saying, "You're arguing with the expert in the field. We recruited her here because this procedure is her area of expertise. We should trust her." Knowing that she shut him down, Jain went on to ask, "Do you have a technical question related to what she's saying? She seems to be explaining things appropriately." By doing so, Jain got him to stop complaining, and they were able to focus on the best treatment and care plan for the patient.

People might argue with experts or ask off-topic questions to test presenters, undermine someone's credibility, and make themselves look smart in the process. It's a power play that's been used for years. It can be incredibly distracting, forcing someone who was in a position of authority at the beginning of the meeting to suddenly defend their expertise.

Derailing experts in meetings can also take the form of veiled insults. I spoke with a staff member at a hospital in London who shared an example of this behavior. As an immigrant who speaks English with an accent, he admits he can feel nervous if he's invited to a meeting full of people who were born and raised in the United Kingdom. At one such meeting, he mispronounced a word, and one of his colleagues interrupted him with, "I'm sorry, what's that, my love?" This happened a few more times until another colleague stepped in with, "Excuse me, but what is it that you don't understand?" Their show of allyship was powerful for this man. Even though he speaks with an accent, he knows he can express himself clearly and should participate in the meetings he attends.

Yet, at times it can be hard to speak up because of the pecking order.

Dr. David Brown, the associate professor of otolaryngology you heard from in Chapter 5, told me about a time this happened to him. A leader within his organization publicly scolded him for calling on someone who raised their hand during a presentation *he* was giving. They said, "This is my meeting, and I call on whoever is going to speak next." No one spoke up when this leader rebuked him, which Brown attributes to the power dynamics in the room. And he felt devalued, shut down during a conversation he was leading.

Later on, during a bystander training session (that the leader was not attending), the facilitator asked for an example of non-inclusive behavior. Brown spoke up with, "I have an example that we all know," and then relayed what happened during that previous meeting, adding that no one said a thing to the leader who had scolded him. Well, it came out that a few people did talk to that leader afterward, though they hadn't felt comfortable saying anything in the moment.

Brown acknowledges that, given the hierarchy, it can be challenging to be an ally during meetings. "But, why didn't they let me know? I was left thinking that no one cared."

As allies, we can point out someone's non-inclusive behavior to them after the meeting has wrapped up, but let's remember to check in with our colleagues. Let them know we noticed and did something about it. Don't just offer them a "What happened earlier today was awful. I'm so sorry." But also add, "and here's what I said to them afterward."

Here's one more thing. Allies, let's be sure not to showboat ourselves. On an episode of the *Docs With Disabilities* podcast, Dr. Diana Cejas shared the guidance she gives to medical students about how they can use their own platform to advocate for others. She explained, "Sometimes the best thing you can do is be quiet and pass the mic. So, if there is something that's coming up and you're like, 'Oh, I really want to comment on this…' look and see if there are other people around, particularly those that belong to these marginalized groups, who are doing work already."[158]

In other words, ask yourself if you really need to comment on something, and if you don't, avoid the temptation to grab the spotlight yourself.

Missing invites

Dr. VK Gadi, the medical oncology director you heard from in earlier chapters, admits that he's still learning to speak up when he sees non-inclusive behavior in meetings he attends. Recently, a senior official at his institution invited Gadi and a select group of physicians, data scientists, and other specialists to a meeting. The discussion focused on a new technology they could integrate into their research to achieve better results. He told me, "I was one of the first to arrive. I watched as people started filtering in and greeting each other. Then, when the door closed, I realized I was in a manel. Not a single woman or nonbinary person in the mix."

Uncomfortable with what was happening, Gadi stayed for about half the meeting before deciding to leave. Afterward, he made plans to talk to the organizer, knowing he needed to point out the obvious. "It's 2022 at a university that purports to break down these barriers and be inclusive. But that meeting was uniformly just senior dudes."

Gadi suspects that a lot of the men in the room noticed the lack of diversity as well. "I bet they ended up leaving that meeting thinking, Huh, this feels like 20 years ago." He emphasized to me, "Unless more people focus intentionally on being inclusive, it'll keep happening, right?" I couldn't agree more.

Allies, let's review the invite lists for meetings and take steps to ensure that people, especially those from underrepresented groups, aren't missing.

Don't insist on cameras

Dr. Kelly Paradis, the associate professor of medical physics you heard from in previous chapters, told me about a meeting she joined soon after she gave birth to her daughter. It was an American Association of Physicists in Medicine (AAPM) task force call with mostly men. In discussing the plans for an upcoming virtual meeting, someone insisted that attendees should turn their cameras on. Paradis explained, "He wanted to ensure that everyone was paying attention." She pushed back, explaining there might be individual circumstances that prevent someone from turning on their camera. She told them, "For example, because I have an infant that I need to feed, I need to turn my camera off from time to time." Immediately, one of the men said, "Whoa, TMI". (As I'll bet you know, TMI stands for "too much information.") What followed was an awkward silence where no one said anything before the conversation moved on. As a result, Dr. Paradis felt she had made them all uncomfortable and that she had done something wrong.

Paradis wishes an ally had spoken up in the meeting. A simple "I agree with what Kelly just said" would have made all the difference. Even better would have been to mention a few other reasons why people might not be able to turn on cameras, such as children in the background, not having enough bandwidth to support video, or simply not wanting to broadcast their personal space with others.

It might also be because they're dealing with a medical issue.

I remember attending a virtual meeting with a potential client who had invited me to speak about *Better Allies* at their law firm.

They didn't turn on their camera, and as I had done countless times before, I joked, "Are you having a bad hair day?" Usually, this question got a laugh, followed by an explanation that their camera was on the fritz or they hadn't showered yet. But not on this day. The person explained they were undergoing chemo and didn't feel up to having their camera on.

As you might imagine, I felt terrible and apologized immediately. I also pledged never to make that "bad hair" joke again.

Allies, if someone has their camera off, trust that they have a good reason, and skip the teasing.

The role of professional associations

At the end of the previous chapter, I explored the role professional associations can play in reshaping the representation of their field, including ensuring that there are diverse speaker lineups. Similarly, other aspects of conferences and annual meetings might not be inclusive today that professional associations can and should address. Let's take a peek at some of the problems and opportunities ahead.

Hold Hybrid Events

In Oregon, most of the state's population lives in a corridor along Interstate 5, between the cities of Portland and Eugene, that takes about two hours to drive. But physicians and clinicians are practicing all over the state, and some face up to an eight-hour drive to attend state chapter meetings of a national medical society. Not surprisingly, during the COVID-19 pandemic, they switched to an all-virtual format, which meant it was easier for all to attend.

During a planning discussion in 2022, Dr. Avital O'Glasser, an associate professor of medicine you heard from previously, made a plea. "If we decide to go back to holding in-person meetings, should we offer a hybrid component? We don't want to exclude anyone who can't make the drive, or members with young kids who still can't get vaccinated, or breastfeeding parents." O'Glasser pointed out that by slowing down and being intentional about supporting people who are underrepresented in their group or at specific events, they're making more inclusion possible. It's not just a superficial platitude of "I'm striving for inclusion," but actually making changes.

Her hope is that conferences and professional events will embrace a hybrid structure moving forward. Many people can't travel because they are immunocompromised, have mobility challenges, don't feel safe traveling because of a family member's condition, or have caregiving responsibilities at home. O'Glasser emphasized, "We may all be tired of video meetings, but we have the tech and we should really put it to use."

Offer childcare and financial assistance

As the entire world recently learned, access to childcare is an issue that impacts millions of workers. A recent *Harvard Business Review* article summarized this revelation: "When the Covid-19 pandemic removed the safety net of schooling and employee-paid childcare for working families, the damage was cataclysmic. Without a stable form of childcare as part of the business infrastructure, the world stopped working for the vast majority of working parents around the world."[159] As of 2020, only 6 percent of companies in the United States offered any childcare benefits,[160] with the rest putting the financial and logistical burden back onto their employees. Although this impacts parents of all genders, women continue to shoulder most household responsibilities, including caring for young children, so it frequently forces women to choose between work and caregiving.[161] Black and multiracial parents are more likely than white parents to experience childcare-related job disruptions, according to the Center for American Progress. Since many have negligible financial cushions, the ability for parents to work full-time and access affordable childcare is more urgent for many families of color than it is for non-Hispanic white families.[162] Parents struggling to secure reliable childcare is an equity issue, and an important one.

Fortunately, several prominent healthcare organizations are beginning to recognize this fact. In 2017, the American Association of Physicists in Medicine (AAPM) ran a survey regarding the childcare needs of its members when attending its events. Of the respondents, 19 percent indicated that the lack of adequate childcare caused them to miss AAPM conferences or participate for a shorter period than they desired.[163] As a result, the organization started offering childcare at their annual meeting.

More recently, the Society of Clinical Ultrasound Fellowships decided to do the same for their yearly conference. Their conference website provided information about a local childcare provider. While they weren't able to cover the cost of the care, they did arrange to have the enrollment fee waived.

As Dr. Resa E. Lewiss shared on Twitter, "I would love this to be a standard for … all medical conferences."[164] Me, too. Even better would be to find a sponsor to cover some or all of the cost.

Speaking of conference-related costs, professional associations could also provide reduced registration fees and travel stipends for students and others early in their careers who might be struggling with student loan debt. Doing so could help attract a more diverse set of attendees.

Make events accessible

If an event is being held in the United States, it's likely that the rented space already complies with the Americans with

Disabilities Act (ADA). Still, there's so much more that's needed to make an event — in-person or virtual — truly inclusive. Many disabilities are invisible, and others are not related to physical needs, but all merit respect and accommodation. Are ramps clearly marked? Are pathways wide enough that people with wheelchairs and scooters can navigate them? Is type large and high-contrast? Will simultaneous sign language translation and closed captions be offered? The ADA offers a comprehensive document titled "A Planning Guide for Making Temporary Events Accessible to People with Disabilities" online.[165] It's definitely worth a look.

Planning an event and not sure what accommodations you should provide? On your event registration form, provide a point of contact and invite attendees to let you know their needs in advance — and be prepared to respond to and meet whatever needs the attendees specify. I appreciate how Change Catalysts, a DEI consulting firm, explains their accessibility support on their registration page for their events: "We'll have ASL interpreters and Live Captioning. Do you have any other accessibility needs? (We'll do our best!)" Underneath is a text box where you can type what you need.

And here's a reminder from Chapter 6: For people who are speaking at events, Tara Robertson, a DEI coach, recommends the Digital Library Federation's Guide to Creating Accessible Presentations.[166]

Have (and enforce) a code of conduct

Everyone deserves to feel comfortable and safe within a community, especially at meetings and gatherings where social capital is often at stake. A code of conduct is one indicator that an organization wants to provide a harassment-free experience for everyone at all of its sponsored activities. Yet, this concept may be new to some professional associations. For example, only recently did the American College of Physicians (ACP) establish an anti-harassment policy and reporting process that defines professional behavior at ACP meetings.[167] An encouraging step, but one that has come late in the game.

As allies, we can encourage more meeting and event hosts to create and distribute codes of conduct. Why are these codes so important? Because most of the problematic behaviors at meetings and events aren't illegal, and many are subtle and social in nature. When it comes to curbing microaggressions and harassment, a code of conduct can make a huge difference.

The purpose of a code of conduct is to protect members of a community from harm by other members of the community, even if that harm is unintended. In fact, thoughtful and impactful codes of conduct address behaviors that the general population may view as socially acceptable but unacceptable within a particular community, group, or professional context.

Here's an example from tech company Mapbox:

> Events Code of Conduct
> All attendees, speakers, sponsors, vendors, partners and volunteers at our conferences/events are required to adhere to the following Code of Conduct. Mapbox event organizers will enforce this Code throughout the event.
>
> Our aim in hosting events is to build community. To that end, our goal is to create an environment where everyone feels welcome to participate, speak up, ask questions, and engage in conversation. We invite all those who participate in this event to help us create safe and positive experiences for everyone.
>
> Every Mapbox event/conference is dedicated to providing a harassment-free environment for everyone, regardless of gender, gender identity and expression, age, sexual orientation, disability, physical appearance, body size, race, ethnicity, or religion (or lack thereof). We do not tolerate harassment of participants in any form. Sexual language and imagery is not appropriate during any aspect of the event/conference, including talks, workshops, parties, social media such as Twitter, or other online media.

Expected Behavior

Participate in an authentic and active way. In doing so, you contribute to the health and longevity of the community.

Exercise consideration and respect in your speech and actions.

Attempt collaboration before conflict.

Refrain from demeaning, discriminatory, or harassing behavior and speech.

Be mindful of your surroundings and of your fellow participants. Alert community leaders if you notice a dangerous situation, someone in distress, or violations of this Code of Conduct, even if they seem inconsequential.

Conference participants violating these rules may be sanctioned or expelled from the event/conference without a refund at the discretion of the organizers. Participants asked to stop any harassing behavior are expected to comply immediately.

Reporting an Incident

If you see, overhear or experience a violation of the Code of Conduct during an event, please seek out the nearest Mapbox team member to escalate your complaint. If you cannot find a team member, or would like to report a violation after an event, you may email events@mapbox.com.[168]

Note the essential components:

- A statement that the event organizers will not tolerate certain behaviors
- A description of the inappropriate behaviors and who they might target
- An explanation of the possible actions or sanctions that will be taken against offenders
- Directions on what to do if one experiences or sees unacceptable behavior
- A list of the ways the organizers will support anyone who has been targeted

- Indication that anyone unwilling to comply should not attend

Codes of conduct can be considerably more detailed if there is a need, which may be the case for events with a history of inappropriate behavior. However, all that's really needed are these six elements to create a clear, enforceable code of conduct.

In their book *How to Respond to Code of Conduct Reports*, Valerie Aurora and Mary Gardiner pointed out several elements that should be *omitted* from codes of conduct. Don't call out behaviors that aren't common in a community (e.g., juggling in the aisles during events), and don't call out crimes or behaviors that are universally unacceptable (e.g., stealing money). Doing this distracts from what's essential about the code and insults your attendees. Finally, don't list rules that won't or can't be enforced. Codes of conduct must be backed up with action.[169]

A code of conduct needs to prove that actions have consequences. It will only be an effective tool for protecting conference attendees and participants if everyone knows it will be enforced.

Allies can help enforce codes of conduct. Allies can and should work harder to ensure that the events they sponsor and attend feel safe for all, including people from underrepresented groups. Together, we can force those numbers downward until professional gatherings become the welcoming, equitable, uplifting events they ought to be.

Actions for Better Allies:
Create More Inclusive Meetings

As allies, let's ensure that the voices of members of underrepresented groups are heard and valued in the shift huddles, morning rounds, administrative meetings, and events we attend, large or small.

- Challenge yourself to notice and take action when interruptions happen.
- Cultivate a culture of credit: Encourage everyone around you to acknowledge the originators of ideas as often as possible.
- Be vigilant and push back on off-topic questions, showboating, and splaining.
- Don't insist that colleagues turn on their video cameras for virtual meetings.
- Hold professional societies accountable for hosting inclusive events.

DISRUPTING GLUE WORK

If I had a nickel for every time I was in a meeting where someone asked a woman to take notes, even though it wasn't part of her job responsibilities, I'd definitely have a lot of nickels.

Here's one outstanding example. I was attending a monthly planning meeting for a women's group at a tech company where I was doing a consulting project. It started with the chairperson reviewing a file on her laptop to figure out who would take notes. (I later learned that they had made a rotation schedule for note-taking and a few other administrative tasks at the beginning of the year.) When she announced it was Brian's turn, the only male committee member declared, "I'm not very good at taking notes, so someone else should do that."

While this was several years ago, I remember being taken aback, but not so much that I couldn't think of something to say in the moment. In fact, I believe I had a spot-on response. I told Brian, "Practice makes perfect, and this is the perfect place to practice." There was no way I was going to let him get away with not doing his fair share of this undervalued but necessary work — especially given the research on this topic.

Multiple studies have found that women take on undervalued tasks such as note-taking more than men and that, because of gender stereotypes, women face a backlash if they opt out. Furthermore, women are not only expected to engage in more of this work, but they receive less recognition and rewards than their male counterparts.[170] It's even worse for women of color, who are tasked with more of this "glue work" than their white male peers.[171]

What is glue work?

Every workplace and professional society has glue work: administrative or volunteer duties that aren't part of anyone's job description but need to get done for the health of the organization. Tanya Reilly coined this term to capture the less glamorous — and often less-promotable — work that needs to happen to make a team successful.[172] I've also heard it called office or meeting housework, citizenship tasks, undervalued work, non-promotable tasks, and invisible work.

Some of these tasks may take only a small amount of time and can be crossed off to-do lists quickly. Others may require dedicated effort, often during off-hours on nights and weekends.

The most obvious example of glue work is taking the minutes and recording action items at a meeting if that's not part of one's job description. (As a former program manager and epic note-taker, I know the value of good notes and documented next steps. I'm not diminishing this role at all. I'm simply calling it out as a housework task if it's not part of a team member's assigned responsibilities.)

Yet, glue work goes beyond note-taking and task-tracking. When I spoke to Dr. Dawn Haut, who you've heard from before in this book, she mentioned an all-too-common scenario in staff lunchrooms everywhere: Forgotten lunch leftovers and expired condiments. Cleaning out an overcrowded communal fridge is a task that almost inevitably falls to admin staff, women employees, or women admins. At Haut's health centers, some of the managers have set up a rotation where everyone takes a turn cleaning out the fridge, with guidance to toss out anything and everything left behind.

Glue work can also show up as unreasonable expectations, such as being expected to answer the majority of questions from coworkers. I heard about a medical assistant who asked a woman physician about the dose for that year's flu vaccine (which they could have easily found by searching online). It turns out this phenomenon has been studied; researchers found that women primary care physicians (PCPs) receive 24 percent more messages from staff via electronic medical record systems than men PCPs.[173]

Here's why that extra burden can happen. When a patient sends a message, a nurse screens it and then forwards it. If the patient's PCP is on vacation, the nurse will forward it to another physician. The nurse might know that a certain physician will answer it quickly or won't complain about it. They might think, Dr. Xu didn't give me a hard time the last time I asked her a similar question, so I'm going to ask her again. Or there may be unconscious bias at play, where women are perceived to be nicer and more nurturing, leading a nurse to forward more messages to their in-baskets.

There are plenty of other examples that many people might not immediately recognize as glue work, especially if they've never been asked to do them before. Here are some other administrative and undervalued tasks that I've collected from my coaching clients, heard from audiences at my keynotes, and gathered while doing research for this book:

- Do the dishes after a staff event.
- Deep clean the lab or the emergency room.
- Plan a team-building event.
- Join a DEI committee. Bonus points for volunteering to be the chairperson.
- Serve on a hiring board to improve the diversity of the interview team.
- Set up for a health fair and clean up afterward.
- Educate the community about COVID-19 vaccines and treatments.
- Volunteer at a vaccination clinic.
- Pose for pictures for a newsletter or brochure.
- Organize a baby shower or going away party.
- Be the only mentor for people of your underrepresented gender, race, or ethnicity.
- Join a project to improve billing or coding accuracy.
- Schedule a project meeting.
- Track down people who are late to a meeting.
- Order food or make reservations at a restaurant.
- Clean whiteboards and clear coffee mugs as a meeting wraps up.
- Become the interim leader or department chairperson when the organization is in bad shape.

In addition to raising their hands to handle glue work, women are also often perceived as "enjoying" this work simply because they are more likely to do it. I remember leading a workshop in San Francisco a few years ago. During a discussion of glue work, one of the men in attendance asked, "But what if someone enjoys doing these tasks? Like Jess, who frequently washes mugs left in the sink?" He went on to add, "I think she likes cleaning up because it helps her handle stress." I immediately asked if Jess was also in the workshop. She was. And was it true that she enjoyed washing the mugs? She vehemently answered, "No." She did this task only because she hated seeing a sink full of mugs a lot more than she minded washing them.

Organizing a baby shower, serving on a DEI committee, or cheerfully answering nurses' questions may or may not be enjoyable for those who take on these responsibilities. It doesn't actually matter. Regardless of whether someone likes doing these things or not, they can create a negative impact.

How glue work can stunt a career

Chances are glue work doesn't lead to career growth; it may even impede it. After all, the person doing these tasks is saddled with busy work that may prevent them from getting their regular responsibilities done efficiently. Sliding into a role where they are in service to others, they might be perceived to be at a lower level than their colleagues or have less authority to make decisions. Furthermore, those taking the meeting notes are often a step behind the conversation, documenting what has been said instead of making important points themselves.

By helping everyone else, the good citizen is putting themselves at a distinct disadvantage. They might work on these projects or clear their in-baskets after-hours, which can lead to burnout. For academics, glue work tasks take valuable time away from research, grant writing, paper publishing, and other responsibilities that will help them advance in their careers.

There's also the "minority tax" phenomenon to be considered. This arises when people from underrepresented racial groups are asked to serve on committees and hiring boards to improve the diversity of those efforts. There is a demand and supply problem: People from underrepresented racial groups are in high demand to provide their input on diversity initiatives, but they are often in short supply within any given organization. This leads to a small group of individuals being tapped for service more often than their white counterparts. And because they are underrepresented, they risk being overburdened with providing service to others.[174]

That's not all. The minority tax is even greater for people who are members of multiple intersecting underrepresented groups. For example, women of color receive more service requests and engage in service that requires more time than men of color.[175]

The time spent on glue work can be substantial. A recent survey of women physicians found that most respondents reported spending between one and five hours per week on work-related citizenship tasks. For some, it was even worse; 12 percent said they spent six or more hours weekly on them.[176]

Overall, these unrewarded and undervalued responsibilities impact how someone is perceived, the work they need to deliver, and potentially the patients they need to care for. In other words, they can negatively impact a career.

Disrupting the status quo

Be on the lookout for glue work. I guarantee that it's happening in your workplace and the professional societies to which you belong. Once you spot it, there are many ways you can act as an ally to disrupt the norms around how such tasks are handled. Depending on your position within a department or organization, you can impact the distribution of this work using a variety of tactics:

- If you're part of a new committee or working group that's forming, **set up a rotation schedule** for any administrative tasks that aren't part of someone's job description. Think scheduling meetings, taking notes, timekeeping, and ordering food. (And if you end up with

a "Brian," like the man in the story at the beginning of
this chapter, be prepared to push back and enforce the
schedule despite complaints.)

- If you're a supervisor or committee chairperson, **spread
  glue work among the team**. For example, if you notice
  one person is always tasked with setting up for the health
  fair, say something like, "Amara's great at getting us
  organized. But it's the perfect stretch assignment for
  Chad, who has never done it before."

- **Increase the value of the work** that needs to get done
  for the health of the group or organization. Recommend
  that it be recognized as part of your promotion process
  or in applications for leadership roles in your
  professional society. (More on this in Chapter 10.)

- If you're a man, **model better behavior yourself**. Offer
  to message people who are late for a meeting. Volunteer
  to collect contributions for a colleague's baby shower
  gift. As in-person discussions break up, look around. If
  mugs, pastry boxes, or other post-meeting detritus are
  left on the table, take a minute to throw out the trash and
  bring the rest to the nearest kitchen — especially if
  you're in a position of privilege or authority. If you don't,
  chances are someone will ask a woman. Or a woman will
  feel compelled to roll up her sleeves and get the task
  done.

- If you're a woman, **be a role model for others** by
  downsizing the amount of glue work you take on.

- If you're a manager or mentor, **coach anyone who
  frequently volunteers to step back**. Let them know
  that you're concerned about the toll that undervalued
  tasks will have on their career growth. Encourage them
  to get involved in more impactful projects, and offer a
  few examples to nudge them in the right direction.

Here are some phrases that your mentees or others you work closely with can use when people ask them to do glue work:

- **"I'll have to ask my manager about prioritizing it."** Unless the person making the request *is* the manager, it can be helpful to postpone agreeing to accept glue work until it's been discussed with a supervisor or boss. Their input will provide cover for saying no.
- **"I'd like to understand why you think I'm the right person to handle that."** Forcing someone to articulate specific talents or credentials related to ordering lunch or scheduling a meeting often makes them realize their bias.
- **"Remember, I volunteered last time. Let's spread the wealth."** The person making the request may need reminding that they should distribute glue work more evenly among team members.

If you have the ability to impact your organization's policies, consider holding a discussion *about* glue work. You could facilitate a brainstorming session about which tasks qualify, discuss why it's detrimental to foist them on women and other marginalized employees, and identify approaches for disrupting how your team handles glue work.

There are many more ideas for effectively responding to inequitable requests in Ruchika Tulshyan's article, "Women of Color Get Asked to Do More 'Office Housework.' Here's How They Can Say No."[177] In preparation for your brainstorming session, consider circulating that article so attendees will have some background on the dynamics that will be discussed.

Relying on certain people or groups to handle tasks that don't drive business impact or lead to career growth is a prime example of unconscious bias. Most people who assume that women will clean the fridge in the staff lounge don't even realize they're being chauvinistic until someone points it out. Allies can and should educate colleagues, helping to change how glue work is distributed and eradicating this erosive and harmful prejudice.

Last but not least, look to reward people when they do take on undervalued but necessary work. Offer to write a recommendation letter or provide mentoring for someone earlier in their career. Sing their praises and sponsor them for a career-growing opportunity. Invite them to co-author a paper. Advocate for bonus pay. Provide administrative support or protected time for doing service work.

In other words, make sure people get something in return for taking on these much-needed but lowly tasks.

Actions for Better Allies:
Disrupt the Burden of Glue Work

Office housework and citizenship tasks aren't just aggravating. Calling exclusively on women, people of color, and members of other marginalized groups to perform glue work means preventing them from tackling more meaningful work. With that in mind:

- Share the work among the team. For example, if you notice one person is always tasked with setting up for meetings, say something like, "Amara's been handling meeting setup for too long. Let's ask Chad, who has never done it before."
- Set up a rotation for tasks like taking minutes or scheduling upcoming meetings.
- If you're in a position of privilege or authority, model better behavior yourself by cleaning the fridge or tracking down people who are late to a meeting, rather than letting someone else take care of it.
- Never assume that certain coworkers are shouldering glue work because they "enjoy" it or find it "rewarding."
- Reward people who take on these tasks with bonus pay, letters of recommendation, administrative support, mentoring, and sponsorship for career-growing opportunities.

PART THREE

INCREASING
YOUR
IMPACT

9

GIVING FEEDBACK

Imagine how a medical student might feel when receiving their clerkship evaluation from a supervising physician. Knowing it would feed into letters of recommendation for residency programs, I bet they'd feel excited and a bit nervous.

Then consider how that student would feel if they discovered their assessment was not objectively based on their performance during the clinical rotation but tainted by bias.

Unfortunately, this is an issue facing women and other students who are members of underrepresented groups. I learned about it during a planning session for a Better Allies event at the University of California, San Francisco (UCSF). One of the hosts told me about an article she'd co-authored on language differences in third-year medical student evaluations. Their research found that personal attributes such as "lovely" appeared more frequently in assessments of women, while competency-related behaviors, such as "scientific," appeared more often in letters for men. Students from underrepresented racial groups also received notably different evaluations. "Pleasant" appeared more often in their reviews, whereas their white counterparts were more likely to be called "knowledgeable."[178]

It turns out that giving feedback based on someone's personality is a well-documented problem.

The producers of *1001 Cuts*, a film about women surgeons, summarized some of the anecdotes they'd heard in their interviews:

> A man raises his voice in the operating room and is viewed as commanding; a woman is perceived as shrill. A man asks for a specific instrument and is viewed as competent; a woman is perceived as being demanding. A man takes extra time on a procedure and is congratulated on his technical skill on a difficult case; a woman is perceived as being less competent.[179]

There are also extensive research studies exploring differences in performance feedback in the workplace. Textio, a company that creates tools to analyze and augment writing for inclusion, conducted a cross-industry survey about job performance feedback. They coupled it with an analysis of performance documents given to more than 25,000 people. Perhaps not surprisingly, they found that different groups of people get different kinds of feedback at work — with women, Black people, Latinx people, and older workers receiving the lowest-quality feedback.[180]

Textio's report is full of insight into how feedback can be biased. Here are some highlights:

- Feedback to men tends to focus on the substance of their work, whereas women tend to receive feedback on their personalities.
- Women are seven times more likely to report being described as "opinionated" and 11 times more likely to report being labeled as "abrasive."

- Men are three times more likely to report being described as "confident."
- Asian people are described as "brilliant" more than twice as often as white people and more than four times as often as Black or Latinx people.
- Groups receiving the least actionable feedback tend to be least represented, especially in leadership. For example, Black women receive almost nine non-constructive comments for every one received by white men.

Similarly, by analyzing thousands of annual performance reviews, researchers at Stanford University's Clayman Institute uncovered some telling differences in the kind of feedback given to men versus women. They found that women were less likely than men to receive specific feedback tied to outcomes. This was true for both praise and constructive feedback. By contrast, men were offered a clearer picture of what they were doing well, how their performance was making a positive impact, and what they needed to do to get promoted. Women also got shorter reviews, which means they received less feedback to act upon.[181]

As the Textio researchers pointed out, "Why does this matter? Specific and constructive feedback about someone's work performance offers them more opportunities to grow."[182]

How race and identity affect professional growth

Within Black communities, it's common for people to coach each other on the fact that they need to be "twice as good" as their white counterparts to achieve the same levels of success, and research shows that this is not far off.

An investigation by *STAT* found that Black residents either leave or are terminated from training programs at far higher rates than white residents. When interviewed, many said they received unclear communication about what they had done wrong and were written up for transgressions that went unpunished when white residents committed them.[183]

Furthermore, as I mentioned in Chapter 3, a study of the overall labor market found that Black workers receive extra scrutiny from their supervisors, which can lead to less favorable or constructive performance reviews, increased nervousness, lower wages, and even job loss.[184]

On top of undue scrutiny, Black women frequently receive less support from their managers than their white coworkers. A study by LeanIn.Org found that only 36 percent of Black women surveyed agreed that "My manager provides opportunities for me to showcase my work," compared to 39 percent of white women and 43 percent of white men.[185]

Gender identity and sexual orientation also affect career growth and pay. In a survey of LGBTQ Americans conducted by Harvard's T.H. Chan School of Public Health, 22 percent reported that they were not paid equally or promoted at the same rate as their straight and cisgender peers.[186] According to a nationally representative survey of transgender people in the United States by the National Center for Transgender Equality, 27 percent of respondents said they had experienced being not hired, fired, or passed over for promotions due to their gender identity or expression.[187] And an in-depth report on the financial penalty for LGBT women in America — co-authored in 2020 by the Center for American Progress and the Movement Advancement Project — stated that for every dollar a man in a married-opposite-sex couple earns, a woman in a same-sex couple earns $0.79 whereas a man in a same-sex couple earns $0.98.[188] Clearly, this lack of actionable feedback is impacting earning potential.

The bottom line? When stereotypes and bias play into performance appraisals and feedback, it can lead to inaccuracy and unfair treatment based on age, gender, race, ability, religion, appearance, sexual orientation, and other traits. Members of all underrepresented groups may struggle to obtain constructive, actionable feedback. And this means they will have a harder time improving their performance and advancing in their careers, keeping them from moving into higher-paying roles and leadership positions.

As you read the rest of this chapter, think about when you give feedback to the people around you. Perhaps you are a supervisor responsible for writing performance reviews. You might provide informal feedback and offer suggestions to help fellow doctors, nurses, or aides improve. As a trusted advisor, you might write letters of recommendation. Regardless of the situation, realize that bias may unknowingly creep in. Fortunately, there are strategies to employ so that your feedback is both effective and equitable.

Revisiting professionalism

A study published in the journal of the Association of American Medical Colleges found that faculty rated internal medicine residents from underrepresented racial and ethnic groups lower than white trainees on five of six core competencies. One notable theme? Professionalism.[189]

In an interview with *STAT*, Dr. Sheri-Ann Burnett-Bowie, a co-author of the study, explained, "Professionalism can be used to tell people they are too loud, or too quiet, or that they need to dress or look a certain way." She also shared, "Many Black residents report an uncomfortable focus on their hair and whether they can wear locks or twists."[190]

Fortunately, there's support (in the United States at least) for banning hair discrimination in workplaces. In 2022, the American Medical Association adopted a policy against natural hair and cultural headwear discrimination.[191] And the CROWN

Act (Creating a Respectful and Open World for Natural Hair) passed in the US House of Representatives and, as of this writing, was headed to the Senate.

Yet, professionalism is measured more broadly than hairstyles. It also includes such customs as speaking in a mainstream dialect, not having visible tattoos or piercings, following certain table manners, and wearing specific styles of clothes.[192] All of which tend to be centered on whiteness and Westernness in white-majority countries.

Allies, let's look out for comments about someone's lack of professional semblance. Are they being judged simply because their appearance, clothing, hair, or speaking style differs from the norm? Does any of this impact their ability to do their job?

I have a feeling the answer will be "No" or "Not really."

Disrupting "prove it again" bias

Earlier in her career, Dr. Lorna Rodriguez (the vice chair of surgery you heard from in earlier chapters) was planning a big site visit for some prominent scientists she'd met at meetings the previous year. It was the first time she had organized such a visit, and, in hindsight, she admits that she was somewhat naive about how much time and effort it would take. Yet, that naiveté gave her the courage to boldly invite highly respected scientists, and they all said yes.

However, when her new boss heard about the visit and reviewed the list of guests, he became concerned about her ability to pull it off. He also saw an opportunity for himself and decided he would make the opening remarks at the dinner, not she. "I think he wanted to look good in front of them," she told me. "But, I invited all of these people, and they expected to see me at that dinner to welcome them."

Rodriguez approached some of her colleagues, asking for their support. One by one, she heard the same story. While they thought she should speak at the dinner, they weren't willing to say anything to their boss. When she asked them why, each one asked if she had done something like this before and why she thought she would be able to pull it off by herself. Rodriguez couldn't believe it. "I thought they were my friends. I thought they respected me scientifically. But no one backed me up."

What happened to Rodriguez was a form of "prove it again" bias. Before speaking up on her behalf, her peers wanted to know if she had successfully hosted such an event previously.

Groups that have been stereotyped as less competent or hardworking often have to provide a larger, more compelling body of evidence to be judged as equally competent. Groups that have to "prove it again" include women, Black people, Latinx people, individuals with disabilities, and Asian Americans.[193] While a white man may only need to show promise to be given some new responsibility, a Latina may need to make a long and convincing case for herself to even be considered ready.

If you hear someone giving feedback about certain coworkers and describing them as "not ready," ask point-blank what it would take to prove their competence. Then ask if they'd hold a white man to the same standard.

By the way, Rodriguez decided on a different approach for that dinner. Without allies willing to advocate for her to make the official opening remarks, she decided to arrive early and work the room. "After all, my reputation was on the line," she explained to me. "It was important for me to speak to everyone I invited." I love it.

Giving better feedback

In 2016, McKinsey and LeanIn.Org performed a survey and found that women are less likely than men to receive difficult feedback — almost 20 percent less likely.[194]

More recently, Dr. Shelley Correll of Stanford University's Clayman Institute analyzed performance reviews and found that leaders often gave male employees specific (and sometimes harsh) feedback that would help them achieve specific goals. Women? Not so much.[195]

Why would this happen? Both studies cited several reasons, including:

- It can be difficult to give constructive feedback because we don't want to upset someone. And this is especially true for male managers giving feedback to women employees.

- It can also be uncomfortable to give feedback to someone different from us — not just another gender, but a different race, sexual orientation, or educational background. We might think, If I point out how Aliyah, an immigrant who studied nursing overseas, could have done a better job with that patient, she might think I'm biased against people from other countries. To avoid this perception, we might soften the feedback.

In her book *Radical Candor*, Kim Scott explored why it may be harder for men to be radically candid with women. She wrote, "Most men are trained from birth to be 'gentler' with women than with men. Sometimes this can be very bad for the women who work for them."[196] In other words, men might hold back from criticizing women employees because they're afraid they might cry.

Scott reminds us that criticism is a gift and must be given out in equal measures to all employees. Sounds good, but how do we actually make it so? Here are some suggestions from the Clayman Institute for how supervisors can be more effective in evaluating employees equitably and giving them feedback:

- Identify the criteria you'll use to evaluate employees at each level, and apply those criteria consistently.
- With each employee, discuss how their work has impacted your organization's goals.
- Tie all feedback, both positive and constructive, to goals. For example, instead of just "Become a more strategic leader," you could say, "Become a more strategic leader by better understanding our community's needs and addressing them on a daily, weekly, and monthly basis."
- Tell employees about the expertise you see them already exhibiting and how they can develop more job-related skills.
- Write reviews of similar lengths so that you give roughly the same level of detailed feedback to all employees.[197]

Researchers at Textio suggest these straightforward ways to provide less biased, more useful feedback to all:

- Avoid commenting on employees' personality traits. Instead, focus on their behaviors.
- With every piece of feedback, provide concrete examples.
- Recommend specific changes in employee behavior that would bring about better outcomes.
- Suggest new ways to approach challenging situations.[198]

Giving feedback frequently

In her book *The Waymakers*, equity strategist Tara Jaye Frank shared a jaw-dropping data point from a survey she ran: 80

percent of the respondents did not receive feedback on their performance until it became a barrier to advancement. As Frank wrote, "If you wait until I'm 100 miles out of the way to guide me, I'm going to be a lot more stressed and feel more defeated than if you tell me I'm about to take a wrong turn."[199]

Whether we're a supervisor who's in a position to give feedback to people who report to us, or a peer who can provide feedback to a teammate, let's be sure we do so frequently.

One of my favorite approaches to giving frequent feedback is to "name one thing," which I learned years ago from the book *Thanks for the Feedback* by Douglas Stone and Sheila Heen.[200] Consider when someone asks, "How did I do on the presentation/report/project? Do you have any feedback for me?" It can be tempting to reply, "You were great." After all, it can be a lot of work to reflect on someone's performance, package up a comprehensive collection of our thoughts, and share it all effectively. By contrast, if we focus on naming one thing, we can give feedback quickly while helping them to learn and grow. Here's one example: "To have an even bigger impact, here's one thing you can do the next time you give a presentation."

I've also come across the notion of "fast feedback." Instead of letting feedback fester or delaying it in the hope you'll figure out the perfect way to express it, you share what's top of mind. Teams who adopt this approach share their observations immediately after attending a presentation or reviewing a project. For example, while walking out of a meeting, someone might say, "Are you open to receiving some fast feedback on your approach?"

That said, asking if someone wants feedback is essential. As Kim Scott wrote in *Radical Candor,* "If the other person is hungry, angry, or tired, or for some other reason not in a good frame of mind, it's better to wait."[201]

The "name one thing" and "fast feedback" approaches lower the barrier to giving feedback, and I'll bet they'd help the 80 percent of Frank's survey respondents get the feedback they need to grow in their careers. Your own coworkers will likely appreciate these tactics, too.

Seeking common ground, then educating

At times, we may need to give people feedback on how they can be better allies. Perhaps we spot someone acting in a non-inclusive way. Or hear a biased or prejudiced remark. Or read a well-intentioned yet denigrating comment in an email.

I recently received a newsletter from a friend with the subject line, "I'm opening the kimono. Marketing consultants, open this!"

I gave a big sigh, made myself a cup of tea, and then sent her an email that included this message:

> I used to use the phrase 'Open the kimono' somewhat regularly. I think I had a boss who said it a lot, and I liked the impression it gave – that I'm going to be honest and share some things with you I don't tell everyone. But, I've since learned it's both misogynistic and racist. FYI, as I know the importance you place on being inclusive.

(In my email, I also included a link to an article explaining the assumptions behind this loaded phrase.[202] While its origin isn't known, many Western people associate kimonos with women sex workers in Japan, whose job is providing pleasure to others.[203])

Stepping back from the details, did you notice how I gave her this feedback? I used one of my favorite techniques for Upstanders: **Seek common ground, then educate.** I first connected with her, explaining I used to use the phrase, too, and then I shared what I've learned. It's a powerful approach we can bring to many situations to speak up about someone's behavior without shaming or blaming them.

And it works. After receiving my email, my friend thanked me, mentioned that she had no idea, and sent out an apology to her newsletter list later the same day. What's cool is that, in addition to learning something herself, she passed it along to her subscribers. I love seeing the ripple effects caused by everyday acts of allyship.

Addressing patient slurs

In medical school, Dr. Benito Nieves (who you heard from in previous chapters) remembers being on a rotation when a patient used a racist slur against a Black classmate. No one said anything in the moment, but afterward, he and his classmate talked about it. As Nieves shared with me, "I think back on that day sometimes and wonder if I should have done anything differently. I still don't know." He added, "If a similar scenario were to happen outside the hospital, I would likely disrupt that behavior. As healthcare professionals, we're often in a position to build trust with patients so that we can learn more in building their care plan. While it can seem like calling out or disrupting that behavior would create more conflict, I believe it's important for hospital systems to have clear zero-tolerance policies around racism that help guide clinicians' actions during these moments. We can both disrupt racist behaviors from patients and provide them excellent care."

I heartily agree. I also believe it's possible to call out racist, sexist, or other derogatory remarks in a respectful way to minimize conflict. The trick? Speak up, but don't try to change their views. For example, "We don't say things like that here; let's put it aside and focus on your treatment plan."

Being an ally is a journey, and we're bound to miss opportunities or make mistakes as we strive to create more inclusive workplaces. We can and should check in with co-workers and let them know we're working to become a better ally for underrepresented groups. Consider soliciting feedback by asking, "What's one thing I could be doing differently to support you better or to create a more inclusive workplace?" And then take action.

Actions for Better Allies:
Give Equitable and Effective Feedback

Feedback can be tricky to give, but it truly is a gift to receive. Without clear feedback, members of marginalized groups will have a much harder time succeeding and advancing. So, as an ally, remember:

- When giving feedback, make it actionable. What should they keep doing because it's effective? What new skills should they learn? How should they improve?
- Don't ease up just to avoid hurt feelings. Remember, vague feedback holds people back from growing in their careers.
- Tell them about the expertise you see in them right now, and how to develop more job-related skills for the future.
- Use objective criteria to evaluate trainees and employees in similar roles.
- Give feedback on someone's skills, not their personality or professional semblance.
- Write reviews of roughly the same length for everyone on your staff.
- Give feedback frequently.
- When pointing out how someone can be more inclusive, seek common ground and then educate.
- Ask for feedback on how you can be a better ally.

FINDING AND SELECTING TALENT

Even though it's been proven across industries by multiple studies that diverse workforces deliver better results,[204] the progress feels glacial.

Going back to 2004, the Institute of Medicine (now the National Academy of Medicine) noted, "Evidence regarding race- and ethnicity-based disparities in health status is mounting, and the need to increase diversity in the health workforce as a strategy for improving the nation's health is both logical and clear."[205]

This observation isn't just about the "optics" of hiring more women, people of color, immigrants, and other members of underrepresented groups. It's about patient care. For example, a recent study found that women treated by women surgeons were 15 percent less likely than patients treated by male surgeons to have complications, readmission to the hospital, or death.[206]

The call to action is clear, but is enough being done to diversify the healthcare workforce?

The hiring pipeline is an easy scapegoat for why many workforces and academic programs lack diversity. Plenty of

healthcare organizations and hospitals still claim that they are
trying their best to diversify their employee pools but just don't
receive enough applications from qualified people from underrepresented groups. You've probably heard the excuses. Maybe
you've even made some of them yourself. I know I have.

- "There aren't enough women candidates." (For male-
  dominated specialties and leadership roles)
- "We don't get many Black, Latinx, or Indigenous people
  applying for our program."
- "We'd hire them/accept them if we could find them."

The list goes on.

Yet people who are members of these underrepresented
groups are often bewildered when these excuses filter back to
them. Many eager and qualified candidates — working hard to
get selected for a training program, hired, or promoted — are
passed over. They feel unnoticed. Invisible, even.

And certain leaders within healthcare have proven that the
pipeline isn't the problem. They've prioritized attracting and
hiring staff from underrepresented groups, and their organizations are thriving because of their efforts.

Here's a great example. When Kayla Cook (the leader at a
large community healthcare system you heard from in Chapter 7)
started her career, less than 4 percent of registered nurses in the
United States were Black. Today, that number has grown to
almost 10 percent, but get this: 30 percent of the nursing staff in
Cook's department are Black people.

How did Cook accomplish this? Instead of blaming the hiring
pipeline for failing to provide her with enough qualified Black
candidates, she examined that pipeline. Closely.

Cook noticed that her organization didn't hire nurses who
obtained degrees from specific schools with large populations of
Black nursing students because they didn't offer the same

curriculum as other schools. To address this difference, she created a more robust onboarding and training process to supplement what those schools taught. By doing so, she cast a wider net and was able to attract more Black talent. A lot more.

Organizations that are truly dedicated to hiring diverse talent can take a page out of Cook's book.

The rest of this chapter explores strategies for finding and selecting healthcare talent equitably, whether you are hiring employees or admitting trainees to a program. Specifically, I've combined approaches from my book *The Better Allies*® *Approach to Hiring* with insight from my interviews and research in the healthcare field. You'll find strategies for attracting talent from underrepresented groups, growing the hiring pipeline, understanding and mitigating bias during interviews, and advocating for pay equity, as well as stories and statistics underlining the importance of such policies.

Read on to find out how to adopt an ally mindset as you search for and hire new talent.

Attracting talent online

To research anything these days, the first thing most of us do is head online. Students looking for graduate schools will explore the information about programs and faculty on school websites. Job seekers will click on an organization's careers page to learn more about open roles, workplace culture, benefits, and advancement opportunities.

If you are serious about attracting a diverse pool of candidates for your program or job openings, make sure your website, especially the pages where you hope to attract talent, welcomes them.

Showcase diversity with images

First, look at the photos on your admissions or recruiting pages. Do the images show people of all kinds thriving? Or are they full of young white people without any visible disabilities? In researching this chapter, I took a peek at the admissions page for a medical school in Jackson, Mississippi, a city where more than 80 percent of residents are Black. Guess what I found? One photo of one white person and a preview image for a promotional video showcasing a white woman.[207]

Before you decide your own page is perfectly fine, put yourself in the shoes of an applicant from an underrepresented group. Imagine how a woman, a person of color, an older worker, or a person living with a disability would feel seeing the images on your recruiting or admissions page. Would they see people who look nothing like them, engaging in activities that broadcast an uninviting culture? Or would they see people from a variety of backgrounds in settings that showcase their enjoyment of being there and value to the organization or school? Candidates need to be able to envision themselves being somewhere, and seeing their own experience reflected through photos is a crucial way to do that.

That said, be genuine and authentic. As I explained in Chapter 6, use photos of your actual staff, students, and faculty in a way that represents your demographics. In other words, don't try to deceive candidates by showcasing more diversity than you actually have. If you have only one (or a small number of people) of a given demographic, don't feature them as though they were the norm.

To be fully transparent, consider putting your diversity statistics on your recruiting or admissions page, along with an explanation of what you're doing to improve them. Do this not just for the overall employee or student base but also for your leadership team. If your executives or department chairs are mostly "male and pale," explain any goals you have for improving representation there, too.

Wondering what to do if you don't have a diverse workforce?

First up, don't use stock photography. It may be a tempting solution, but candidates can easily do an image search online and find that your "employees" are models who appear on many job sites. Yes, this happens. In doing research for this book, I quickly spotted a stock photo of a diverse group of people featured as though they were employees on a large managed healthcare provider's career page. I found the same photo featured on the Diversity, Equity, and Inclusion page of a software company.[208]

Second, you're going to have to emphasize how welcoming and inclusive you are through text, not photos. I'll explore this in the next section.

One last thing about photos. As I shared in Chapter 6, people may use assistive technology such as screen readers. Add descriptions with HTML alt tags or in captions underneath the pictures to help candidates understand what your images depict.

Use inclusive language

While photos are important, don't forget about the power of language in making people feel like they belong — or not.

I was curious to see how healthcare graduate programs measure up in their use of inclusive language. When I checked out the UCLA School of Nursing application page, I noticed an Equity, Diversity, and Inclusion tab. In addition to a statement about their commitment to diversity and its benefits to nursing, that page had a list of affinity groups for Latinx, Asian and Pacific Islander, LGBTQ+, and men nursing students.[209]

By contrast, another University of California campus with a world-famous medical school had almost no messaging about diversity. Their admissions page for the MD program had information about supporting students' well-being and disability-related needs, but nothing else.

Whether you're recruiting students, residents, or employees, think about how you describe the kind of candidates you're looking for. Are you being welcoming to people from diverse backgrounds, genders, ethnicities, sexual orientations, ages, and abilities?

One way to show a commitment to diversity is by offering resource groups for underrepresented demographics, as the UCLA School of Nursing does. If these exist at your organization, be loud and proud about them. For example, here's how the Great Ormond Street Children's Hospital in London describes its inclusive culture and its resource groups on its careers page:

> We know that a diverse and inclusive workforce can help us to develop new ways of thinking leading to improvement and innovation in the way we work. For us, it is vital that all colleagues are treated fairly and are enabled to reach their full potential. We are dedicated to eliminating discrimination, valuing diversity and promoting equality of opportunity, to build and sustain an inclusive environment to deliver and receive care.
>
> We are proud to be a Disability Confident Employer and have active Black, Asian and minority ethnic, LGBT+ and Allies, Disability and Long Term Health Conditions and Women's staff forums.[210]

When hiring, most organizations in the United States include an Equal Employment Opportunity Commission (EEOC) statement on their website or in job descriptions to comply with the law, yet not all EEOC statements are created equal. Some are short and sweet (e.g., "We are an equal opportunity employer"), while some are more extensive. For example, I appreciate this one from Peer Health Exchange, a nonprofit focused on helping youth make healthy choices:

> At Peer Health Exchange, we celebrate difference and are committed to providing equitable opportunities, addressing the effects of power and privilege. PHE is proud to be an equal employment opportunity workplace. We are committed to equal employment opportunity regardless of race, color, ancestry, religion, gender, gender identity, national origin, sexual orientation, age, citizenship, marital status, physical disability, veteran status or length of time spent unemployed.[211]

Did you notice that last phrase? "Length of time spent unemployed." This organization encourages job seekers to apply even with résumé gaps. Here's why I like that a lot.

Between 2008 and 2013, one in four Americans in their fifties lost their jobs. Many gave up looking after that economic downturn because they assumed a lapse in employment would be held against them.

More recently, we've seen the devastating impact of the COVID-19 pandemic on employment. As I mentioned in the Introduction to this book, the healthcare field lost millions of workers during the height of COVID-19, and job recovery has been slow, especially in long-term care. Health aides and assistants, workers from underrepresented racial and ethnic groups, and women with young children have also been slow to return to jobs in healthcare.[212]

To attract workers who may have been forced out of work during that time — as well as others who have taken a break in their career for any other reason — make it clear that you won't hold it against them.

Here's one more idea for employers and admission committees. (I've saved the best for last.) Encourage candidates to apply for positions even if they don't meet all the criteria.

You may have heard about an internal Hewlett-Packard study that found that women applied for a promotion only when they believed they met 100 percent of the qualifications listed for the job, while men applied when they thought they could meet 60 percent of the job requirements.[213]

Hewlett-Packard's findings have been validated by other research. In *How to Lead*, Jo Owen described how men applied for head teaching roles when they thought they were 50 percent ready, while women wanted to be nearer to 100 percent ready before taking on the responsibility.[214]

Of course, there can also be problems with the requirements themselves. Requiring high test scores can favor those who can afford prep classes. Publication requirements can favor those who have been tapped to join research projects or have connections to journal editors. Extracurricular expectations can favor those who aren't primary caregivers, living with a disability, or handling other health concerns. As Dr. Vanessa Grubbs wrote for the *New England Journal of Medicine*:

> As the only Black member of division-chief search committees, I often heard colleagues remark that the Black candidate's CV was thinner than the White man's — fewer manuscripts, leadership positions, and grants — without acknowledging that the White man had been groomed, sponsored, and uplifted by people who looked like him throughout his 400-year head start. And without ascribing value to the time and energy Black candidates had dedicated to recruiting and mentoring people who look like them.[215]

Want to attract more candidates from underrepresented groups for your training programs and open roles, especially for those that are hard to fill? Step one: Simplify the criteria, removing "preferred" skill sets and other requirements that aren't truly required. Step two: Consider adding this one sentence: "We'd love to hear from you — even if you don't meet 100 percent of the criteria listed here."

Let's also make sure our organization's career pages or job descriptions clearly state how candidates who are living with disabilities can request accommodations during the interview process. Here's an example of how to do so from JAN, the Job Accommodation Network:

> [Employer] is committed to the full inclusion of all qualified individuals. As part of this commitment, [Employer] will ensure that persons with disabilities are provided reasonable accommodations. If reasonable accommodation is needed to participate in the job application or interview process, to perform essential job functions, and/or to receive other benefits and privileges of employment, please contact [include name and/or department, telephone, and e-mail address].[216]

Whether through photos or the language used to describe your culture and expectations, people from underrepresented groups will evaluate you by your careers and admissions pages. They may self-select out before even applying.

So, think about the messages you want to send, and ensure that your website reinforces them.

Growing the pipeline

One of the things that frustrates me about hearing organizations blame "the pipeline" for failing to supply them with diverse applicants is the assumption that candidates should do all the legwork. Many are willing to pay headhunters to track down ideal candidates for some positions and yet resist investing any resources in actively recruiting women, people of color, older workers, people living with disabilities, and others from underrepresented groups.

This is especially troubling considering how many bias barriers already exist for members of these groups, both as they apply and after being hired. In *Narrative Inquiry in Bioethics*, Dr. Gloria A. Wilder, vice president at Centene Corporation and CEO of Core Health and Wellness Centers, wrote about how those in positions of privilege in healthcare can marginalize talent who are members of racial minority groups. Wilder provided this list of concerning, non-inclusive practices (I like to think of them as the *opposite* of best practices):

- Creating criteria for promotion that do not give credit for diverse achievements,
- Devaluing community-based scholarship,
- Giving preferential recognition of specialties and procedure-based care,
- Allowing social interactions and networking to influence advancement,
- Creating dress codes that are narrow or purposely limit diverse cultures, and
- Using prescriptive policies to impede the progress of marginalized groups.[217]

There are, of course, some organizations and individual leaders who are being mindful and active about their hiring policies and recruitment tactics. In Boston, where the population has shifted over time from being largely white to majority-minority, the city's large cluster of elite academic healthcare institutes are still primarily staffed by white people. To address this disparity, as well as the long-standing shortage of healthcare professionals, Dana-Farber Cancer Institute (DFCI) created the Office of Workforce Development. It offers programs to ensure that youth and adults from underserved and underrepresented Boston neighborhoods have the necessary access, skills, and resources to pursue healthcare careers. This strategic program has resulted in DFCI filling its workforce pipeline with highly skilled and prepared individuals.[218]

This program also helps DFCI's workforce look more like their patients, which leads to patients trusting the healthcare providers, which leads to better patient outcomes. It's a win–win all around.

I've also seen medical schools create pathways for students from underrepresented groups. For example, the University of Minnesota has a six-week "Native Americans into Medicine" summer program for college sophomores and juniors interested in pursuing health careers. They study Tribal public health issues and get involved with projects benefiting Native American communities.[219]

I love seeing efforts like this pop up across the industry. After all, the pipeline isn't going to grow itself. When organizations create programs and support systems that encourage people from underrepresented groups to apply, join, or learn, they are taking responsibility in a meaningful way. They are helping the entire healthcare field become more diverse by welcoming new populations into the existing pipeline.

Of course, actively widening the pipeline is an activity that may ruffle some feathers, especially if doing so means including immigrants who trained in other countries. Cynthia Walsh, who you've heard from in previous chapters, told me about an online article she read on the shortage of nurses in the United States and how to encourage more people to go into nursing. In the comments, Walsh responded, "This conversation is great, but you're ignoring all these women who trained as nurses in other countries who are here now. We make it impossible, or expensive, for them to be nurses. We make them start all over again, giving them no credit for what they already learned." Walsh received many negative comments back from people who insisted that the US programs were better or that there was no way to gauge the caliber of non-US-based nursing training.

This wasn't the first time Walsh had advocated for foreign-trained nurses. While working at The Boston Home, Walsh made sure some of their CNAs, who had been nurses in other countries, could be recognized as licensed practical nurses. Working with her HR director and an organization that assesses and validates foreign-educated nurses, Walsh helped her staff through this arduous process.

Other countries also seem resistant to hiring foreign-trained nurses. The United Kingdom is also facing a nursing shortage, needing to hire an estimated 50,000 nurses by 2024.[220] To grow their pipeline, the UK government recruits nurses from other countries. Yet, they are treated like second-class workers until they can pass an exam and be added to the Nursing and Midwifery Council register. Even then, they have to start from the bottom of the ladder, regardless of the knowledge and experience they bring to their roles. They may also be tied by contract to a specific trust unit within the National Health Service (NHS), limiting their personal and career choices.[221] This is the opposite of allyship and a very short-sighted way to cope with a nursing shortage.

Although populating and diversifying the nursing profession is critically important, especially right now, growing the pipeline also applies to other specialties and positions within healthcare. This is especially true of leadership roles at universities, hospitals, and elsewhere.

While the overall pipeline of women going into medicine is promising, leadership roles still tend to be filled by men. To get more women into leadership roles in radiology, Dr. Cheri Canon believes the key is sponsorship, explaining, "Sponsors are people at the proverbial table and invite you to join them at that table."[222] To ensure that there's a pipeline of talent who are visible to sponsors, she helped create the Leading, Empowering and Disrupting (LEAD) Program, a joint initiative of the Society of Chairs of Academic Radiology Departments (SCARD) and GE Healthcare. It provides training, networking, and mentoring for 20 emerging women leaders from academia and industry each year.

LEAD is another great example of allies actively working to encourage and include more people from underrepresented groups. Instead of blaming the pipeline, I love to see people and organizations dedicating resources to widening it. Doing so will help ensure that healthcare becomes a truly diverse field.

Understanding bias in interviews

Bias can easily creep into the process of interviewing candidates, and the impact is substantial. For example, overweight or obese applicants to master's and doctoral programs are less likely to receive an offer of admission than thinner applicants.[223] Résumés with African American–sounding names receive 50 percent fewer callbacks than résumés with white-sounding names.[224] And women who don't have children were two times more likely to be called for an interview, compared to similarly qualified women who referenced children or parent-teacher associations on their application.[225]

There are more examples than just these. In fact, more than can possibly be mentioned here. Especially since interview bias tends to be unconscious, making it harder to flag and a flashpoint for defensiveness. The following sections will highlight some key areas of interview bias so you and your colleagues can be on the alert when screening candidates.

Motherhood bias

Unfortunately, there seems to be an ingrained bias against mothers in healthcare. In a study of the 2015 and 2016 Medical Physics Residency Match, women candidates were twice as likely as men to be asked about having children or plans to have children. Not surprisingly, most were uncomfortable answering the question.[226]

And it's not limited to residency programs. A survey of almost 6,000 physician mothers found that four in five report discrimination in the workplace, much of it related to maternal concerns. As Dr. Resa E. Lewiss (the emergency medicine professor you've heard from previously) shared with me, "I was applying to one of my first jobs, and the interviewer said he'd had bad luck with hiring women because they tended to get pregnant."

Another person I spoke to shared this frustrating conversation from a recent candidate debrief session. One of her colleagues said, "Are we really sure that she should have this role? She has small kids and may not be able to devote the time needed to be successful."

Then there's this anecdote from Courtney Burns, a second-year medical student, who tweeted:[227]

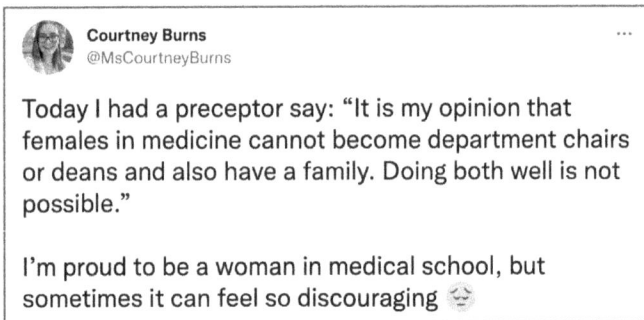

> **Courtney Burns**
> @MsCourtneyBurns   ...
>
> Today I had a preceptor say: "It is my opinion that females in medicine cannot become department chairs or deans and also have a family. Doing both well is not possible."
>
> I'm proud to be a woman in medical school, but sometimes it can feel so discouraging ☹

I'm going to state the obvious here. Don't ask candidates if they have children or plan to start a family. In many US states, making a hiring decision based on family responsibilities is illegal, so there is no reason for these questions to come up.

Also, if you're about to comment on someone's eligibility for job success because they might start a family, use the "flip it to test it" approach. (You may remember it from Chapter 3.) Simply ask yourself, Would I make the same comments about someone of a different gender? If the answer is no, acknowledge your bias, and keep your mouth shut.

Extra scrutiny

With any kind of bias can come extra scrutiny. Dr. Kelly Paradis (the associate professor of medical physics you heard from in earlier chapters) told me about some of the things she hears about women during the interview process, including, "She said, 'I' a lot in her presentation. 'I did this, I did that.' Did she really do all that stuff by herself?" Yet, as Paradis pointed out, members of the same review committee didn't question the validity of the men who similarly described their accomplishments.

This additional scrutiny also shows up by questioning someone's credentials. When then-Judge Ketanji Brown Jackson was nominated to serve as a U.S. Supreme Court justice, one conservative news host demanded to see her LSAT score. (As you may know, the LSAT is a standardized law school entrance exam.) It shouldn't have mattered. Jackson received her law degree from Harvard 25 years earlier and went on to have an impressive career, including being a district judge in Washington, DC. By contrast, that same news host didn't ask to see the LSAT scores of the previously nominated Justice Amy Coney Barrett before announcing, "There's no question that Barrett is qualified for the job."[228] (I should note that Jackson is Black and Barrett is white.)

Allies, let's reflect on how we evaluate candidates. Ideally, a hiring manager or committee would specify all the qualifications needed for an open position before reviewing the first résumé or application. Once they're in place, look for requests for additional credentials for specific people. If you spot any, there could be some bias at play.

That said, ensure that your qualifications aren't unwittingly designed as gatekeeping hurdles, effectively eliminating people from underrepresented groups. For example, the Atlas system was developed by Tulane University's School of Medicine to purportedly objectively rank applicants for their residency program using factors like their test scores, class ranking, and the perceived quality of their medical school. Yet, it effectively shut out applicants from historically Black medical schools.[229] Be especially wary of algorithms and tools that remove all human judgment and nuance from the vetting process. Objectivity is helpful, but not at the cost of holistic understanding.

Culture fit

UCLA's chair of neurosurgery, Dr. Linda Liau, knows she doesn't look like a typical surgeon. She's a woman and a racial minority. And she's short, measuring just 5'2" tall. In meetings to evaluate faculty candidates, Liau often spots examples of confirmation bias from her male colleagues. As she explained in an interview with Yahoo news, "When they're looking for other faculty members or department chairs, they're looking for themselves. They're looking for people who are like them, and because we've had so many generations of male dominance in academia, there's this perception that it's also equated with excellence."[230]

This bias can show up via veiled comments. I'll bet none of those faculty members say outright, "We can't hire her because she's a woman." Instead, people tend to skirt the issue. For example, "I can't quite put my finger on it, but I just don't think they'd fit in here."

I remember attending a panel where Jeffrey Siminoff, then head of diversity at Twitter, made a truly memorable comment. "If I hear that a candidate isn't a culture fit, I ask if they could be a culture add." I love this and recommend taking it a step further.

Emphasize what they'll bring to your organization that you don't have today and how that will help you achieve your goals or improve patient outcomes.

In a similar vein, tech company Atlassian shifted its hiring focus from "culture fit" to "values fit." It helped recruiters hire people who shared the company's goals but not necessarily the viewpoints or backgrounds of the interview team.[231]

Undervalued DEI Work

While many institutions value DEI initiatives, and some have paid staff to do the work, others expect the work to be done by volunteers who are members of underrepresented groups themselves. This is especially true for women in academia, who end up taking on this "third shift" burden because they are determined to make an impact and fix the systemic gender inequities that are pervasive in healthcare.[232]

Yet, this volunteer work tends to go unrecognized. As Dr. Kelly Paradis, who you heard from above, told me, "Even though institutions say DEI is important, they may not count DEI work towards a promotion." She added, "The burden of this work falls on the people who are most harmed. It takes away their time to do other work that would get them promoted and would get them recognized." It's another example of the "minority tax" I mentioned in Chapter 8.

If you're trying to build a more inclusive environment, why not screen for inclusive attitudes, experiences, and contributions during the selection process? A straightforward way to do this is by asking candidates questions about their past inclusion experiences. Here are a few suggestions:

- How have you contributed to an inclusive culture or community?
- Have you been actively involved in DEI work?

- Tell me about your experience working with diverse teams.
- What have you done to ensure that coworkers feel a sense of belonging?
- Have you had the opportunity to act as someone's ally at work? Tell me about it.

Not recognizing the journey

On Twitter, Dr. Joannie Yeh posted:[233]

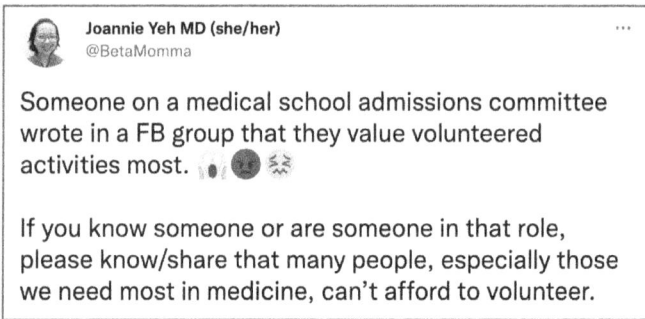

> **Joannie Yeh MD (she/her)**
> @BetaMomma
>
> Someone on a medical school admissions committee wrote in a FB group that they value volunteered activities most. 😠 ● 💢
>
> If you know someone or are someone in that role, please know/share that many people, especially those we need most in medicine, can't afford to volunteer.

Turns out that for decades, medical students have disproportionately hailed from high-income households.[234] Researchers have found that a low socioeconomic status significantly decreases the likelihood that a student interested in healthcare will apply or get accepted to medical school.[235] The high costs are barriers for lower-income students, who are disproportionately Black or Hispanic. The same groups that are underrepresented in medicine.

Instead of favoring a student because of impressive volunteer activities and creating yet another barrier for those from lower-income households, let's realize that not everyone can afford to volunteer their time. Or do unpaid internships. Or get a bachelor's degree without getting some credits via a community college.

Instead of making huge assumptions about candidates who haven't pursued certain experiences, we could ask why. Until you face a situation where one of them says, "Well, I wanted to do that, but here's why I couldn't," you might be unaware of your ingrained bias.

Instead of excluding someone because they didn't hit some mark, let's work to understand their journey.

Eliminating bias

Recognizing bias is tricky, but actually eradicating it can be even more difficult. Especially since, as I mentioned earlier, many people get defensive when asked to keep their biases in check. Every leader will need to handle this differently based on team dynamics and organizational needs, but I recommend offering a reminder that no one is free of bias. We all have them, whether we know and admit it or not, so everyone is in the same boat. Removing bias from your screening and interviewing processes can be presented as a team effort that everyone should actively embrace. This approach helps prevent certain people from feeling singled out for their individual biases.

That said, no one should be excused and no harmful biases should be ignored. Read on for some actionable strategies to help reduce favoritism and unfair judgments in your hiring practices.

Remind people bias may exist

Perhaps one of the easiest ways to eliminate bias from talent selection is to call attention to it. I first learned about this approach from Google. At the start of their talent discussion meetings, everyone is given a brief handout describing common errors and biases that assessors make and how to fix them. Simply reminding managers of potential biases is enough to eliminate many of them.[236]

Some medical schools are taking similar steps and seeing a positive impact on the diversity of their student body.

Prior to the 2012–2013 application cycle, all 140 members of the Ohio State University College of Medicine (OSUCOM) admissions committee took a black-white implicit association test (IAT). Most thought the IAT might help reduce bias, and almost half of the committee members said they were conscious of their individual results when interviewing candidates. As a result, the class that matriculated following the IAT exercise was the most diverse in that institution's history.[237]

If you'd like your hiring or admissions committees to take an IAT, consider leveraging the free, online ones on Harvard's Project Implicit website.[238]

Or, if you want to simply remind them about biases that are common during the talent selection process, consider distributing a handout like Google. You can download their "unbiasing hiring" checklist from the re:Work website.[239]

Be objective

Another effective way to bust bias is to remove personal feelings, opinions, or other subjective measures from the talent evaluation process. Here are some suggestions for introducing more objectivity as you evaluate trainees and job candidates.

- **Create objective criteria for reviewing applications or résumés.** Choose the most critical requirements for your program or job opening, and evaluate candidates on those qualities, not on their child-bearing abilities, ages, volunteer experiences, or other attributes that don't equate to being able to do the work.
- **Use structured interview tactics.** Create questions focused on the skills and abilities you're seeking. Ask each interviewee the same questions in the same order.

- **Share interview questions ahead of time.** Set up candidates for success by telling them the questions to expect. This approach helps minimize performance anxiety, which may especially impact certain groups, including women in a male-dominated field.[240]
- **Create a standardized rubric for evaluating candidates.** Then rank every person on the same scale to help with decision-making and eliminating "gut" feelings.[241]
- **Make voting anonymous.** Discourage group-think or letting the most senior person influence the decision by using paper ballots or a polling tool.[242]

Watch out for biased comments

Here are some frequently used phrases that should raise red flags during discussions of applicants for training programs or job openings. (You saw some of them in Chapter 4.)

All-Too-Common Biased Comments

The candidate doesn't have ... (something not on a job or training program description, but that more privileged candidates tend to have).

They wouldn't want this role because of the travel, long hours, or overnight shifts.

Before selecting them, I'd like to see them prove they're capable (when discussing some responsibility they've done previously).

I don't want to lower the bar.

I'm not racist/sexist/homophobic, but ...

They wouldn't be a culture fit.

If you hear any of them, ask some probing questions. "What makes you say that?" or "Would you say the same thing about a candidate who isn't a member of an underrepresented group?" For more ideas, review the "Being an Upstander" section in Chapter 4.

Diversify your interview or admissions team

When possible, make sure candidates meet at least one interviewer of the same gender, ethnicity, or age. By seeing someone "like them," candidates from underrepresented groups may feel more at ease and do better in the interview process. At tech company Cisco, this practice resulted in a roughly 50 percent increase in the odds that they would hire a woman for a given position.[243]

Furthermore, a diverse committee is more likely to select talent from underrepresented groups. Research shows that women, minorities, and younger people have less implicit racial bias than older white men.[244]

That said, you don't want to burden employees from underrepresented demographics by asking them to do more talent selection work than their peers. Being on an interview panel or admissions committee takes time away from the work that is going to be measured as part of performance assessments. It's a form of glue work, as I covered in Chapter 8. If you are tasking certain people with more than their fair share of interviewing, what can you do to reward them or set them up for success with the rest of their job responsibilities?

Lastly, ensure that everyone on your interview panel has a real and respected voice in evaluating candidates. If you invite someone to join your panel so that candidates can meet with someone "like them," their perspective should matter just as much as everyone else's.

It's impossible to eliminate personal bias completely, but it's imperative to remove as much of it as possible. Especially for those who are truly committed to selecting talent from marginalized groups.

Paying attention to pay

Kara Shafer, the registered nurse you heard from in Chapter 3, told me how she is advocating for a colleague's pay equity. Before immigrating to the United States, this person attended nursing school in Japan and worked as a nurse there for six years. Shafer told me, "Because her nursing school was recognized by the US, she simply had to pass our licensing exam to practice here. Which she did." But, their hospital administration refused to recognize those years of experience and paid her as if she were a first-year nurse. Shafer became outraged. She brought it up at a recent labor-management meeting and told them they were participating in institutional racism. Her next step? She asked her union to add language to their contract that prior experience outside the United States should be recognized if someone attended an approved nursing school.

Of course, pay inequity in healthcare isn't limited to nurses who received their training in other countries. There can be gendered differences, too. As I mentioned in the Introduction, women nurses in the United States earn just 94 percent of what men nurses earn.[245]

Physicians also face pay inequity. Here are a few cases in point: The average salary for radiologists in the United States is $429,000, but women make 21 percent less than men.[246] Women gastroenterologists earn $82,000 less on average.[247] And women surgeons in Ontario received 24 percent less per hour of operating time than their male counterparts.[248] In fact, there are no medical specialties in which women physicians earn the same or more than men.[249]

This problem has also been documented in academic medicine. One cross-sectional study of US physician compensation in academic medicine found women had lower early career earning potential than men in nearly every subspecialty analyzed, primarily due to lower starting salaries for women. In 42 of the 45 subspecialties, women had a median starting salary 10 percent lower than men.[250] As a result, their lifetime earning potential suffers.

For example, imagine two equally qualified physicians, one a man and one a woman, starting their careers at a university. Let's assume the man receives an annual salary of $240,000, and the woman earns 90 percent of that, or $216,000. That means the woman is earning $24,000 less than the man per year, or $2,000 less every month. (Wow.) Now, assume they work for 30 more years, and they both receive exactly a 4 percent increase each year. By the time they retire, the man will earn almost $6,500 more than the woman monthly. Adding up the income difference each year over the 30 years, the man will have earned over $1.4 million more than the woman. That's right — 1.4 MILLION dollars.

Of course, my math doesn't account for salary bumps that come with promotions. Assuming the man and woman received similar support for their research, grant funding, and publishing activities, they might have equal opportunities for advancement. (This is a big assumption.) But the salary inequity will persist.

While hospitals, training programs, academic departments, and other healthcare institutions are held to tight budgets — and, in some cases, need to be run profitably — they also need to treat employees well and pay them equitably.

And there are roles for allies to play to help make it happen. Let's explore a few.

Conduct (or ask for) a pay equity review

When Salesforce CEO Marc Benioff heard concerns in 2015 that his company was paying women less than men, he was initially in denial. Yet, a company audit uncovered a statistical difference in pay between genders. Benioff admitted, "It was everywhere. It was through the whole company, every department, every division, every geography."[251] Over the next two years, Salesforce spent almost $6 million to close the gap.

Many other companies have since followed Salesforce's lead, and I hope healthcare institutions have done or will do so, too. As Dr. Amy S. Gottlieb, editor of the book *Closing the Gender Pay Gap in Medicine: A Roadmap for Healthcare Organizations and the Women Physicians Who Work for Them*, recommends, "The first step [to achieving pay equity] will be to conduct salary audits to understand where women fall relative to the institution's target salary benchmarks compared with male colleagues."[252]

If your organization hasn't already instituted a pay equity review, you have work to do. Do you have the power to make this happen for your team — or, better yet, for your larger function or department? Can you ask your leadership team or union what steps are being taken to ensure pay equity? (Not just for women, but for everyone.) Make sure it's on their radar, ideally with a plan underway to make it happen.

Advocate for salary transparency

When I spoke with Dr. VK Gadi, he emphasized the importance of salary transparency in addressing discrimination. While he has always worked at institutions where salaries are public data, he acknowledges that not every employer shares this information freely. And he recommends total salary transparency as a structural approach to addressing inequities. As he explained, "We don't want to realize after the fact that we offered a woman candidate a contract that is less than the one we gave to a man."[253]

If your employer doesn't already publish salaries (with personally identifying information redacted), ask what it would take to get started. Perhaps the first step can be publishing just the starting salaries for various roles.

You could also do something on a personal level: Share your salary with others.

In an interview for *Forbes*, Sarah Hillware, a global health and development leader, shared a great example of such allyship. "I had an informal conversation with a white male colleague, and he shared how much he made and informed me how much I was eligible to request. I used this information to move to another department and obtain a 20 percent pay raise."[254]

Scrutinize Your Wage Minimum

Some healthcare organizations take pay equity seriously. When I spoke to the head of human resources at a large urban safety net health system, she told me that one of their areas of focus is "the wage minimum" (as opposed to "the minimum wage" which is mandated by their state). A few years ago, they set their wage minimum at $11/hour. Then they moved it to $13/hour. During the fall of 2021, it became $15/hour. And in June of 2022, their wage minimum became $18/hour. They'll keep increasing this number to get to their target of paying a rate that would allow any employee to purchase a home and begin to build wealth. In the state where this organization is based, that would be about $21–$22/hour.

For the record, the US federal minimum wage is $7.25/hour as of the writing of this book. This pay rate is supposed to be a living wage, but it hasn't been raised since 2009 and hasn't been aligned with sustainable pay since the late 1960s. In fact, the earnings of a minimum-wage worker with a family of four fall well below the poverty line.[255]

If your employer simply adopts the government's guidance on minimum wage, consider advocating for an increase that will make a difference to the hourly workers who, frankly, make a difference every day.

This chapter offers some key insights on the topic of allyship in hiring practices, but there's so much more to learn. In fact, I wrote *The Better Allies Approach to Hiring* so I could dig deeper into equitable hiring practices. To learn more — including guidelines for writing inclusive job descriptions and attracting a diverse candidate pool — I hope you'll consider checking out this companion guidebook.

And remember that you don't need to work in HR to be an active ally around issues of finding and selecting talent, hiring people from underrepresented groups, or pay equity. Take small steps, speak up, work together, and do whatever you can to create positive change in your organization and healthcare overall.

Actions for Better Allies:
Select Talent Equitably

Allies can band together to banish the "pipeline" excuses and focus on employing strategies that are proven to attract and select applicants from underrepresented groups. Here are some ways you can make this possible:

- Ensure that your admissions or recruiting web pages use language and images to convey that people from marginalized groups are welcome and belong.
- Advocate for programs to increase the pipeline instead of blaming it.
- Create objective processes to set up candidates for success and prep committee members to be aware of hidden biases.
- Recognize and value the journeys of applicants.
- Pay attention to pay and advocate for salary transparency however you can.

11

OPENING CAREER DOORS

"As you succeed, it's your obligation to bring others along with you." That was the sage advice given by Dr. Mary Mahoney at a webinar hosted by the American Association of Women in Radiology. As the chair of radiology at the University of Cincinnati, Mahoney finds, "One of the most rewarding things is not to be on the podium myself any longer, but to sit in the back and see others that I have mentored speak." She went on to emphasize, "At this point in my career, I get more satisfaction from seeing a woman earlier in her career give a talk than to publish another paper myself."[256]

Regardless of where you are in your career or the position you hold, I hope you will embrace the same mindset: Bring others along with you. This chapter explores ways allies can do exactly that by opening career doors for members of underrepresented groups.

Believing in and boosting

In his book *Work Rules!*, Laszlo Bock described a problem Google was facing: Women employees were less likely to nominate themselves for promotions, despite a policy allowing all employees to do so.[257] The company found that a slight nudge made a huge difference. All it took was senior vice president Alan Eustace sending an email to employees citing research about classroom dynamics, where boys tend to raise their hand to answer any question and girls tend to wait to be certain. With that nudge, not only did women's application rates soar, but the volume of their promotions surpassed those of their male counterparts.[258]

People with multiple underrepresented identities may benefit even more from positive feedback, encouragement, and career-related nudges. Why? Because they receive less of it overall. For example, women of color are less likely to have supervisors who promote their work contributions to others, help them navigate internal politics, or socialize with them outside work. This shuts them out of the informal networks that propel most high-potentials forward in their careers[259] — and it means that allies who offer genuine support and praise can make a huge impact.

Allies don't need to be in a position to award promotions to employees from underrepresented groups. Instead, we can provide support from the sidelines. Just encouraging them, and nudging them to push forward in their careers, can make a huge difference.

Here are some stories I collected during my interviews about the power of such encouragement.

Kessie Davis, the chief human resources officer at an urban safety net health system you heard from previously, is used to being the "only." Growing up, she was the only person in her immediate family who had the opportunity to go to college, and during school, she developed an interest in physical therapy. As she told me, "I was in a predominantly white institution, and I was the only person of color in the study for pre-physical therapy. Although I didn't see people like me, I was able to pursue a degree with the wonderful influence of my advisor. He just really believed in me and told me that it was possible." Her advisor also encouraged her to go to graduate school; Davis subsequently earned a master's degree in physical therapy, where, once again, she was the only person of color in the program.

When I asked Davis what her advisor had done to support her, she was quick to respond. "He would always affirm that I was just as smart, if not smarter than the next person, and that all things were possible for me."

Similarly, I heard from Dr. Resa E. Lewiss (the emergency medicine professor you also heard from in previous chapters) about the encouragement she received. "I didn't start off with a plan and ambition to become a full professor. Yet, I had people pull me aside and say that I should. They encouraged me to apply for academic promotions, given my publications and other accomplishments."

In addition to verbal nudges and other forms of in-person encouragement, allies can also look to create and open doors that may not otherwise exist.

Dr. Dawn Haut, who you may remember inspired me to write this book, told me, "When I was doing my general pediatric residency in the early Nineties, we were essentially presented with two options: go into primary care in private practice or pursue a fellowship to become a specialist." Yet, toward the end of her residency, she met a white man working as a community pediatrician in lower-income neighborhoods. She went on to explain, "This really resonated with me, and he helped show me that it could be a career path. He introduced me to some leaders in the American Academy of Pediatrics (AAP), who set up a community pediatrics 'fellowship' for me. I was able to travel to different parts of the country to see different kinds of models of community pediatrics and meet with providers. It was phenomenal."

Now get this. That single opportunity turned into something larger. The AAP went on to offer this fellowship for many years, introducing other pediatric residents to community health as a career.

It's clear that suggestions around applying for opportunities, words of praise, and consistent verbal support can make a huge difference in the career choices of healthcare workers who might otherwise fly under the radar. So, allies, take opportunities to bolster, nudge, encourage, and open career doors for people from underrepresented groups.

Giving wholehearted and powerful recommendations

Recommendations come in many forms. Student evaluations, formal letters for job seekers, social media endorsements, verbal reference checks, and back-channel casual conversations can all impact the career trajectories of the people they describe. This means that when you're giving any kind of recommendation, you should show complete confidence. No hedging ("she might be good"), faint praise ("she'll do okay"), or other phrases that undermine ("she needs only minimal guidance").

Wondering why I'm calling this out? In a 2018 study of recommendations for academic positions, researchers found that letters about women included more doubt-raising phrases than those about men, and even *one* such phrase can make a difference during a job search.[260,261] This means that a lukewarm recommendation may be more harmful than no recommendation at all.

As inclusion and women's leadership expert Lori Nishiura Mackenzie wrote, "Doubt has others question one's abilities. Doubt is a negative sentiment that we do not intentionally wish to cast on most folks. Yet, often unbeknownst to us, doubt can creep into our assessments and statements of advocacy."[262]

There are also other forms of bias that can creep into narrative evaluations of learners, even for those receiving identical grades.

As you may remember from Chapter 9, a study of almost 90,000 core clerkship evaluations of third-year medical students found that personal attributes such as "lovely" appeared more frequently in evaluations of women, while competency-related behaviors, such as "scientific" appeared more often in men's. The study also found that personal attributes like "pleasant" appeared more frequently in evaluations of students from underrepresented minority groups. In contrast, competency attributes, such as "knowledgeable," appeared more regularly in evaluations of well represented students.[263]

Another study found that Black residency applicants were more likely to be described by tepid terms like "competent," whereas white applicants more frequently received standout descriptors like "exceptional."[264]

I wonder if this research inadvertently highlights one of the reasons that medical students from underrepresented racial and ethnic groups are more likely to leave medical school before graduating than their white peers.[265]

Allies, let's make sure we're getting to know talent from underrepresented groups well enough to recommend them for opportunities. Then, as we write letters or evaluations, make them wholehearted and powerful. Focus on the person's competencies and accomplishments and praise them to the skies. And when describing a woman or a member of an underrepresented racial group, ask yourself, Would I use the same language to commend a white man? Otherwise, you risk shutting a door you intended to open.

Avoiding gatekeeping

In her TEDx talk "A Moonshot for Gender Equity," Dr. Shikha Jain (also interviewed for this book) reflected on her career, wondering if some of the challenges she had faced weren't because she wasn't good enough, but because she was in a system that put barriers in places where they shouldn't be.

Jain shared a few anecdotes she's heard from other women in healthcare. "Maybe you should wait for that leadership position until your kids are in college." And "Why on earth would you go to medical school, take a spot from an equally qualified male candidate, when everyone knows you're just going to get married, have kids, and work part-time or leave medicine all together."[266]

I've also witnessed such gatekeeping firsthand. When I worked as a tech executive, I remember talking with a man on my staff who needed to fill a senior role on his team. When I asked if he planned to promote his top employee into the position, he replied that she had young children at home, and he felt sure that she wouldn't want all the travel that would come with the promotion. As you might imagine, I countered, saying that was her decision, not his. He went on to make her the offer, which she accepted and went on to do an outstanding job.

Allies, as we come across career opportunities, let's not make decisions on someone's behalf because we think we know what's best for them. Instead of gatekeeping, let's tell them about the possibilities, be encouraging, and let them make their own choices.

Giving credit

Dr. Kelly Paradis, the medical physicist you heard from in earlier chapters, feels fortunate to have allies who mention her name when someone starts talking about her area of expertise. She told me it often happens with a simple, "Kelly already knows about that. You should include her." She also appreciates that in her department, there are people who like to go out of their way to recognize the work of others that might otherwise not necessarily come up. I loved hearing about this strong focus on giving credit.

Yet, it's far from universal within academic departments or on social media. Here's a good reminder from Dr. Shivani Misra, a physician and scientist, who tweeted:[267]

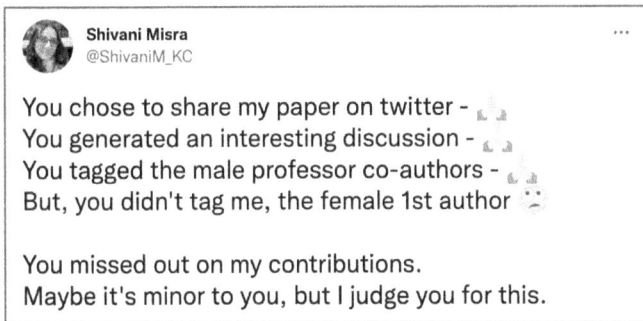

> **Shivani Misra**
> @ShivaniM_KC   ...
>
> You chose to share my paper on twitter -
> You generated an interesting discussion -
> You tagged the male professor co-authors -
> But, you didn't tag me, the female 1st author
>
> You missed out on my contributions.
> Maybe it's minor to you, but I judge you for this.

While Misra believes it's often done unconsciously, she wants to raise more awareness because, as she wrote, "It's super annoying for #WomenInSTEM."

I'd go one step further: Not crediting someone is not just annoying, it also minimizes their visibility in their field, across their organization, or even within their team. And visibility is a significant predictor of career growth for women.[268] It's also needed to build a national reputation, a prerequisite for the academic promotion process.

The importance of giving credit extends far beyond academia, of course. Several studies have found that Black women's statements were remembered less quickly and less accurately than those of their white female and male peers,[269] making it all the more important for allies to echo and credit them as often as possible.

Let's be sure to credit everyone when we share a paper on social media, cite someone's research, or mention a team's project in a meeting.

Celebrating accomplishments

In my friend Jo Miller's book, *Woman of Influence: 9 Steps to Build Your Brand, Establish Your Legacy*, she explains how women can face backlash when they advocate for themselves and talk about their achievements. This behavior goes against cultural expectations for women, so people of all genders tend to recoil from it. Yet, women need to talk about their accomplishments to be perceived as competent.

In fact, it's helpful for *all* people to learn how to celebrate their workplace wins openly. One survey found that 86 percent of recruitment decision-makers agree that it's essential for candidates to be able to clearly communicate their achievements.[270] It's much harder to do that if you're working in an environment where colleagues discourage positive discussion of your accomplishments. Socially suppressing discussion of personal wins can literally stunt someone's career growth.

To combat this "damned if you do, doomed if you don't" conundrum, Miller recommends creating a culture where accomplishments are regularly recognized and celebrated. Doing so can normalize it for everyone, not just women. Consider adding "Humble Brags" as a regular agenda item during staff meetings, creating an online forum for sharing wins, or adding a section to an employee newsletter to give shout-outs.

Promoting on potential

In Chapter 9, I explored how "prove it again" bias can show up in feedback we give to colleagues from underrepresented demographics. In a nutshell, we might tell members of groups that have been stereotyped as less competent or hardworking that they're not ready for some responsibility because they have not yet demonstrated they're capable. By contrast, we might see the potential that someone will be successful if they "look the part" and give them more supportive feedback. Loads of research backs this up: When Harvard Business School's David A. Thomas and John Gabarro conducted an in-depth six-year study of leaders, they found that people of color had to manage their careers more strategically than their white peers did and to prove greater competence before winning promotions.[271]

This bias can also show up in the promotion process. Research from McKinsey and LeanIn.Org found that "men get promoted based on potential, and women get promoted based on performance."[272] In other words, women can get stuck on a treadmill, constantly proving and reproving that they're worthy of responsibility and capable of leadership. In fact, when women did all the things they were told would help them get ahead — using the same tactics as men — they still advanced less than their male counterparts and had slower pay growth.[273]

More evidence that men are immune from "prove it again" bias: They're more likely to get what they want without even asking. According to the 2017 "Women in the Workplace" study:

> Women of all races and ethnicities negotiate for raises and promotions at rates comparable to their male counterparts. However, men are more likely to say they have not asked for a raise because they are already well compensated or a promotion because they are already in the right role.[274]

While women are expected to illustrate competence through repeated performance, men get access to advancement opportunities without having to ask for them. While women must prove their worth, men are promoted simply for showing potential.

People of color are frequently targets of "prove it again" bias, too. This can be especially true for Black people, who may be inadvertently disadvantaged by the glorification of Black exceptionalism. In an article titled "Our Obsession With Black Excellence Is Harming Black People," diversity consultant and author Janice Gassam Asare wrote, "No matter how good or excellent a Black person is, it never seems to be enough. Nikole Hannah-Jones experienced this firsthand after a public tenure battle with the University of North Carolina at Chapel Hill. Despite being a Pulitzer Prize-winning journalist who writes for the *New York Times*, and having a wealth of other accomplishments, she was initially denied tenure by a board of trustees at the university."[275]

So how do allies recognize potential, regardless of gender, background, or identity? How can allies combat "prove it again" bias and learn to see promise in the people they work closely with on a daily basis?

Psychologists Tomas Chamorro-Premuzic and Seymour Adler, along with Robert B. Kaiser, found that traits like enthusiasm and success-centric mindsets are considered desirable by hiring managers, but don't actually indicate that an individual has high potential. Their study showed that the following three markers of high potential are the ones to look for:

- **Ability.** Is the candidate capable of doing the job in question? Is the candidate clearly able to learn and master the requisite knowledge and skills needed to perform this job?
- **Social skills.** Does the candidate excel at teamwork and collaboration? Can the candidate manage both themselves and others?
- **Drive.** Is the candidate willing to work hard, achieve, and do whatever it takes to get the job done?[276]

Clearly, people of all genders and backgrounds can possess all three of these traits. "Ability" only becomes dicey if a promoting manager insists that a certain candidate prove again and again that they have what it takes. If you are an ally who is advocating for a promotion for a colleague from an underrepresented group, consider these three criteria instead of relying entirely on your gut. (Guts can be biased.) And if you are in a position to sit on a calibration or promotions board, and you don't know all of the candidates, take the time to get to know them. Once you do, find ways to scope and recognize their potential instead of insisting they prove their worthiness by already doing the same job.

Stepping back

I wish everyone had the same mindset as Dr. VK Gadi, the director of medical oncology you heard from in earlier chapters. During his training, he had mentors who were already thinking inclusively. "They modeled behavior for me to model going forward. And if anything, I've just expanded on what they modeled."

Gadi went on to elaborate, saying, "As I built my career, I figured out how to promote people from underrepresented groups. It's not that I will ever say no to a male, but I go out of my way to give a step up to folks who are not commonly invited to the table. In fact, some would argue I've handed out more opportunities than I've kept for myself." He added, "My instinct is to always find somebody junior, give them a seat at the table, and promote them. I'd rather do that ten times over than do anything for myself."

What does this look like in practice? As the PI (principal investigator) of his lab, Gadi could claim credit for all the emerging research being done by scientists in his lab. But he doesn't. "As soon as someone dominates an area of thought, it's theirs. Instead of taking it over myself, I go find something new to work on." Otherwise, he'd be usurping their research base, which would make it that much harder for them to grow in their careers.

Gadi also steps back from other opportunities to make room for people who are at earlier stages in their careers. He told me he feels fortunate that he is in a position to offer many people "step-ups." For example, when asked to speak or join a committee, Gadi immediately recommends someone in their mid-career. He tells the organizer, "They have the gravitas. You just don't know it yet."

To repeat the call-to-action I shared at the start of this chapter, let's bring others along with us as we succeed. Even if it means sometimes stepping back from opportunities ourselves.

Sponsoring

Dr. David Brown, the associate professor of otolaryngology you heard from in Chapters 5 and 7, is biracial and the first in his family to go to college. When he was applying to match for residency programs, two mentors wrote recommendation letters on his behalf. While he's grateful to both of them, one had a much bigger impact than the other. This person clearly believed in Brown and put their reputation on the line to endorse him. Here's what happened.

During the match process, Brown hoped to be invited to interview at three top-rated schools for his specialty. It turns out he got interviews at two and was placed on the waiting list for the third. One of his mentors told him not to worry about that third interview and that everything would be fine. That he'd get into a good program. "Basically, he was dismissive of my concerns," Brown told me. By contrast, the other mentor sprang into action. The next day, Brown received a call from that third school. They told him, "We had you on a waiting list for an interview. And today, we sent you a letter denying you an interview. But all of a sudden, we have an opening. And we want to know if you can come this Thursday." Brown ended up matching there. Today, he proudly displays both the rejection letter and his diploma from that school on his office wall.

Brown's story is one example of an ally acting as a sponsor. I appreciate how Dr. Matthew Chow, president of the professional association Doctors of BC, describes sponsorship as an elevated form of allyship. In a webinar on advancing women in healthcare leadership, he shared that when an equity-seeking person runs a race, an ally can come up alongside them, pass them water, and cheer them on. Compare that to sponsorship, where "you get into a bulldozer, and you drive that bulldozer in front of that equity-seeking person, and … you push away the things that are getting in the way of that person so that they can succeed."[277]

While the "sponsor as bulldozer" is a powerful metaphor, it's not the only option for allies who want to embrace sponsorship. London Business School professors Herminia Ibarra, PhD, and Kathleen O'Connor, PhD, have identified a spectrum of sponsorship styles, some of which are more impactful than others. Here are their five archetypes:

Classic mentor: provides personal advice and support privately, with no more at stake than the time invested.

Strategizer: shares insider knowledge about how to advance in the organization, outlining a strategy that will help fill any developmental gaps that may be a barrier to advancement.

Connector: makes introductions to influential people in their network and "talks up" the sponsored employee with peers.

Opportunity giver: offers the sponsored employee high-visibility projects or roles (for example, giving a key presentation or running an important meeting).

> **Classic advocate:** the sponsor advocates publicly for an individual, typically in a succession contest for a significant role, with their reputation at stake.[278]

Now, reflect on the kind of sponsor you are for people who are members of underrepresented groups. As Ibarra and O'Connor explain, unless you know someone well, you will likely to be at the start of this list. That's a fine place to begin, but what would it take to move to the next level and have a more significant impact?

Here's a pro tip: Get to know them well enough so that you're willing and eager to use your privilege and reputation to sing their praises with gusto.

In her 2018 TEDWomen talk, which has been viewed over 4 million times, Carla Harris delivered an important message about meritocracy — or lack thereof. She debunked the myth that to get ahead, you just need to do great work so that it will be recognized and rewarded. Instead, she points out that you need a sponsor who will speak your name when you're not in the room. Someone who is invited to decision-making meetings and is willing to spend some of their hard-earned social capital advocating on your behalf. Someone with privilege who has your back.[279]

Journalist Sherrell Dorsey has echoed this sentiment, saying, "My best opportunities have come at the hands of white males referring to the quality and impact of my work in rooms I have never stepped into."[280]

To be an effective sponsor, our first step is getting to know trainees and colleagues from underrepresented groups so we can speak about them when they're not around. Then, let's praise the quality and impact of their work and enthusiastically describe their potential. Doing so can open career doors and other opportunities that otherwise might be sealed off.

Actions for Better Allies:
Don't Be a Gatekeeper, Be a Door Opener

Helping people from underrepresented groups achieve their goals and advance their careers is one of the most powerful things allies can do. Here's how:

- Nudge colleagues from marginalized groups to pursue opportunities.
- Speak positively about colleagues when they're not around.
- Give wholehearted and powerful recommendations and evaluations.
- Don't make career decisions on someone's behalf because you think you know what's best for them.
- Increase visibility by crediting people, being sure to mention everyone involved.
- Create a culture where accomplishments are regularly recognized and celebrated.
- Promote on potential without expecting people to prove themselves over and over again.
- Step back yourself and recommend others for opportunities.
- Sponsor people who are not like you. Remove barriers getting in their way. Share insider knowledge. Make introductions. Recommend them for high-visibility projects. Endorse them publicly.

12

CONTINUING THE JOURNEY

We're nearing the end of *Belonging in Healthcare*. Thanks for sticking with me.

Starting off, we explored privilege, ally archetypes, and examples of everyday discrimination with actions to take to address each one. We then moved into ways we can diversify our professional networks, reshape representation to be more diverse, transform meetings to be more inclusive, and disrupt undervalued glue work. To have an even bigger impact, we then looked at giving more equitable and effective feedback, being more inclusive when hiring and selecting talent, and how to open career doors for people from underrepresented groups.

Together, we covered a lot of ground. Yet, on the journey to be better allies, there will always be more to learn. Here are a few more ideas for allies on how to show up and continue the learning.

If you weren't the first, be the "second courageous"

In her book *The Wake Up*, Michelle MiJung Kim lays out this common scenario: "You're in a meeting, and someone makes a racist or sexist joke or uses offensive terminology. A courageous soul intervenes, using the tactics they learned in a bystander training. Everyone shifts in their seats; the air thickens with an awkward tension." Kim then provides the most likely response: "'Oh, stop being so sensitive. It's just a joke,' or 'Come on, lighten up,' followed by a few chuckles in the room."[281]

Kim calls the individual who speaks up the "first courageous," a title I adore. She goes on to explain, "The moment will quickly pass, and the group will move on to a different topic, with everyone desperately wanting to forget the momentary discomfort. … That quick dismissal of the first courageous will signal to the rest of the people in the room to abandon future attempts to shake the status quo." Chances are, everyone leaves the meeting reminding themselves to keep quiet.

That's not all. She adds, "Sideliners who watch the first courageous without also jumping into the arena have an irritating habit of engaging in what I call delayed camaraderie." You may have experienced this phenomenon yourself. It takes place when someone reaches out after witnessing active allyship with, "Hey, what you did in the meeting was really brave and inspiring." Or, "I totally agree with what you said back there."

Allies, instead of being a sideliner to the first courageous, be the *second courageous* who doubles down on the intervention in the moment, when your support will have the greatest impact. Kim shared how a simple comment like, "Hey, I didn't find it funny either," will validate the original intervention and send a powerful signal that the behavior isn't welcome.

And as Kim pointed out, "maybe next time, someone else will try on the role of the first courageous, knowing they can count on the support of others."

Leave loudly

We've all got them: Personal things we need to do during work hours, such as attending children's school events or appointments with our healthcare providers. We might need to be home for a repair person or to care for a sick family member.

While not all healthcare workers have the privilege and flexibility to take time off as needed to handle such commitments, some do. If you're one of them, do you try to slink away from your office or lab, hoping no one notices? Each time we might do so, we miss an opportunity to "leave loudly" and tell people why we're heading out or going to be unavailable for a while. We miss the chance to message that it's okay (and frequently required) to prioritize personal needs and our health and utilize flexible, family-friendly policies.

Here's one way to do it. Dr. Félix Manuel Chinea shared:[282]

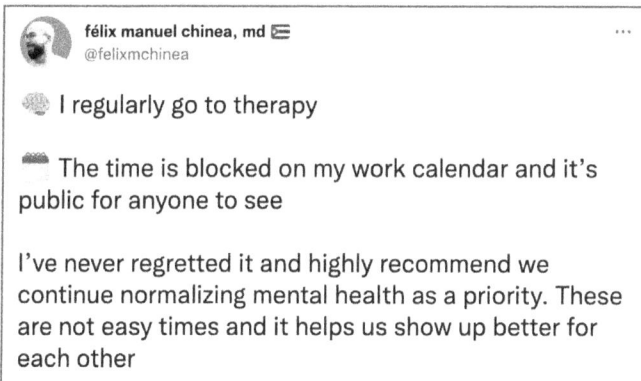

---

félix manuel chinea, md 🔖
@felixmchinea

⋯

🧠 I regularly go to therapy

🕰️ The time is blocked on my work calendar and it's public for anyone to see

I've never regretted it and highly recommend we continue normalizing mental health as a priority. These are not easy times and it helps us show up better for each other

---

We can all normalize taking advantage of benefits and flexible work arrangements (if available) by being transparent about these things on our calendars, like Chinea, or with out-of-office automated email responses. Doing this sends social signals to our colleagues that they, too, can utilize their benefits without shame or fear of censure. For example,

- "Working remotely to care for a sick child"
- "Out of the office volunteering today"
- "At home waiting for a plumber"
- "On parental leave"

That last one is especially important for guys to be loud about. Many American men don't take advantage of parental leave, perhaps because they're concerned they'll be seen as less committed employees.[283] The more men who utilize this benefit, the more accepted it will be for all caregivers.

As allies, we can also push for our organizations to encourage everyone to prioritize wellness and personal needs. For example, Dr. Ally Flessel, who you heard from in Chapter 3, told me that her residency program emphasizes the importance of taking time off for therapy and other health-related appointments. It's a no-questions-asked situation. I love it.

Conduct stay interviews

During a talk I gave about being a better ally, someone in the audience asked me how they could identify why people from underrepresented groups decide to leave an organization.

I decided to answer a slightly different question: How to identify why someone *might* leave before they leave. And I shared a best practice I learned from Angel Uddin, director of diversity, equity, and inclusion at Blue Cross and Blue Shield of Minnesota (BCBSMN). During a webinar hosted by Jennifer Brown Consulting, Uddin told us how this health insurance company has embarked on a journey to tackle disparities in healthcare and make the organization more inclusive and equitable for all employees. Just one of their initiatives is to conduct "stay interviews."[284]

You've probably heard of "exit interviews," which are meetings conducted after someone resigns to understand why they're leaving and gather feedback.

"Stay interviews" are the opposite, intending to identify what needs to improve or change to keep someone at your organization. In BCBSMN's case, they utilized stay interviews specifically to understand how to retain Black employees as part of their goal to become an anti-racist organization. Here's the process they followed.

After George Floyd's murder in May 2020, BCBSMN ran their annual employee audit, but they also collected employee demographic data for the first time. After using the audit to identify key areas they needed to improve, they conducted a series of stay interviews to gather stories to round out the quantitative data collected. (I believe these were conducted in small groups of associates from underrepresented groups, not with individuals.) At each interview, they showed the drivers of engagement from the survey. For example, "We heard you collectively say that there is a lack of opportunity for advancement" or "We heard you collectively say that you don't feel your voice is heard." They emphasized that it was a safe place to share stories and to help the organization improve. And then they listened.

The stories collected during these stay interviews helped BCBSMN identify specific programs to roll out and changes to their business processes to move the company toward a more anti-racist stance. For example, they created a "Lead In Circles" program that matched executives with leaders of their employee resource groups and other employees. These cohorts met monthly, using discussion guides to facilitate conversations. The net result? The executives were blown away by the valuable insight they gained about the barriers and concerns facing these employees, people they otherwise would never have had contact with.

Can you do something similar for your team? Would "stay interviews" help you and your organization understand the needs of employees from underrepresented groups and learn to support them more equitably?

Provide a platform

Rick Neitzelt, who chairs the Rehab Diversity Task Force at The Ohio State University Wexner Medical Center, told me about a simple yet powerful approach to helping coworkers from underrepresented groups access opportunities to build their reputations.

"One of our task force members, who identifies as a Black woman, has a goal of building a new DEI lead position in our department," he said. "In addition to her full-time job, she actively participates in national, state, and university DEI committees. During our monthly leadership meetings, which include top directors and key leaders in our department, I created a standing meeting agenda for her to highlight the work she is doing for, and outside of, our department."

As Neitzelt emphasized to me, "This way, she speaks directly in front of decision-makers. Her work speaks for itself, and her direct manager and I continue to look for other ways to recognize and provide a platform for her outside of our department to accomplish her career goals."

Furthermore, Neitzelt said that this standing agenda item has other benefits. "It enriches our leadership meetings, continues to drive our group's objectives, and promotes collaboration across all levels of our department."

While Neitzelt is focused on amplifying one person, I've also heard of using standing agenda items to highlight diversity more broadly. During an American Association for Women in Radiology webinar in April 2022, I learned that the Radiology Department at the University of Cincinnati added a "Diversity Moment" to their regular meetings. People use this time to share something of interest about diversity and inclusion, perhaps something they recently learned about or a resource they found helpful.[285]

Now it's your turn. How will you create a platform to further learning around diversity, inclusion, and allyship?

Avoid performative allyship

Dr. Paul Haut, the former hospital COO you heard from in earlier chapters, advises other leaders to focus on more than just sound bites. Even if you don't know exactly how you're going to proceed or don't yet have the new diversity plan finalized, don't be tempted to use a bunch of platitudes. Don't make shallow remarks, like "I wrote a column on Martin Luther King's importance to me." Instead, he challenges all of us to demonstrate our awareness of the issues, openly and transparently talking about how things can and should change in the future.

He also cautions against becoming a white cheerleader for racial equity. "In their enthusiasm for showing support for Black team members, some people end up filling space by agreeing with things or jumping into a conversation with 'yeah, we need to be allies,' without adding anything helpful."

Instead, Haut wants more people to share what they've learned and how they are acting differently. Most importantly, he wants people to feel comfortable sharing their failures and what they're going to do differently the next time.

I heartily agree. With each incident of non-inclusive behavior, harassment, or bullying, allies have a choice: Do something or stay silent. Yet, as Brené Brown, PhD, noted in *Dare to Lead*,

> People are opting out of vital conversations about diversity and inclusivity because they fear looking wrong, saying something wrong, or being wrong. Choosing our own comfort over hard conversations is the epitome of privilege, and it corrodes trust and moves us away from meaningful and lasting change.[286]

Now that you've read this book, I hope you feel a new or renewed sense of responsibility to speak up, speak out, and take action.

Keep learning

I firmly believe that you don't have to be a leader or have the words "Diversity," "Inclusion," or "Belonging" on your business card to make a difference. There are everyday actions we all can take to create more inclusive workplaces. There are myriad ways we can be allies.

I hope you've found this book helpful, though it is just one resource. I also have a weekly newsletter, "5 Ally Actions," where I share ideas curated from the week's news and my interactions with clients, audience members, and Twitter users from around the world. I'm on a mission to be a better ally myself, and I learn new approaches all the time. And when I make mistakes, I write about them in the newsletter so others can learn with me. You can subscribe at *www.betterallies.com*.

If you prefer social media, I'd love to have you follow @betterallies on Twitter, Instagram, or Medium.

Being an ally is a journey, and I'm thrilled you're joining me. I also hope you feel a sense of urgency to do this work. Together, we can — and will — make a difference.

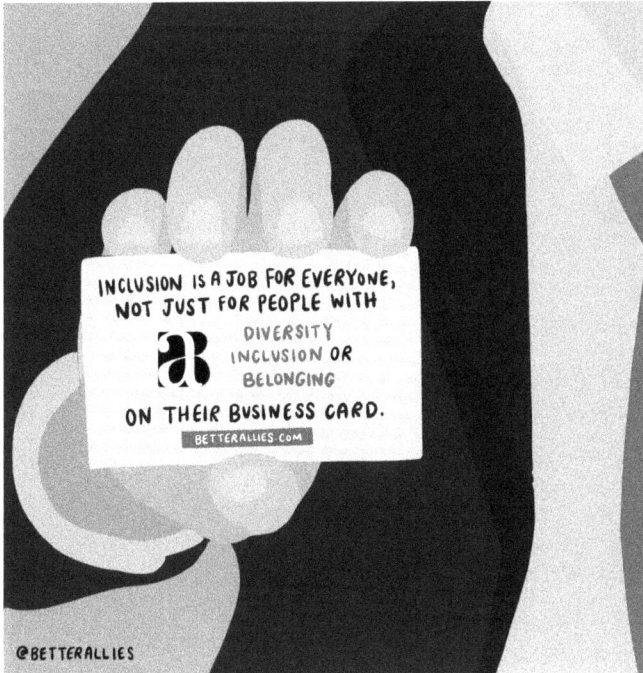

INCLUSION IS A JOB FOR EVERYONE, NOT JUST FOR PEOPLE WITH DIVERSITY INCLUSION OR BELONGING ON THEIR BUSINESS CARD.

BETTERALLIES.COM

@BETTERALLIES

RECAP: ACTIONS FOR BETTER ALLIES

Here's a compilation of the actions included at the end of each chapter.

Understand Your Privilege and Use It for Good

An essential part of allyship is being open to learning, improving, and taking action.

- Review the list of 50 potential privileges in Chapter 1. How many apply to you? What benefits or obstacles do you face at work because of each privilege you have or don't have?
- Identify at least one way you can be a better ally, using the archetypes in this chapter.
- Understand that being an ally is a journey. We all make mistakes. Don't let that hold you back from taking action. Don't opt out.

Be an Ambassador for Change

Helping individuals is laudable, but the larger responsibility of allies is to take actions that will have lasting, beneficial effects on systems (as often as possible).

- When lending a hand to a single person, step back to look for systemic changes that will benefit many.
- Suggest new processes to shift ingrained behaviors and create a more inclusive culture.
- Pay attention to your motivations: Focus on what will authentically support marginalized people over the long-term, rather than actions that will make you feel or look good in the moment.

Speak Up Against Microaggressions

Microaggressions are all around us, and they have a powerful cumulative effect. Speaking out against them at first can be uncomfortable, but it becomes less so with practice. Having a few simple strategies in your back pocket helps, too. Here are seven from this chapter to get you started.

- Use people's titles or refer to their expertise when introducing them.
- Stand up to bullies with "We don't do that here," "We're better than that," or "Not cool."
- In response to a racist or sexist comment, say, "I don't get it. What makes you say that?"
- Use the seek-common-ground-and-educate approach. For example, "I used to think that, too, but I have since learned ..."
- Learn to pronounce people's names.
- Say, "I am concerned. I am uncomfortable. This is a safety issue." (CUS)
- Move closer to someone who's being discriminated against.

Listen, Believe, Learn

Being an effective ally includes the less forceful but equally important activities of listening to alternative perspectives, believing the information that people from under-represented groups share, and learning from their stories and our own mistakes.

- Be vulnerable and honest when you open discussions with colleagues who have less power and privilege than you.
- Resist the urge to get defensive.

- Review the list of red-flag phrases in this chapter, and speak out when you hear them.
- Take action when you see or hear about bigotry, harassment, or discrimination. Be an upstander, not a bystander.
- Recommend organization-wide learning opportunities.
- Accept that, yes, prejudice does exist in your workplace.

Diversify Your Network

Most of us have largely homogeneous networks. Here are some tips for ensuring that your network is diverse and more effective:

- Do a network inventory. List out the people you feel to be your top ten contacts. Are any of them marginalized in ways that you are not? If not, start in your own backyard: Who within your own organization could be a great addition to your current network?
- Seek out people who disagree with you and engage them in respectful conversation. Listen and learn.
- The next time you attend an event of any kind, introduce yourself to someone who doesn't look like you.
- Seek out media, including podcasts and blogs, by people who are different from you.
- Remember to network with your current coworkers and colleagues as a way to foster respect and trust. Be mindful of doing this across functions, racial boundaries, and power differentials.
- As you diversify your network, be generous with your inside knowledge and talk about the unwritten rules for growth and success.

Ensure Equitable Representation

Representation matters. We can and should take steps to ensure that people from underrepresented groups are represented in the awards we give, the content we create, the journals and educational material we consume, and the caregiving teams we're on.

- If you're in a position to select imagery for your hospital or organization's website or publications, make sure photos reflect the diversity of your employee and patient populations.
- Refuse to participate in "manels" or "wanels." When you see them, call them out.
- Share your pronouns. If you use the wrong pronoun for someone, apologize without making it all about yourself.
- Hold up role models from underrepresented groups every chance you get.
- Hold your professional associations accountable for reshaping representation.

Create More Inclusive Meetings

As allies, let's ensure that the voices of members of under-represented groups are heard and valued in the shift huddles, morning rounds, administrative meetings, and events we attend, large or small.

- Challenge yourself to notice and take action when interruptions happen.
- Cultivate a culture of credit: Encourage everyone around you to acknowledge the originators of ideas as often as possible.
- Be vigilant and push back on off-topic questions, showboating, and splaining.
- Don't insist that colleagues turn on their video cameras for virtual meetings.

- Hold professional societies accountable for hosting inclusive events.

Disrupt the Burden of Glue Work

Office housework and citizenship tasks aren't just aggravating. Calling exclusively on women, people of color, and members of other marginalized groups to perform glue work means preventing them from tackling more meaningful work. With that in mind:

- Share the work among the team. For example, if you notice one person is always tasked with setting up for meetings, say something like, "Amara's been handling meeting setup for too long. Let's ask Chad, who has never done it before."
- Set up a rotation for tasks like taking minutes or scheduling upcoming meetings.
- If you're in a position of privilege or authority, model better behavior yourself by cleaning the fridge or tracking down people who are late to a meeting, rather than letting someone else take care of it.
- Never assume that certain coworkers are shouldering glue work because they "enjoy" it or find it "rewarding."
- Reward people who take on these tasks with bonus pay, letters of recommendation, administrative support, mentoring, and sponsorship for career-growing opportunities.

Give Equitable and Effective Feedback

Feedback can be tricky to give, but it truly is a gift to receive. Without clear feedback, members of marginalized groups will have a much harder time succeeding and advancing. So, as an ally, remember:

- When giving feedback, make it actionable. What should they keep doing because it's effective? What new skills should they learn? How should they improve?

- Don't ease up just to avoid hurt feelings. Remember, vague feedback holds people back from growing in their careers.
- Tell them about the expertise you see in them right now, and how to develop more job-related skills for the future.
- Use objective criteria to evaluate trainees and employees in similar roles.
- Give feedback on someone's skills, not their personality or professional semblance.
- Write reviews of roughly the same length for everyone on your staff.
- Give feedback frequently.
- When pointing out how someone can be more inclusive, seek common ground and then educate.
- Ask for feedback on how you can be a better ally.

Select Talent Equitably

Allies can band together to banish the "pipeline" excuses and focus on employing strategies that are proven to attract and select applicants from underrepresented groups. Here are some ways you can make this possible:

- Ensure that your admissions or recruiting web pages use language and images to convey that people from marginalized groups are welcome and belong.
- Advocate for programs to increase the pipeline instead of blaming it.
- Create objective processes to set up candidates for success and prep committee members to be aware of hidden biases.
- Recognize and value the journeys of applicants.
- Pay attention to pay and advocate for salary transparency however you can.

Don't Be a Gatekeeper, Be a Door Opener

Helping people from underrepresented groups achieve their goals and advance their careers is one of the most powerful things allies can do. Here's how:

- Nudge colleagues from marginalized groups to pursue opportunities.
- Speak positively about colleagues when they're not around.
- Give wholehearted and powerful recommendations and evaluations.
- Don't make career decisions on someone's behalf because you think you know what's best for them.
- Increase visibility by crediting people, being sure to mention everyone involved.
- Create a culture where accomplishments are regularly recognized and celebrated.
- Promote on potential without expecting people to prove themselves over and over again.
- Step back yourself and recommend others for opportunities.
- Sponsor people who are not like you. Remove barriers getting in their way. Share insider knowledge. Make introductions. Recommend them for high-visibility projects. Endorse them publicly.

DISCUSSION GUIDE

The benefits of book clubs are almost too numerous to count. They deepen friendships, improve emotional intelligence, promote the exchange of opinions, and encourage critical thinking. Since so many healthcare work environments are fast-paced and stressful, creating a book club among your colleagues is a fabulous way to reinforce trust outside the hospital, clinic, or research lab. It may also create the opportunity to bring together coworkers from different backgrounds and with different life experiences.

Since the book you've just finished includes dozens of concepts and action items, bringing it to your book club for discussion may help you process what you've read. And make concrete plans to begin implementing what you've learned in your workplace.

Here are questions to consider. Some require pre-work, so send them to participants ahead of time. You can download a PDF of this discussion guide at *www.betterallies.com*.

Icebreaker: How would you complete this sentence? "Inclusion in healthcare is important to me because _____ ."

Question 1: How well do you know your own privilege? Using the list in Chapter 1, examine your privilege. As you review this list, keep a tally. Note any items that surprise you and make you wonder, Does anyone actually face this challenge? Discuss these items with the group.

Question 2: In Chapter 1, you'll find descriptions of roles that allies can play. Which one sounds most like you? Which one do you admire most? If you were to push yourself to take on another ally role in addition to the one you play naturally, what would it be?

Question 3: Chapter 3 dives into examples of everyday discrimination and suggestions for taking action as an ally. Discuss a recent experience in which you saw discriminatory or inappropriate behavior and didn't step in or speak up. What held you back? Do you feel more equipped to intervene now?

Question 4: Chapter 4 explores scenarios of when someone could have moved from being a bystander to an upstander. Put yourself in the shoes of one of those bystanders. Can you imagine using the guidelines offered in this chapter to become an upstander? If not, what's the heart of the issue? Be honest, and ask for help and input from your book club members.

Question 5: Think about your professional and personal networks. Are they "just like" you? Think about gaps and how a more diverse network could have a positive impact on your professional goals and the patients you care for. Consider asking other book club members to help you broaden your network through introductions.

Question 6: Chapter 6 focuses on why representation matters and how it might be lacking in many situations. What action can you take in your workplace, training program, private practice, pharmacy, or professional association to improve the representation of people who are members of underrepresented groups?

Question 7: Think about your workplace culture. Do you regularly experience or witness idea hijacking, "manterruptions," show-boating, splaining, or golf course decision-making? What's one thing you can do in the coming week to shift the culture in a more inclusive direction?

Question 8: Chapter 8 is all about the necessary but undervalued work that tends to fall to women, especially women of color. What examples of "glue work" do you see in your workplace? If they aren't equitably assigned, what changes can you make or advocate for?

Question 9: "Fast feedback" and "just one thing" are two approaches that enable allies to offer constructive input on a regular basis. Do you feel comfortable with these formats? Could you and your fellow book club members commit to providing fast feedback at least three times in the coming month as a shared goal?

Question 10: Before the club meets, review the admissions or careers page on your organization's website. Using the best practices in Chapter 10, identify ways you are set up to attract a diverse candidate pool, and brainstorm ideas for improvement.

Question 11: Are you now (or have you been) a mentor to someone with a very different background, lifestyle, or identity than you? If not, how can you get connected to someone from an underrepresented group you're not part of?

Final Lightning Round: What action will you take to improve the sense of belonging in your healthcare setting? (Consider asking someone to be your "accountability buddy" to check in and help ensure that you make progress.)

ACKNOWLEDGMENTS

When I first decided to write this book, I reached out to two of my friends: Dawn Haut and Resa E. Lewiss. Both are physicians and champions of diversity and inclusion, and they enthusiastically supported my idea to write a version of *Better Allies* for healthcare. Throughout the writing process, they were by my side, cheering me. I'm forever grateful.

I am more than honored by all the people who generously shared their time and wisdom with me in my interviews for this book. Many thanks to David Brown, Suzanne Brown, Alaettin Carikci, Marina Del Rios Rivera, Ally Flessel, VK Gadi, Dawn Haut, Paul Haut, Shikha Jain, Resa E. Lewiss, Rick Neitzelt, Avital O'Glasser, Kelly Paradis, Chris Phung, Lorna Rodriguez, Marva Serotkin, Kara Shafer, Cynthia Walsh, and many others who requested anonymity.

To my editing and proofreading team, I deeply appreciate your partnership. Many thanks to my editor, Sally McGraw; you're the best! I couldn't have brought this book to life without you, and I'm so happy to have you on my team. Thank you to my sister, Cindy Smith, for painstakingly reviewing and editing the extensive list of endnotes and to Mark Rhynsburger for his detailed proofreading.

Many thanks to the early reviewers who provided invaluable feedback on my manuscript and to everyone who wrote testimonials to help me spread the word about my book.

I also want to acknowledge my newsletter subscribers and many supporters on social media. You've helped me evolve the Better Allies approach to what it is today. Not only do you help amplify my work, but you point me to new research and resources and kindly give me feedback when I could have (and should have) done better.

Last but not least, this book and all of my work on the Better Allies approach wouldn't exist without the encouragement and support of my husband, Tim, and our children, Emma and Ted. Thank you for believing in me. I love you.

ABOUT THE AUTHOR

After spending 25 years building software products and serving as a vice president of engineering at Macromedia and Adobe, Karen Catlin witnessed a sharp decline in the number of women working in tech. Frustrated but galvanized, she knew it was time to switch gears.

Today, Karen is a leadership coach and a highly acclaimed author and speaker on inclusive workplaces. She coaches women to be stronger leaders and people of all gender identities to be better allies. Her client roster includes Airbnb, DoorDash, Google, and Intuit, as well as entrepreneurs and individuals. Karen's coaching offerings include tactics for increasing visibility, being more strategic, managing stakeholders, negotiation, and cultivating ally skills. Her writing on these and related topics has appeared in *Inc.*, the *Daily Beast*, *Fast Company*, and *The Muse*, and she's consulted on articles for the *Wall Street Journal*, *Forbes*, and the *New York Times*.

In late 2014, Karen started the Twitter handle @betterallies to share simple, actionable steps that anyone could take to make their workplaces more inclusive. That Twitter handle became the inspiration for three books: *Better Allies®: Everyday Actions to Create*

Inclusive, Engaging Workplaces, *The Better Allies® Approach to Hiring*, and *Belonging in Healthcare*. She also emails a roundup of "5 Ally Actions" to over 30,000 newsletter subscribers every week.

A self-professed public speaking geek, Karen is a highly sought-after and engaging presenter who has delivered talks at hundreds of conferences and corporate events. Her TEDx talk, "Women in Tech: The Missing Force," explores the decline in gender diversity in tech, why it's a problem, and what can be done about it. In addition to speaking herself, Karen is determined to change the ratio for who is onstage giving keynotes and other presentations. To support her goal of bringing more diversity to speaker lineups at tech industry events, she co-authored the book *Present! A Techie's Guide to Public Speaking* with engineer and entrepreneur Poornima Vijayashanker.

Karen is a graduate and active alum of Brown University, mentoring women computer science students on how to launch their careers. She's also a member of the board of directors of Digital NEST and on the advisory boards for the Women's CLUB of Silicon Valley and WEST (Women Entering & Staying in Technology). In 2015, the California State Assembly honored Karen with the Wonder Women Tech Innovator Award for outstanding achievements in business and technology and for being a role model for women.

Karen and her husband, Tim, live in San Mateo, California. They're the proud parents of Emma and Ted.

Learn more at *www.karencatlin.com* and *www.betterallies.com*.

NOTES

Inroduction

1   Lynda Laughlin et al., "Who Are Our Health Care Workers?,"
     United States Census Bureau, April 05, 2021, https://www.census.
     gov/library/stories/2021/04/who-are-our-health-care-workers.html.

2   "Healthcare support occupations had employment of 6.4 million in
     May 2020," U.S. Bureau of Labor Statistics, April 2, 2021,
     https://www.bls.gov/opub/ted/2021/healthcare-support-
     occupations-had-employment-of-6-4-million-in-may-2020.htm.

3   Samantha Artiga et al., "COVID-19 Risks and Impacts Among
     Health Care Workers by Race/Ethnicity," KFF (Kaiser Family
     Foundation), November 11, 2020, https://www.kff.org/racial-
     equity-and-health-policy/issue-brief/covid-19-risks-impacts-health-
     care-workers-race-ethnicity.

4   Kirsten Wilbur et al., "Developing Workforce Diversity in the
     Health Professions: A Social Justice Perspective," *ScienceDirect*,
     Volume 6, Issue 2, June 2020, pp. 222-229, https://www.science
     direct.com/science/article/pii/S245230112030016X.

5   Enrique Rivero, "Proportion of Black physicians in U.S. has changed
     little in 120 years, UCLA research finds," UCLA Newsroom, April
     19, 2021, https://newsroom.ucla.edu/releases/proportion-black-
     physicians-little-change.

6   "Labor Force Statistics from the Current Population Survey," U.S.
     Bureau of Labor Statistics, last modified January 20, 2022, accessed
     June 1, 2022, https://www.bls.gov/cps/cpsaat11.htm.

7   Patrick Boyle, "Nation's physician workforce evolves: more women,
     a bit older, and toward different specialties," AAMC News, February
     2, 2021, https://www.aamc.org/news-insights/nation-s-physician-
     workforce-evolves-more-women-bit-older-and-toward-different-
     specialties.

8   Alex Kacik, "Few women reach healthcare leadership roles," *Modern Healthcare*, May 22, 2019, https://www.modernhealthcare.com/operations/few-women-reach-healthcare-leadership-roles.

9   "Women in Medicine" Twitter Space, February 3, 2022, accessed February 5, 2022.

10   "Registered Nurse Demographics and Statistics In The US," ZIPPIA, accessed June 1, 2022, https://www.zippia.com/registered-nurse-jobs/demographics/.

11   "Licensed Practical Nurse Demographics and Statistics In The US," ZIPPIA, accessed June 1, 2022, https://www.zippia.com/licensed-practical-nurse-jobs/demographics/.

12   William H. Frey, "Less than half of the US children under 15 are white, census shows," BROOKINGS, June 24, 2019, https://www.brookings.edu/research/less-than-half-of-us-children-under-15-are-white-census-shows/.

13   Jonathan Vespa et al., "Demographic Turning Points for the United States: Population Projections for 2020 to 2060," U.S. Census Bureau, February 2020, https://www.census.gov/content/dam/Census/library/publications/2020/demo/p25-1144.pdf.

14   Bianca D.M. Wilson and Ilan H. Meyer, "Nonbinary LGBTQ Adults in the United States," UCLA School of Law Williams Institute, June 2021, https://williamsinstitute.law.ucla.edu/publications/nonbinary-lgbtq-adults-us/.

15   Rachel Minkin and Anna Brown, "Rising shares of U.S. adults know someone who is transgender or goes by gender-neutral pronouns," Pew Research Center, July 27, 2021, https://www.pewresearch.org/fact-tank/2021/07/27/rising-shares-of-u-s-adults-know-someone-who-is-transgender-or-goes-by-gender-neutral-pronouns/.

16   "Racial and Ethnic Disparities Continue in Pregnancy-Related Deaths," CDC, September 5, 2019, https://www.cdc.gov/media/releases/2019/p0905-racial-ethnic-disparities-pregnancy-deaths.html.

17   Daniel Wood, "As Pandemic Deaths Add Up, Racial Disparities Persist — And In Some Cases Worsen," NPR, September 23, 2020, https://www.npr.org/sections/health-shots/2020/09/23/914427907/as-pandemic-deaths-add-up-racial-disparities-persist-and-in-some-cases-worsen.

18   "Ashley McMullen: Storyteller and Human Doctor," episode 66, *The Visible Voices* podcast, January 31, 2022, https://www.thevisible voicespodcast.com/episodes/dzqoKwIuj4iL3MuMm-HqiQ.

19   Bianca K. Frogner and Janette S. Dill, "Tracking Turnover Among Health Care Workers During the COVID-19 Pandemic: A Cross-sectional Study," *JAMA Health Forum*, 2022;3(4):e220371. April 8, 2022, https://jamanetwork.com/journals/jama-health-forum/ fullarticle/2790961.

20   Deidra C. Crews et al., "Distinguishing Workforce Diversity From Health Equity Efforts in Medicine," *JAMA Health Forum*, 2021;2(12):e214820, December 2, 2021, https://jamanetwork.com/journals/jama-health-forum/fullarticle/ 2786975.

Chapter 1: The Ally Journey

21   "What Is Intersectionality?," Grinnell College, accessed October 1, 2018, http://haenfler.sites.grinnell.edu/subcultural-theory-and-theorists/intersectionality/.

22   Kittu Pannu, "Privilege, Power, and Pride: Intersectionality Within the LGBT Community," Impakter, August 14, 2017, https:// impakter.com/ privilege-power-and-pride-intersectionality-within-the-lgbt-community/.

23   Kimberlé Crenshaw. "Mapping the Margins: Intersectionality, Identity Politics, and Violence against Women of Color." *Stanford Law Review*, July 1991, https://doi.org/10.2307/1229039.

24   Sian Ferguson, "Privilege 101: A Quick and Dirty Guide," Everyday Feminism, September 29, 2014, https://everydayfeminism.com/ 2014/09/what-is-privilege/.

25   "Effective Allyship: Advancing Women in Healthcare Leadership," webinar hosted by Sanokondu and Equity in Medicine, November 23, 2021, https://media1.cc.umanitoba.ca/legacy/bann/events/ Allyship_2021_11_23.mp4.

26   Renzo Guinto (@RenzoGuinto), "Just declined an invite to speak in a #COVID19 webinar…," Twitter, March 30, 2020, 7:10 a.m., https://twitter.com/RenzoGuinto/status/1244628121090838529.

27 "The Lancet Group's commitments to gender equity and diversity,"
    The Lancet, Volume 394, ISSUE 10197, P452-453, August 10, 2019,
    https://www.thelancet.com/journals/lancet/article/PIIS0140-
    6736(19)31797-0/fulltext.

28 "The Power of Allyship," webinar hosted by American Association
    of Women in Radiology, November 11, 2021, https://www.aawr.
    org/Events/Webinar-Archives.

29 "Jenna Lester and Susan Chon: Skin Color and Representation in
    Dermatology," episode 69, *The Visible Voices* podcast, March 4, 2022,
    https://www.thevisiblevoicespodcast.com/episodes/6ctjLBHrm14A
    KLynmcuSYA.

30 Fahima Dossa et al., "Sex Differences in the Pattern of Patient
    Referrals to Male and Female Surgeons," *JAMA Surgery*, November
    10, 2022;157(2):95–103, https://jamanetwork.com/journals/
    jamasurgery/article-abstract/2786065.

31 Vidya (@vidyapdermody), "For the first time in my 21 years in the
    NHS…," Twitter, February 16, 2022, 11:54 a.m.,
    https://twitter.com/vidyapdermody/status/1494037369846128641.

32 David Leonhardt, "Pundit Accountability," *New York Times*, January
    10, 2022, https://www.nytimes.com/2022/01/10/briefing/pundit-
    accountability-covid-predictions.html.

33. Megan Carpenter, "Get it wrong for me: What I need from allies,"
    LinkedIn, May 28, 2020, https://www.linkedin.com/pulse/get-
    wrong-me-what-i-need-from-allies-megan-carpenter/.

Chapter 2: Knights Versus Allies

34 Better Male Allies, "Male Allies: The Tech Industry Needs You,"
    Opensource.com, June 13, 2017, https://opensource.com/article/
    17/6/male-allies-tech-industry-needs-you.

35 Jason van Gumster, "Haters Gonna Hate: 7 Ways to Deal with
    Criticism," Opensource.com, April 27, 2017, https://opensource.
    com/article/17/4/haters-gonna-hate.

36 Corey Ponder, "Allyship is Not the Hero's Journey," *Corey Ponder*
    blog, July 15, 2019, https://www.coreyponder.com/post/allyship-is-
    not-the-hero-s-journey.

37 Eileen Barrett, "A More Inclusive Medical School Graduation Ceremony," Women in Medicine, March 17, 2022, https://www. womeninmedicinesummit.org/blog/a-more-inclusive-medical-school-graduation-ceremony.

38 Barrett, "A More Inclusive Medical School Graduation Ceremony."

39 Dr. Ijeoma Opara (@IjeomaOparaPHD), "Mentors: be aware of your need to control and take …," Twitter, April 5, 2022, 12:12 p.m., https://twitter.com/IjeomaOparaPHD/status/15114215954698977 31.

Chapter 3: Everyday Discrimination

40 Zaiba Jetpuri et al., (2021). Full Collection of Personal Narratives. *Narrative Inquiry in Bioethics*, Winter 2021, https://doi.org/10.1353/nib.2021.0087.

41 Derald Wing Sue, "Microaggressions: More Than Just Race," *Psychology Today*, November 17, 2010, https://www.psychologytoday.com/us/blog/microaggressions-in-everyday-life/201011/micro aggressions-more-just-race.

42 Uché Blackstock, MD (@uche_blackstock), "For the umpteenth time, I was asked again…," Twitter, September 12, 2021, 4:53 p.m., https://twitter.com/uche_blackstock/status/1437202726304288768.

43 Uché Blackstock, MD (@uche_blackstock), "At this point, I smile and ask them…," Twitter, September 12, 2021, 4:54 p.m., https://twitter.com/uche_blackstock/status/1437202901873659905.

44 Amy Diehl and Leanne M. Dzubinski, "When People Assume You're Not In Charge Because You're a Woman," *Harvard Business Review*, December 22, 2021, https://hbr.org/2021/12/when-people-assume-youre-not-in-charge-because-youre-a-woman.

45 "Ashley McMullen: Storyteller and Human Doctor," episode 66, *The Visible Voices* podcast.

46 Daytheon Sturges, (@daytheon), "So yesterday on my flight there was a medical emergency…," Twitter, February 16, 2022, 5:39 p.m., https://twitter.com/daytheon/status/1494124203213144064.

47 "International Women's Day: Personalised scrub caps for women surgeons," *BBC News*, March 8, 2020, https://www.bbc.com/news/uk-england-shropshire-51723693.

48   Amee Vanderpool (@girlsreallyrule), "Trump defers to the doctors on a question…," Twitter, March 31, 2020, 4:14 p.m., https://twitter.com/girlsreallyrule/status/1245127379854536705.

49   Patricia Friedrich, "Women really do get called by their first names more than men—even doctors," Quart at Work, July 20, 2022, https://qz.com/work/1763651/why-it-matters-when-people-ignore-a-womans-title/.

50   Friedrich, "Women really do get called by their first names more than men—even doctors."

51   Christina C. Huang and Fumiko Chino. "Introducing Dr. Smith, Dr. Wang, and Emily," *Digestive Diseases and Science* 67, 1085–1087 (2022), https://link.springer.com/article/10.1007/s10620-021-07139-3.

52   Sophia Kogan, MD, PhD (@SophiaKogan1), "Just received group work email…," Twitter, December 9, 2019, 12:53 p.m., https://twitter.com/SophiaKogan1/status/1204141990578991105.

53   Oni Blackstock (@oni_blackstock), "Agh. This has happened to me…," Twitter, December 9, 2019, 1:58 p.m., https://twitter.com/DrOniBee/status/1204158423413211143.

54   Arghavan Salles, MD, PhD (@arghavan_salles), "Just last week was in a mtg…," Twitter, December 9, 2019, 2:05 p.m., https://twitter.com/arghavan_salles/status/1204160193140912128.

55   Nancy "Very Asian" Yen Shipley, MD, FAAOS (@_NancyMD), "Unconscious bias - two orthopaedic partners…," Twitter, January 22, 2020, 12:23 p.m., https://twitter.com/_NancyMD/status/1220079611087708160.

56   "Area Female Physician Changes First Name to 'Doctor,'" *GomerBlog*, November 2018, https://gomerblog.com/2018/11/area-female-physician-changes-first-name-to-doctor/.

57   "Dr. Diane Cejas and Dr. Justin Bullock," episode 39, *Docs With Disabilities* podcast, November 29, 2022, https://www.docswith disabilities.org/docswithpodcast/episode/2c57ae08/episode-39-part-i-dr-diana-cejas-and-dr-justin-bullock.

58   Calvin Moorley, "Nursing while Black: Why is racism killing nurses?," *Nursing Times*, April 27, 2022, https://www.nursingtimes.net/opinion/nursing-while-black-why-is-racism-killing-nurses-27-04-2022/.

59 Gillian B. White, "Black Workers Really Do Need to Be Twice as Good," *Atlantic*, October 7, 2015, https://www.theatlantic.com/business/archive/2015/10/why-black-workers-really-do-need-to-be-twice-as-good/409276/.

60 "#metoo in surgery: narratives by women surgeons," Foundation for Narrative Inquiry in Bioethics, 2020, https://nibjournal.org/wp-content/uploads/2020/04/VOICES_2020_METOO_FINAL.pdf

61 Kristen Pressner, "Are You Biased? I Am," filmed August 20, 2016 at TEDxBasel, video, https://www.youtube.com/watch?v=Bq_xYSOZrgU.

62 Susanne Täuber and Morteza Mahmoudi. "How bullying becomes a career tool," *Nature Human Behaviour*, February 6, 2022, https://doi.org/10.1038/s41562-022-01311-z.

63 Zaiba Jetpuri et al., "Full Collection of Personal Narratives."

64 "#metoo in surgery: narratives by women surgeons."

65 Mark Wright et al., "Prominent Black doctor talks about resignation from Seattle Children's, citing racism," *King 5,* August 27, 2021, https://www.king5.com/article/news/community/facing-race/doctor-ben-danielson-seattle-childrens-hospital-systemic-racism-health-care/281-94b16198-3c41-4db8-96d1-1dfc257d98e5.

66 "#metoo in surgery: narratives by women surgeons."

67 Zaiba Jetpuri et al., "Full Collection of Personal Narratives."

68 "Mati Hlatshwayo: Davis Health Director," episode 71, *The Visible Voices* podcast, April 25, 2022, https://www.thevisiblevoicespodcast.com/episodes/Ppve8zdA4skLORWUWLiPiA.

69 Zaiba Jetpuri et al., "Full Collection of Personal Narratives."

70 Zaiba Jetpuri et al., "Full Collection of Personal Narratives."

71 Ruchika Tulshyan, "If You Don't Know How to Say Someone's Name, Just Ask," *Harvard Business Review*, January 9, 2020, https://hbr.org/2020/01/if-you-dont-know-how-to-say-someones-name-just-ask.

72 Shaun Lintern, "Minority NHS staff told to use 'western' sounding names by line managers," *Independent Digital News*, August 4, 2021, https://www.independent.co.uk/news/health/nhs-bristol-minority-western-names-b1896897.html.

73 Nneka M. Okona (@afrosypaella), "A tip: if you have no idea how to pronounce…," Twitter, November 27, 2020, 7:31 p.m., https://twitter.com/afrosypaella/status/1332527427365560322.

74 Bridget Balch, "Oversized and overlooked: Women surgeons struggle to find equipment that fits," AAMC, April 22, 2022, https://www.aamc.org/news-insights/oversized-and-overlooked-women-surgeons-struggle-find-equipment-fits.

75 Lindsey C Valone et al., "Breast Radiation Exposure in Female Orthopaedic Surgeons," *Journal of Bone and Joint Surgery*, November 2, 2016, https://doi.org/10.2106/JBJS.15.01167.

Chapter 4: Listening, Believing, and Learning

76 "Discussing Discrimination," American Psychological Association, accessed October 1, 2018, https://www.apa.org/topics/racism-bias-discrimination/keita.

77 Dwight Smith, "The 10 R's of Talking about Race: How to Have Meaningful Conversations," *Net Impact*, June 3, 2020, https://netimpact.org/blog/talking-about-race.

78 Michelle MiJung Kim, *The Wake Up: Closing the Gap Between Good Intentions and Real Change* (New York: Hatchett Go, 2021).

79 Robin DiAngelo, "How White People Handle Diversity Training in the Workplace," Medium, June 27, 2018, https://medium.com/s/story/how-white-people-handle-diversity-training-in-the-workplace-e8408d2519f.

80 "Quotable Quote," Goodreads, accessed October 19, 2020, https://www.goodreads.com/quotes/7273813-do-the-best-you-can-until-you-know-better-then.

81 Jeff Olsen, "Mayo Clinic Minute: Assume Positive Intent," Mayo Clinic, December 18, 2015, https://newsnetwork.mayoclinic.org/discussion/mayo-clinic-minute-assume-positive-intent/.

82 "Assuming Positive Intent," University of Virginia, accessed June 15, 2022, https://www.medicalcenter.virginia.edu/wwp/positive-practices-to-enhance-resilience-and-improve-interpersonal-communication-individual-techniques-1/positive-habits/assuming-positive-intent/.

83 Melinda Briana Epler, *How to Be an Ally* (New York: McGraw Hill, 2021).

84   "Six Steps to Speak Up," Teaching Tolerance, 2005,
      https://www.tolerance.org/magazine/publications/speak-up/six-steps-to-speak-up.

85   "Six Steps to Speak Up," Teaching Tolerance.

86   Andrew Gregory, "NHS risks losing black and Asian doctors over
      'intolerable' racism levels – report," *Guardian*, June 15, 2022,
      https://www.theguardian.com/society/2022/jun/15/nhs-risks-losing-black-asian-doctors-racism-bma-report.

Chapter 5: Diversifying Your Network

87   Sarah Temkin (@temkins), "Over a generation of women have been
      trained…," Twitter, April 16, 2022, 5:57 a.m., https://twitter.com/
      temkins/status/1515313537337466880.

88   Tiffany Burns et al., "Women in the Workplace 2021," McKinsey &
      Company, September 27, 2021, https://www.mckinsey.com/
      featured-insights/diversity-and-inclusion/women-in-the-workplace.

89   Terry Stone et al., "Women In Healthcare Leadership 2019," Oliver
      Wyman, 2019, https://www.oliverwyman.com/women-in-healthcare-leadership.html.

90   "Magazine Editor Demographics and Statistics In The US," ZIPPIA,
      updated April 18, 2022, https://www.zippia.com/magazine-editor-jobs/demographics/.

91   Simge Andı and Rasmus Kleis Nielsen, "Women and Leadership in
      the News Media 2020: Evidence from Ten Markets," Reuters
      Institute, March 8, 2020, https://reutersinstitute.politics.ox.ac.uk/
      women-and-leadership-news-media-2020-evidence-ten-markets.

92   Ana-Catarina Pinho-Gomes et al., "Representation of Women
      Among Editors in Chief of Leading Medical Journals," JAMA
      Network Open, September 8, 2021, https://doi.org/10.1001/
      jamanetworkopen.2021.23026.

93   Devon Magliozzi, "Building Effective Networks: Nurturing Strategic
      Relationships, Especially for Women," The Clayman Institute for
      Gender Research, April 26, 2016, https://gender.stanford.edu/
      news-publications/gender-news/building-effective-networks-nurturing-strategic-relationships.

94   Shikha Jain, "A Moonshot for Gender Equity," filmed March 20, 2022 at TEDxRushU, video, https://www.ted.com/talks/shikha_jain_a_moonshot_for_gender_equity.

95   Drake Baer, "Why You Need a Diverse Network," August 13, 2013, *Fast Company*, https://www.fastcompany.com/3015552/why-you-need-a-diverse-network.

96   Allison Scott et al., "The Leaky Tech Pipeline: A Comprehensive Framework for Understanding and Addressing the Lack of Diversity across the Tech Ecosystem," Kapor Center for Social Impact, February 2018, http://www.leakytechpipeline.com/wp-content/themes/kapor/pdf/KC18001_report_v6.pdf.

97   Amy Nauiokas, "How to Diversify Your Professional Network," *Harvard Business Review*, August 29, 2018, https://hbr.org/2018/08/how-to-diversify-your-professional-network.

98   Paul Gompers and Silpa Kovvali, "The Other Diversity Dividend," *Harvard Business Review*, July 2018, https://hbr.org/2018/07/the-other-diversity-dividend.

99   Forbes Coaches Council, "11 Practical Ways To Build A Diverse Network Of Professional Connections," *Forbes*, October 8, 2020, https://www.forbes.com/sites/forbescoachescouncil/2020/10/08/11-ways-to-build-a-diverse-network-of-professional-connections.

100 Forbes Coaches Council, "11 Practical Ways To Build A Diverse Network Of Professional Connections."

101 "Dr. Diane Cejas and Dr. Justin Bullock," episode 39, *Docs With Disabilities* podcast.

102 Y-Vonne Hutchinson, *How to Talk to Your Boss About Race: Speaking Up Without Getting Shut Down* (New York: Portfolio/Penguin, 2022).

103 Joann S. Lublin, "Employee Resource Groups Are on the Rise at U.S. Companies," *Wall Street Journal*, October 31, 2021, https://www.wsj.com/articles/why-ergs-are-on-the-rise-11635532232.

104 Lublin, "Employee Resource Groups Are on the Rise at U.S. Companies."

105 Erin Finelli, "Addressing and Combatting Gender Inequities on Social Media," *Physician's Weekly*, November 13, 2021, https://www.physiciansweekly.com/addressing-and-combatting-gender-inequities-on-social-media.

106 Nikki Graf, "Sexual Harassment at Work in the Era of #MeToo," Pew Research Center, April 4, 2018, http://www.pewsocialtrends. org/2018/04/04/sexual-harassment-at-work-in-the-era-of-metoo/.

107 "Men, Commit to Mentor Women," LeanIn.Org, accessed October 20, 2020, https://leanin.org/mentor-her.

108 Harris O'Malley, "Treating Men like Idiots Is the Wrong Way to Stop Sexual Harassment," *Washington Post*, February 1, 2018, https://www.washingtonpost.com/news/post-nation/wp/ 2018/02/01/for-men-in-the-metoo-era-the-mike-pence-rule-is-the-easy-way-out/.

109 David G. Smith and W. Brad Johnson, *Good Guys: How Men Can Be Better Allies for Women in the Workplace* (Boston, MA: Harvard Business Review Press, 2020).

Chapter 6: Reshaping Representation

110 Nell Greenfieldboyce, "Academic Science Rethinks All-Too-White 'Dude Walls' Of Honor," NPR, August 25, 2019, https://www.npr.org/sections/health-shots/2019/08/25/ 749886989/academic-science-rethinks-all-too-white-dude-walls-of-honor.

111 Elizabeth Fitzsousa et al., "'This institution was never meant for me': the Impact of Institutional Historical Portraiture on Medical Students," *Journal of General Internal Medicine*, July 3, 2019, https:// doi.org/10.1007/s11606-019-05138-9.

112 Dowin Boatright et al., "Racial disparities in medical student membership in the Alpha Omega Alpha Honor Society," *JAMA Internal Medicine*, May 2017, https://jamanetwork.com/journals/ jamainternalmedicine/fullarticle/2607210.

113 "STATEMENT," Snow Medical, March 7, 2022, https://snowmedical.org.au/wp-content/uploads/2022/03/Snow-Medical-Statement-regarding-University-of-Melbourne-FINAL.pdf.

114 "Nine Cambridge scientists among the new Fellows announced today by the Royal Society," University of Cambridge, May 10, 2022, https://www.cam.ac.uk/research/news/nine-cambridge-scientists-among-the-new-fellows-announced-today-by-the-royal-society.

115 Ebereillustrate (@ebereillustrate), Instagram, November 24, 2021, https://www.instagram.com/p/CWqnIAHg9hT.

116 Ni-ka, (@NikaFord_), "Amazing to see so much awareness being brought…," Twitter, December 6, 2021, 7:41 a.m., https://twitter.com/NikaFord_/status/1467881856674717696.

117 LaShyra Nolen, "How Medical Education Is Missing the Bull's-eye," *New England Journal of Medicine*, June 25, 2020, https://www.nejm.org/doi/10.1056/NEJMp1915891.

118 Patricia Louie and Rima Wilkes, "Representations of race and skin tone in medical textbook imagery," *Social Science & Medicine*, April 2018, https://doi.org/10.1016/j.socscimed.2018.02.023.

119 Jenna C. Lester, "Why skin disease is often misdiagnosed in darker skin tones," filmed August 2, 2021 at TEDMonterey, video, https://www.ted.com/talks/jenna_c_lester_why_skin_disease_is_often_mis diagnosed_in_darker_skin_tones.

120 Ademide Adelekun et al., "Skin color in dermatology textbooks: An updated evaluation and analysis," *Journal of the American Academy of Dermatology,* April 23, 2020, https://doi.org/10.1016/j.jaad.2020.04.084.

121 "About this project," VICE Gender Spectrum Collection, accessed June 15, 2022, https://genderphotos.vice.com/guidelines.

122 Chromatic Vision Simulator, accessed January 10, 2022, https://asada.website/cvsimulator/e/.

123 Eleanor Dickson et al., "Guide to Creating Accessible Presentations," Digital Library Federation, October 2016, https://www.diglib.org/dlf-events/2016forum/guide-to-creating-accessible-presentations/.

124 "'Manels' still rife at medical conferences with over a third of panels only featuring men," scimex, September 29, 2020, https://www.scimex.org/newsfeed/manels-still-rife-at-medical-conferences-with-over-a-third-of-panels-only-featuring-men.

125 Yvonne Coghill, (@yvonnecoghill1), "And then this. The 6th European nursing congress…," Twitter, June 24, 2022, 11:40 p.m., https://twitter.com/yvonnecoghill1/status/1540585592442032131.

126 "Shifting Demographics," United Nations, accessed July 10, 2022, https://www.un.org/en/un75/shifting-demographics.

127 Francis S. Collins, "Time to End the Manel Tradition," NIH, June 12, 2019, https://www.nih.gov/about-nih/who-we-are/nih-director/statements/time-end-manel-tradition.

128 ManelWatchUS (@ManelWatchUS), "#manels end when men refuse to serve on them," Twitter, November 2, 2021, 6:17 p.m., https://twitter.com/ManelWatchUS/status/1455705632045101059.

129 "Jennifer Freyd Kevin Webb: Institutional Trauma Betrayal and Courage," episode 67, *The Visible Voices* podcast, February 10, 2022, https://www.thevisiblevoicespodcast.com/episodes/dL8AoezxeSB UmBvTis3oVQ.

130 Cynthia Vialle-Giancotti, "You've been DARVOed and you don't even know it," Stanford University, December 13, 2021, https://gender.stanford.edu/news-publications/gender-news/you-ve-been-darvoed-and-you-don-t-even-know-it.

131 Resa E. Lewiss et al., "Who's Really the Victim Here?," MedPage Today, June 2, 2022, https://www.medpagetoday.com/opinion/second-opinions/99015.

132 Usha Lee McFarling, "'Health equity tourists': How white scholars are colonizing research on health disparities," STAT News, September 23, 2021, https://www.statnews.com/2021/09/23/health-equity-tourists-white-scholars-colonizing-health-disparities-research/.

133 Usha Lee McFarling, "Even as medicine becomes more diverse, main authors in elite journals remain mostly white and male," STAT News, March 31, 2022, https://www.statnews.com/2022/03/31/main-authors-in-elite-medical-journals-remain-mostly-white-and-male/.

134 McFarling, "Even as medicine becomes more diverse, main authors in elite journals remain mostly white and male."

135 Alan McElligott (@AMCELL), "It would be great if Everyone could…," Twitter, April 28, 2022, 7:00 a.m., https://twitter.com/AMCELL/status/1519678016976302082.

136 Merriam-Webster, s.v. "they (pro.)," accessed November 1, 2018, https://www.merriam-webster.com/dictionary/they.

137 Jeannie Gainsburg, *The Savvy Ally: A Guide for Becoming a Skilled LGBTQ+ Advocate* (Maryland: Rowman & Littlefield, 2020).

138 Laurel Wamsley, "A Guide To Gender Identity Terms," NPR, June
     2, 2021, https://www.npr.org/2021/06/02/996319297/gender-
     identity-pronouns-expression-guide-lgbtq.

139 Kathia Ramos, "I Am Neither," *The Bridge*, September 9, 2020,
     https://blog.kaporcenter.org/i-am-neither-78a5a79e88f9.

140 Jaclyn F Hill et al., "Residents' perceptions of sex diversity in
     orthopaedic surgery," *Journal of Bone & Joint Surgery*, October 2, 2013,
     https://doi.org/10.2106/JBJS.L.00666.

141 Kanu Okike et al., "Orthopaedic Faculty and Resident Racial/Ethnic
     Diversity is Associated With the Orthopaedic Application Rate
     Among Underrepresented Minority Medical Students," *Journal of the
     American Academy of Orthopaedic Surgeons*, March 15, 2020, https://
     doi.org/10.5435/JAAOS-D-19-00076.

142 Paula Magee, "For minority students, the pipeline to an M.D. is
     leaky. Here's how I managed to make it through," STAT News,
     January. 14, 2019, https://www.statnews.com/2019/01/14/
     minority-students-physician-leaky-pipeline/.

143 Usha Lee McFarling, "Orthopedic surgeons pride themselves on
     fixing things. Can they fix their own field's lack of diversity?," STAT
     News, December 14, 2021, https://www.statnews.com/2021/12/
     14/orthopedic-surgeons-fixing-their-fields-lack-of-diversity/.

144 Blackgirlsinhealthcare, Instagram, June 29, 2022, https://www.
     instagram.com/tv/CfZnAkaFdda/.

145 "Our Racial Reckoning Statement," ANA, June 11, 2022, https://
     www.nursingworld.org/practice-policy/workforce/racism-in-
     nursing/RacialReckoningStatement/.

146 Jim Key, "Why seeing marginalized communities in pop culture
     matters," USC, February 14, 2019, https://dornsife.usc.edu/news/
     stories/2954/marginalized-communities-in-popular-culture/.

Chapter 7: Transforming Meetings

147 Shikha Jain, "A Moonshot for Gender Equity."

148 Claire Landsbaum, "Obama's Female Staffers Came Up with a
     Genius Strategy to Make Sure Their Voices Were Heard," The Cut,
     September 13, 2016, https://www.thecut.com/2016/09/heres-how-
     obamas-female-staffers-made-their-voices-heard.html.

149 Naykky Singh Ospina et al., "Eliciting the Patient's Agenda-Secondary Analysis of Recorded Clinical Encounters," *Journal of General Internal Medicine*, July 2, 2018, https://doi.org/10.1007/s11606-018-4540-5.

150 "How often are women interrupted by men? Here's what the research says," Advisory Board, republished on October 30, 2018, https://www.advisory.com/daily-briefing/2017/07/07/men-interrupting-women.

151 Deborah Tannen, "The Truth about How Much Women Talk—and Whether Men Listen," *Time*, June 28, 2017, http://time.com/4837536/do-women-really-talk-more/.

152 Alexa Renee, "Crowd Erupts at World Science Festival after Moderator Is Called Out for 'Mansplaining,'" *ABC 10*, June 10, 2017, https://www.abc10.com/article/news/uc-davis-professor-had-her-theories-mansplained-during-science-panel/103-446300388.

153 Judith A. Hall and Debra L. Roter, "Do patients talk differently to male and female physicians? A meta-analytic review," *Patient and Education Counseling*, December 2002, https://doi.org/10.1016/s0738-3991(02)00174-x.

154 A/Prof Tasha Stanton (@Tash_Stanton), "Friends at conferences - please do not assume…," Twitter, October 19, 2019, 6:31 a.m., https://twitter.com/Tash_Stanton/status/1185549050260537344.

155 John Plunkett, "This chap tried to mansplain the difference between vulva and vagina and the takedowns were brutal," The Poke, updated December 30, 2020, https://www.thepoke.co.uk/2019/02/11/chap-tried-mansplain-difference-vulva-vagina-takedowns-brutal/.

156 Jennifer Brown, *How to Be An Inclusive Leader*, (California: Berrett-Koehler, 2019).

157 Kim Goodwin, "Mansplaining, explained in one simple chart," BBC, July 29, 2018, https://www.bbc.com/worklife/article/20180727-mansplaining-explained-in-one-chart.

158 "Dr. Diane Cejas and Dr. Justin Bullock," episode 39, *Docs With Disabilities* podcast.

159 Alicia Sasser Modestino et al., "Childcare Is a Business Issue," *Harvard Business Review*, April 29, 2021, https://hbr.org/2021/04/childcare-is-a-business-issue.

160 "Only 6% of U.S. Businesses Offer Any Child Care Benefits, Highlighting Significant Challenges for Working Parents," PR Newswire, January 9, 2020, https://www.prnewswire.com/news-releases/only-6-of-us-businesses-offer-any-child-care-benefits-highlighting-significant-challenges-for-working-parents-300984033.html.

161 Leila Schochet, "The Child Care Crisis Is Keeping Women Out of the Workforce," American Progress, March 28, 2019, https://www.americanprogress.org/article/child-care-crisis-keeping-women-workforce/.

162 Cristina Novoa, "How Child Care Disruptions Hurt Parents of Color Most," American Progress, June 29, 2020, https://www.americanprogress.org/article/child-care-disruptions-hurt-parents-color/.

163 Kristi Hendrickson, PhD et al., "AAPM CHILDCARE SURVEY FOLLOW UP," AAPM, May|June 2017, https://w3.aapm.org/newsletter/posts/2017/may-june/4203_8.php.

164 Resa #GetVax Lewiss MD (@ResaELewiss), "Childcare! Amazing work offering this…," Twitter, April 29, 2022, 2:05 p.m., https://twitter.com/ResaELewiss/status/1520147186104864769.

165 "A Planning Guide for Making Temporary Events Accessible to People with Disabilities," ADA National Network, 2015, https://adata.org/publication/temporary-events-guide.

166 Eleanor Dickson et al., "Guide to Creating Accessible Presentations," Digital Library Federation, October 2016, https://www.diglib.org/dlf-events/2016forum/guide-to-creating-accessible-presentations.

167 "ACP Details Efforts to Support Commitment to Diversity, Equity and Inclusion," ACP, April 28, 2022, https://www.acponline.org/acp-newsroom/acp-details-efforts-to-support-commitment-to-diversity-equity-and-inclusion.

168 "Our Commitment to Our Community," Mapbox, accessed November 1, 2018, https://www.mapbox.com/events/code-of-conduct/. Creative Commons Attribution-ShareAlike 4.0 International (CC BY-SA 4.0) license. Reformatted in publishing.

169 Valerie Aurora and Mary Gardiner, *How to Respond to Code of Conduct Reports* (San Francisco: Frame Shift Consulting, 2018).

Chapter 8: Disrupting Glue Work

170 Priscila Rodrigues Armijo et al., "Citizenship Tasks and Women
     Physicians: Additional Woman Tax in Academic Medicine?," *Journal
     of Women's Health*, July 12, 2021, https://doi.org/10.1089/jwh.2020.
     8482.

171 Joan C. Williams, "Sticking Women with the Office Housework,"
     Washington Post, April 16, 2014, https://www.washingtonpost.com/
     news/on-leadership/wp/2014/04/16/sticking-women-with-the-
     office-housework/.

172 Tanya Reilly, "Being Glue," *No Idea* blog, accessed June 30, 2022,
     https://noidea.dog/glue.

173 Eve Rittenberg et al., "Primary Care Physician Gender and
     Electronic Health Record Workload," *Journal of General Internal
     Medicine*, January 6, 2022, https://doi.org/10.1007/s11606-021-
     07298-z.

174 Tiffany L. Carson et al., "A Seat at the Table: Strategic Engagement
     in Service Activities for Early Career Faculty From
     Underrepresented Groups in the Academy," *Academic Medicine*,
     August 2019, https://doi.org/10.1097/ACM.0000000000002603.

175 Misra Joya, et al.., "Gender, Work Time, and Care Responsibilities
     Among Faculty," *Sociological Forum*, May 30, 2012, https://online
     library.wiley.com/doi/10.1111/j.1573-7861.2012.01319.x.

176 Priscila Rodrigues Armijo et al., "Citizenship Tasks and Women
     Physicians: Additional Woman Tax in Academic Medicine?"

177 Ruchika Tulshyan, "Women of Color Get Asked to Do More
     'Office Housework.' Here's How They Can Say No," *Harvard
     Business Review*, April 6, 2018, https://hbr.org/2018/04/women-of-
     color-get-asked-to-do-more-office-housework-heres-how-they-can-
     say-no.

Chapter 9: Giving Feedback

178 Alexandra E. Rojek et al., "Differences in Narrative Language in
     Evaluations of Medical Students by Gender and Under-represented
     Minority Status," *Journal of General Internal Medicine*, April 16, 2019,
     https://doi.org/10.1007/s11606-019-04889-9.

179 1001cuts Newsletter, Winter 2022, accessed June 16 2022, https://docs.google.com/document/d/1WqPXHKx0j6RgvSCB7rzaemlvQHuLm1cjeKKz1A8wEhU.

180 Kieran Snyder and Aileen Lee, "No more 'abrasive,' 'opinionated,' or 'nice': Why managers need to stop giving women and people of color feedback on their personality," *Fortune*, June 15, 2022, https://fortune.com/2022/06/15/performance-reviews-bias-gender-race-language-textio-kieran-snyder-aileen-lee/.

181 Shelley Correll and Caroline Simard, "Research: Vague Feedback Is Holding Women Back," *Harvard Business Review*, April 29, 2016, https://hbr.org/2016/04/research-vague-feedback-is-holding-women-back.

182 Snyder and Lee, "No more 'abrasive,' 'opinionated,' or 'nice': Why managers need to stop giving women and people of color feedback on their personality."

183 Usha Lee McFarling, "'It was stolen from me': Black doctors are forced out of training programs at far higher rates than white residents," STAT News, June 20, 2022, https://www.statnews.com/2022/06/20/black-doctors-forced-out-of-training-programs-at-far-higher-rates-than-white-residents/.

184 White, "Black Workers Really Do Need to Be Twice as Good."

185 "The State of Black Women in Corporate America 2020," LeanIn.Org, accessed October 1, 2020, https://leanin.org/research/state-of-black-women-in-corporate-america/introduction.

186 "Discrimination in America: Experiences and Views of LGBTQ Americans," Harvard T.H. Chan School of Public Health, Robert Wood Johnson Foundation, and National Public Radio (NPR), November 2017, https://www.rwjf.org/content/dam/farm/reports/surveys_and_polls/2017/rwjf441734.

187 Sandy E. James et al., "The Report of the 2015 U.S. Transgender Survey," National Center for Transgender Equality, 2016, https://transequality.org/sites/default/files/docs/usts/USTS-Full-Report-Dec17.pdf.

188 Dayana Yochim, "Pride Month: 12 key numbers highlighting the economic status, challenges that LGBTQ people face," MSNBC, June 22, 2020, https://www.nbcnews.com/know-your-value/feature/pride-month-12-key-numbers-highlighting-economic-status-challenges-lgbtq-ncna1231820.

189 Robin Klein et al., "Association Between Resident Race and Ethnicity and Clinical Performance Assessment Scores in Graduate Medical Education," *Journal of Academic Medicine*, May 17, 2022, https://doi.org/10.1097/ACM.0000000000004743.

190 McFarling, "'It was stolen from me': Black doctors are forced out of training programs at far higher rates than white residents."

191 "AMA supports natural hair & cultural headwear anti-discrimination policies," AMA, June 14, 2022, https://www.ama-assn.org/press-center/press-releases/ama-supports-natural-hair-cultural-headwear-anti-discrimination.

192 Drake Baer, "Professionalism is a bias-making machine that needs to end. Here's how to dismantle it," *Business Insider*, March 26, 2022, http://www.businessinsider.com/professionalism-is-a-bias-making-machine-how-to-dismantle-it-2022-3.

193 "Interrupting Bias in Performance Evaluations," Bias Interrupters, accessed November 1, 2018, https://biasinterrupters.org/interrupting-bias-in-performance-evaluations/.

194 Lareina Yee et al., "Women in the Workplace 2016," LeanIn.Org and McKinsey & Company, 2016, https://womenintheworkplace.com/2016.

195 Francesca Fontana, "The Reasons Women Don't Get the Feedback They Need," *Wall Street Journal*, October 12, 2019, https://www.wsj.com/articles/the-reasons-women-dont-get-the-feedback-they-need-11570872601.

196 Kim Scott, *Radical Candor: Be a Kick-Ass Boss without Losing Your Humanity* (New York: St. Martin's Press, 2017).

197 Correll and Simard, "Research: Vague Feedback Is Holding Women Back."

198 Snyder and Lee, "No more 'abrasive,' 'opinionated,' or 'nice': Why managers need to stop giving women and people of color feedback on their personality."

199 Tara Jaye Frank, *The Waymakers* (Virginia: Amplify Publishing, 2022).

200 Douglas Stone and Sheila Heen, *Thanks for the Feedback* (New York: Penguin Books, 2014).

201 Scott, *Radical Candor.*

202 Joy Ohm, "Open the Kimono: 11 Assumptions Behind a Misogynist and Racist Business Phrase," Catalyst Inc., March 22, 2021, https://www.catalyst.org/2021/03/22/racism-misogyny-asian-american-women-workplace.

203 Steve Haruch, "Why Corporate Executives Talk About Opening Their Kimonos," NPR, November 2, 2014, https://www.npr.org/sections/codeswitch/2014/11/02/360479744/why-corporate-executives-talk-about-opening-their-kimonos.

Chapter 10: Finding and Selecting Talent

204 Vivian Hunt et al., "Why diversity matters," McKinsey & Company, January 1, 2015, https://www.mckinsey.com/business-functions/people-and-organizational-performance/our-insights/why-diversity-matters.

205 Brian D. Smedley et al., *In the Nation's Compelling Interest: Ensuring Diversity in the Health-Care Workforce*, (Washington, D.C.: National Academies Press, 2004).

206 Christopher J. D. Wallis et al., "Association of Surgeon-Patient Sex Concordance With Postoperative Outcomes," *JAMA Surgery*, December 8, 2021, https://doi.org/10.1001/jamasurg.2021.6339.

207 "School of Medicine Admissions," University of Mississippi Medical Center, accessed June 23, 2022, https://www.umc.edu/som/Departments%20and%20Offices/SOM%20Administrative%20Offices/SOM%20Admissions/SOM%20Admissions.html.

208 Better Allies (@betterallies), "I don't use stock photos to represent diversity on my careers page…," Twitter, June 23, 2022, 1:57 p.m., https://twitter.com/BetterAllies/status/1540076604587511808.

209 "Equity, Diversity & Inclusion," UCLA School of Nursing, accessed June 10, 2022, https://nursing.ucla.edu/student-organizations.

210 "Diversity and inclusion at GOSH," Great Ormond Street Hospital for Children NHS Foundation Trust, accessed April 5, 2022, https://www.gosh.nhs.uk/about-us/diversity-and-inclusion/.

211 Peer Health Exchange job description, accessed June 24, 2022, https://phe.bamboohr.com/jobs/view.php?id=182.

212 Bianca K. Frogner and Janette S. Dill, "Tracking Turnover Among Health Care Workers During the COVID-19 Pandemic: A Cross-sectional Study," *JAMA Network Health Forum*, April 8, 2022, https://doi.org/10.1001/jamahealthforum.2022.0371.

213 Original study unavailable. See summaries in: Sheryl Sandberg, *Lean In: Women, Work, and the Will to Lead*, with Nell Scovell (New York: Alfred A. Knopf, 2013); Katty Kay and Claire Shipman, *The Confidence Code: The Science and Art of Self-Assurance—What Women Should Know* (New York: HarperCollins, 2014).

214 Jo Owen, *How to Lead* (Upper Saddle River, NJ: Prentice Hall, 2011).

215 Vanessa Grubbs, "Diversity, Equity, and Inclusion That Matter," *New England Journal of Medicine*, July 23, 2020, https://doi.org/10.1056/NEJMpv2022639.

216 Tracie DeFreitas, "Making a Statement – About Reasonable Accommodation and Equal Opportunity," JAN, Consultants' Corner: Volume 11, Issue 2, accessed May 20 2021, https://askjan.org/publications/consultants-corner/vol11iss02.cfm.

217 Gloria A. Wilder, "Experiencing Racism in Health Care: Stories from Health Care Professionals," *Narrative Inquiry in Bioethics*, Winter 2021, https://doi.org/10.1353/nib.2021.0098.

218 "Student Traning Program Impact Report," Dana Farber Cancer Institute, accessed April 8, 2022, https://www.dana-farber.org/legacy/uploadedFiles/Library/careers/diversity-and-inclusion/workforce-development-impact-report.pdf.

219 Alyssa Dindorf, "Early Pathways: 'Native Americans Into Medicine' Inspires Future Careers in Tribal Health," University of Minnesota, August 18, 2021, https://med.umn.edu/news-events/early-path ways-'native-americans-medicine'-inspires-future-careers-tribal-health.

220 Moorley, "Nursing while Black: Why is racism killing nurses?"

221 Moorley, "Nursing while Black: Why is racism killing nurses?"

222 "The Power of Allyship," American Association of Women in Radiology.

223 Anna Miller, "Body size matters in graduate school admissions, study suggests," American Psychological Association, *gradPSYCH* magazine, November 2013, https://www.apa.org/gradpsych/2013/11/body-size.

224 Marianne Bertrand and Sendhil Mullainathan, "Are Emily and Greg More Employable than Lakisha and Jamal? A Field Experiment on Labor Market Discrimination," National Bureau of Economic Research, July 2003, https://www.nber.org/papers/w9873.

225 Lesley Evans Ogden, "Working mothers face a 'wall' of bias—but there are ways to push back," *Science*, April 19, 2019, https://www.science.org/content/article/working-mothers-face-wall-bias-there-are-ways-push-back.

226 Kristi R. G. Hendrickson et al., "Ethical violations and discriminatory behavior in the MedPhys Match," *Journal of Applied Clinical Medical Physics*, August 20, 2017, https://aapm.onlinelibrary.wiley.com/doi/10.1002/acm2.12135.

227 Courtney Burns (@MsCourtneyBurns), "Today I had a preceptor say: "It is my opinion that females in medicine…," Twitter, February 23, 2022, 12:19 p.m., https://twitter.com/MsCourtneyBurns/status/1496580458158727176.

228 Dominique Stewart, "What the Term 'Diversity Hire' Gets Wrong," *Anti-Racism Daily*, https://the-ard.com/2022/03/22/what-the-term-diversity-hire-gets-wrong/.

229 Stephanie M. Lee, "A Black Doctor Tried To Diversify Medicine. Then She Lost Her Job," *BuzzFeed News*, May 19, 2022, https://www.buzzfeednews.com/article/stephaniemlee/tulane-medical-school-racial-reckoning.

230 Adriana Belmonte, "A very well-kept secret: Women doctors detail widespread sexism in medicine," *Yahoo! Finance*, March 17, 2021, https://sports.yahoo.com/culture-of-silence-women-in-medicine-detail-crushing-effects-of-sexism-150036336.html.

231 Lydia Dishman, "How Google, Pinterest, and Others Use Internships to Push Their Diversity Initiatives," *Fast Company*, May 23, 2016, https://www.fastcompany.com/3060118/how-google-pinterest-and-others-use-internships-to-push-their-diversity-i.

232 Lekshmi Santhosh et al., "The 'Third Shift:' A Path Forward to Recognizing and Funding Gender Equity Efforts," *Journal of Women's Health*, November 12, 2020, https://doi.org/10.1089/jwh.2020.8679.

233 Joannie Yeh MD (@BetaMomma), "Someone on a medical school admissions committee wrote…," Twitter, March 6, 2022, 4:26 a.m., https://twitter.com/BetaMomma/status/1500447780447342597.

234 Arman A. Shahriar, BS, et al., "Socioeconomic Diversity of the Matriculating US Medical Student Body by Race, Ethnicity, and Sex, 2017-2019," *JAMA Network Open*, March 15, 2022, https://doi.org/10.1001/jamanetworkopen.2022.2621.

235 Arman A. Shahriar et al., "Comparison of Medical School Financing Plans Among Matriculating US Medical Students From 2017 to 2019," *JAMA Network Open*, July 20, 2021, https://doi.org/10.1001/jamanetworkopen.2021.17704.

236 Laszlo Bock, *Work Rules! Insights from Inside Google That Will Transform How You Live and Lead* (New York: Twelve Books, 2015).

237 Quinn Capers et al., "Strategies for Achieving Diversity through Medical School Admissions," *Journal of Health Care for the Poor and Underserved*, February 2018, https://doi.org/10.1353/hpu.2018.0002.

238 "Project Implicit," Harvard University, accessed November 1, 2018, https://implicit.harvard.edu.

239 "Google's unbiasing hiring checklists," Google re:Work, accessed August 27, 2019, https://docs.google.com/document/d/1_1qvG7ESd2kJj7QJKsUObwMJShswvzurNmpmbM7LE3Y/export?format=pdf.

240 Mary Blair-Loy et al., "Can rubrics combat gender bias in faculty hiring?" *Science*, June 30, 2022, https://www.science.org/doi/10.1126/science.abm2329.

241 Iris Bohnet, "How to Take the Bias out of Interviews," *Harvard Business Review*, April 18, 2016, https://hbr.org/2016/04/how-to-take-the-bias-out-of-interviews.

242 Quinn Capers et al., "Strategies for Achieving Diversity through Medical School Admissions."

243   Lindsay Gellman and Georgia Wells, "What's Holding Back Women in Tech?," *Wall Street Journal*, March 22, 2016, https://www.wsj.com/articles/whats-holding-back-women-in-tech-1458639004.

244   Robert A. Witzburg and Henry M. Sondheimer, "Holistic review—shaping the medical profession one applicant at a time," *New England Journal of Medicine*, April 25, 2013, https://doi.org/10.1056/NEJMp1300411.

245   "Registered Nurse Demographics and Statistics In The US," ZIPPIA.

246   Michael Walter, "Radiology's average salary is $429K, but women make 21% less than men," *Radiology Business*, March 28, 2019, https://www.radiologybusiness.com/topics/economics/radiology-compensation-average-salary-wage-gap.

247   "Effective male allies 'recruit, train and retain' female gastroenterologists," Healio, March 27, 2022, https://www.healio.com/news/gastroenterology/20220327/effective-male-allies-recruit-train-and-retain-female-gastroenterologists.

248   Solarina Ho, "Gender bias against female surgeons fuelling surgical backlogs," *CTV News*, March 26, 2021, https://beta.ctvnews.ca/national/health/2021/3/26/1_5363844.html.

249   "2021 Physician Compensation Report," Doximity, December 2021, https://c8y.doxcdn.com/image/upload/v1/Press%20Blog/Researc h%20Reports/Doximity-Compensation-Report-2021.pdf.

250   Eva Catenaccio et al., "Addressing Gender-Based Disparities in Earning Potential in Academic Medicine," *JAMA Network Open*, February 18, 2022, https://doi.org/10.1001/jamanetworkopen.2022.0067.

251   Marcel Schwantes, "The CEO of Salesforce Found Out His Female Employees Were Paid Less Than Men. His Response Is a Priceless Leadership Lesson," *Inc.*, July 26, 2018, https://www.inc.com/marcel-schwantes/the-ceo-of-salesforce-found-out-female-employees-are-paid-less-than-men-his-response-is-a-priceless-leadership-lesson.html.

252   Jennifer Southall, "Report highlights wide pay gap for women, minorities in medicine," Healio, November 11, 2021, https://www.healio.com/news/hematology-oncology/20211111/report-highlights-wide-pay-gap-for-women-minorities-in-medicine.

253 Ronald Piana, "Bridging the Gender Gap in Oncology," The ASCO Post, July 25, 2021, https://ascopost.com/issues/july-25-2021/bridging-the-gender-gap-in-oncology.

254 Madhukar Pai, "Disrupting Global Health: From Allyship To Collective Liberation," Forbes, March 15, 2022, https://www.forbes.com/sites/madhukarpai/2022/03/15/disrupting-global-health-from-allyship-to-collective-liberation.

255 Andrew Bloomenthal, "Can a Family Survive on the US Minimum Wage?" Investopedia, March 18, 2022, https://www.investopedia.com/articles/personal-finance/022615/can-family-survive-us-minimum-wage.asp.

Chapter 11: Opening Career Doors

256 "A Fireside Chat with Mary C. Mahoney, MD, FACR, FSBI," American Association of Women in Radiology, April 6, 2022, https://www.aawr.org/Events/Webinar-Archives.

257 Bock, *Work Rules!*

258 Cecilia Kang, "Google Data-Mines Its Approach to Promoting Women," *Washington Post*, April 2, 2014, https://www.washingtonpost.com/news/the-switch/wp/2014/04/02/google-data-mines-its-women-problem.

259 Zuhairah Washington and Laura Morgan Roberts, "Women of Color Get Less Support at Work. Here's How Managers Can Change That," *Harvard Business Review*, March 4, 2019, https://hbr.org/2019/03/women-of-color-get-less-support-at-work-heres-how-managers-can-change-that.

260 Colleen Flaherty, "Help That Hurts Women," *Inside Higher Ed*, June 19, 2018, https://www.insidehighered.com/news/2018/06/19/study-finds-recommendation-letters-inadvertently-signal-doubt-about-female.

261 Hebl et al., "How We Describe Male and Female Job Applicants Differently," *Harvard Business Review*, September 27, 2018, https://hbr.org/2018/09/how-we-describe-male-and-female-job-applicants-differently.

262 Lori Nishiura Mackenzie, "How to remove 'doubt' when writing about performance," LinkedIn, April 24, 2022, https://www.linkedin.com/pulse/how-remove-doubt-when-writing-performance-lori-nishiura-mackenzie/.

263 Alexandra E Rojek et al., "Differences in Narrative Language in Evaluations of Medical Students by Gender and Under-represented Minority Status," *Journal of General Internal Medicine*, May 2019, https://doi.org/10.1007/s11606-019-04889-9.

264 David A. Ross et al., "Differences in words used to describe racial and gender groups in Medical Student Performance Evaluations," PLOS One, August 9, 2017, https://doi.org/10.1371/journal.pone.0181659.

265 Mytien Nguyen, MS et al., "Association of Sociodemographic Characteristics With US Medical Student Attrition," *JAMA Internal Medicine*, July 11, 2022, https://doi.org/10.1001/jamainternmed.2022.2194.

266 Shikha Jain, "A Moonshot for Gender Equity."

267 Shivani Misra (@ShivaniM_KC), "You chose to share my paper on twitter…," Twitter, September 4, 2021, 1:27 a.m., https://twitter.com/ShivaniM_KC/status/1434070528994729985.

268 Christine Silva, "The Myth of the Ideal Worker: Does Doing All the Right Things Really Get Women Ahead? (Report)," Catalyst, October 1, 2011, https://www.catalyst.org/research/the-myth-of-the-ideal-worker-does-doing-all-the-right-things-really-get-women-ahead/.

269 Washington and Roberts, "Women of Color Get Less Support at Work. Here's How Managers Can Change That."

270 Micaela Marini Higgs, "How to Accept a Compliment — Even if It's From Yourself," *New York Times*, December 4, 2018, https://www.nytimes.com/2018/12/04/smarter-living/how-to-accept-a-compliment.html.

271 Laura Morgan Roberts and Anthony J. Mayo, "Toward a Racially Just Workplace," *Harvard Business Review*, November 14, 2019, https://hbr.org/2019/11/toward-a-racially-just-workplace.

272 Courtney Connley, "Ambition is not the problem: Women want the top jobs—they just don't get them," CNBC, March 5, 2020, https://www.cnbc.com/2020/03/05/why-women-are-locked-out-of-top-jobs-despite-having-high-ambition.html.

273 Nancy M. Carter and Christine Silva, "The Myth of the Ideal Worker: Does Doing All the Right Things Really Get Women Ahead?," Catalyst, 2011, https://www.catalyst.org/wp-content/uploads/2019/02/The_Myth_of_the_Ideal_Worker_Does_Doing_All_the_Right_Things_Really_Get_Women_Ahead.pdf.

274 Rachel Thomas et al., "Women in the Workplace 2017," McKinsey & Company and LeanIn.Org, 2017, https://womenintheworkplace.com/2017.

275 Janice Gassam Asare, "Our Obsession With Black Excellence Is Harming Black People," *Forbes*, August 1, 2021, https://www.forbes.com/sites/janicegassam/2021/08/01/our-obsession-with-black-excellence-is-harming-black-people.

276 Tomas Chamorro-Premuzic et al., "What Science Says about Identifying High-Potential Employees," *Harvard Business Review*, October 3, 2017, https://hbr.org/2017/10/what-science-says-about-identifying-high-potential-employees.

277 "Effective Allyship: Advancing Women in Healthcare Leadership," webinar hosted by Sanokondu and Equity in Medicine.

278 Herminia Ibarra and Kathleen O'Connor, "Designing leadership programs for women that really work," *I by IMD*, December 27, 2021, https://iby.imd.org/leadership/designing-leadership-programs-for-women-that-really-work.

279 Carla Harris, "How to find the person who can help you get ahead at work," filmed November 29, 2018 at TEDWomen, video, https://www.ted.com/talks/carla_harris_how_to_find_the_person_who_can_help_you_get_ahead_at_work.

280 Courtney Connley, "5 black women on how women, employers and colleagues can work together to close the pay gap," CNBC, August 22, 2019, https://www.cnbc.com/2019/08/22/5-black-women-discuss-solutions-for-closing-the-pay-gap.html.

Chapter 12: Continuing the Journey

281 Kim, *The Wake Up: Closing the Gap Between Good Intentions and Real Change*.

282 félix manuel chinea, md (@felixmchinea), "I regularly go to therapy…," Twitter, June 30, 2022, 7:09 a.m., https://twitter.com/felixmchinea/status/1542510626580246528.

283   Nathaniel Popper, "Paternity Leave Has Long-Lasting Benefits. So Why Don't More American Men Take It?" *New York Times*, April 17, 2020, https://parenting.nytimes.com/work-money/paternity-leave.

284   "DEI Community Call with Angel Uddin," Jennifer Brown Consulting, accessed October 7, 2021, https://bit.ly/JBC_Uddin_Community_Call.

285   "A Fireside Chat with Mary C. Mahoney, MD, FACR, FSBI," American Association of Women in Radiology.

286   Brené Brown, *Dare to Lead* (New York: Random House, 2018).